W9-CTI-343

Suicide in Different Cultures

SUICIDE IN DIFFERENT CULTURES

Edited by
Norman L. Farberow, Ph.D.
Principal Investigator, Central Research Unit
Veterans Administration Wadsworth Hospital Center;
Co-director, Los Angeles Suicide Prevention Center;
Clinical Professor of Psychiatry (Psychology)
School of Medicine
University of Southern California
Los Angeles, California

University Park Press
Baltimore · London · Tokyo

UNIVERSITY PARK PRESS
International Publishers in Science and Medicine
Chamber of Commerce Building
Baltimore, Maryland 21202

Typeset by The Composing Room of Michigan, Inc.

Printed in the United States of America by Universal Lithographers, Inc.

Library of Congress Cataloging in Publication Data
Main entry under title:

Suicide in different cultures.

Includes index.
1. Suicide—Addresses, essays, lectures.
I. Farberow, Norman L. [DNLM: 1. Suicide. 2. Cross-Cultural comparison. HV6545 S9485]
HV6545.S83 364.1'522 75-29247
ISBN 0-8391-0843-5

Contents

Contributors

Kalle A. Achté, Prof. Dr. Med.
Professor of Psychiatry and Chief of the Clinic
Helsinki University Central Hospital
Helsinki, Finland

Maxwell Atkinson, Ph.D.
Faculty of Economic and Social Studies
University of Manchester
Manchester, England

A. Bogdanova, Dr. Med.
Department of History
The Medical Academy
Sofia, Bulgaria

Maurice L. Farber, Ph.D.
Department of Psychology
University of Connecticut
Storrs, Connecticut, U.S.A.

Norman L. Farberow, Ph.D.
Principal Investigator, Central Research Unit
Veterans Administration Wadsworth Hospital Center;
Co-director, Los Angeles Suicide Prevention Center;
Clinical Professor of Psychiatry (Psychology)
School of Medicine
University of Southern California
Los Angeles, California, U.S.A.

Lee Headley, Ph.D.
Family and Child Psychiatric Medical Clinic
Campbell, California, U.S.A.

Mamoru Iga, Ph.D.
Professor, Department of Sociology
California State University, Northridge
Northridge, California, U.S.A.

Richard A. Kalish, Ph.D.
Professor of Behavioral Sciences
Graduate Theological Union
Berkeley, California, U.S.A.

Jouko Lönnqvist, M.D.
Senior Psychiatrist
Psychiatric Clinic
Helsinki University Central Hospital
Helsinki, Finland

K. Milenkov, K.Sc.
Center for Neurology, Psychiatry, and Neurosurgery
The Medical Academy
Sofia, Bulgaria

Pieter Noomen, Drs. T.
Pastoral Counselor
Voormen Psychiatric Clinic
Upland, California, U.S.A.;
Clergyman, Christian Reformed Church of The Netherlands
Amsterdam, The Netherlands

A. Venkoba Rao, M.D., Ph.D., D.P.M., FRC Psych. (Eng.), F.A.P.A.
Professor and Head, Department of Psychiatry
Madurai Medical College and Erskine Hospital
Madurai, India

Nils Retterstøl, Prof. Dr. Med.
Head, Gaustad Hospital
Professor of Psychiatry
University of Oslo
Oslo, Norway

David K. Reynolds, Ph.D.
Assistant Professor
Department of Human Behavior
School of Medicine
University of Southern California;
Research Anthropologist
Veterans Administration Wadsworth Hospital Center
Los Angeles, California, U.S.A.

Hsien Rin, M.D.
Professor, Department of Neurology and Psychiatry
National Taiwan University Hospital
College of Medicine, National Taiwan University
Taipei, Taiwan

Kjell Erik Rudestam, Ph.D.
Department of Psychology
York University
Downsview, Ontario, Canada

Nikola Schipkowensky, Prof. Dr. Med., Dr. Sc.
University Psychiatric Clinic
Higher Medical Institute
Sofia, Bulgaria

Maria Dorli Simon, Ph.D.
Director
City of Vienna School of Social Work
Vienna, Austria

Nico Speijer, Prof. Dr. Med.
Professor Emeritus in Social Psychiatry
University of Leyden
The Hague, The Netherlands

Kichinosuke Tatai, M.D., M.P.H.
Professor
Tokyo Agriculture University
Tokyo, Japan

John P. Webb, M.A.
Med Start
College of Medicine
Arizona Medical Center
Tucson, Arizona, U.S.A.

William Willard, Ph.D.
Division of Social Perspectives in Medicine
College of Medicine
University of Arizona
Tucson, Arizona, U.S.A.

Nasim Yampey, M.D.
Didact, Argentine Psychoanalytic Institute
Buenos Aires, Argentina

INTRODUCTION

NORMAN L. FARBEROW, PH.D.

All deaths in every country undergo a process of classification and certification. Because feelings and attitudes toward death vary markedly, international commissions have tried to provide classifications of deaths that could be easily applied and comprehensive enough to account for all cases. One purpose has been to make the rates reported for modes of death in one part of the world comparable with the rates reported for the same mode in any other part of the world. The degree of success in making reported rates of different modes of death comparable has been inconsistent. It has been apparent that some kinds of deaths, such as physical illness or natural deaths, and some accidents lend themselves to accurate certification with much greater confidence than others. Suicides, especially, have been difficult to certify, so that comparison between countries, and even within countries in which distinct subcultures are found, is unreliable.

Suicide has been particularly troublesome because it is the only mode of death that depends specifically on a psychological motivation; that is, the death results from a conscious initiation of activities by the decedent that were *intended* to bring about his own demise. This motivation is usually exactly opposite to that found in the other modes of death—natural, accident, and homicide—where death is considered to happen *to* the individual, not *by* him. In actuality, of course, there is a gray area for all the modes of death, including suicide, in which intention plays a variable role, both consciously and unconsciously. Examples include the diabetic who disregards his diet or insulin intake or the cardiac patient who shovels off a heavy snowfall. Likewise, the person who drives his car at high speeds with unsafe brakes or who taunts the robber who is holding him up is risking his life and stands a much higher chance of dying than the person who drives only safe cars safely or who obeys every command of the man robbing him. Yet were the diabetic or heart patient to die, his death would be called natural; were the driver to pile up his car against an abutment, his death would be called accident; and the death of the taunting man at the hands of the robber would certainly be called a homicide. Nevertheless, the contribution of each person to his own death is quite evident.

Equivocal deaths occur among suicides, too. There are many persons who live borderline, poorly adjusted lives and whose behavior is readily seen as self-destructive. One example might be the middle-aged woman who spends her lonely evenings drinking and who often takes pills to put herself more quickly to sleep. Many days she has failed to appear at work because of oversleeping, the result of the combination of liquor and pills. One day, she does not waken at all, the heightened impact of both pills and alcohol having finally taken their toll. Was her death suicide or accident? Certifying authorities will vary.

Such questions were matters of concern in the early years of the Los Angeles Suicide Prevention Center and the Veterans Administration Central Research Unit; they continue to be so to this day. When the suicide rates in different countries were compared, or even regions within the same country, it became very clear that the results could not be viewed with much confidence. The certification of a death as suicide was seen to depend not only on different criteria for self-initiated, self-inflicted deaths, but also on the personnel and procedures used in collecting the information and on the variability in training, experience, and attitudes among the medical examiners and coroners who had the final responsibility for making the judgment of suicide. It also became clear that it would be impossible to understand all the factors playing a role in the certifications of the various modes of death unless the cultural framework within which such an event was embedded was equally clear. For example, through correspondence, we learned that a high frequency of suicide deaths in one of the Central American countries occurred as a result of the ingestion of magnesium. This was a highly unusual method and it was not clear why until discussion with a native of the country revealed that magnesium was one of the main elements in the firecrackers used to celebrate the many national holidays. Since firecrackers were popular and available to all, the lethal chemical was readily at hand when self-destructive impulses occurred.

Ask almost any person what are the countries with the highest suicide rates and the answer will almost inevitably be the Scandinavian countries or Japan. Most people are surprised to learn that Hungary has been at the top of the list published by the World Health Organization for a number of years. They are also surprised to learn that Japan's rate had declined after World War II to a point comparable with and about in the middle of the distribution of rates for most Occidental countries. It has recently begun to climb again in Japan, but the rate still remains close to the middle range.

Most people are also surprised to learn that, although the Scandinavian countries of Sweden, Finland, and Denmark score in the upper range of the reporting countries, Norway, a country with the same general culture, has consistently reported rates in the lower half of the distribution. Explanations have been sought in areas such as parental values, industrialization, and religious backgrounds, but the puzzle remains. One of the reasons frequently offered to explain the higher-than-average rates in Sweden, Finland, and Denmark has been their efficient reporting system. However, this can account for it only in part. The attitudes and feelings about the act of suicide, which are a direct reflection of the cultural background of the countries, must also play a significant role in allowing the more effective system to occur. It is within these elements of the culture of each country, then, that one must seek further in order to understand the phenomenon of suicide throughout the world. These data will add the background to the sociological and psychological factors that determine the personal aspects of the event. In summary, culture will define and direct the way in which suicide occurs, is reacted to, and is reported in the countries of the world. This book is a beginning effort to examine these factors within each country and to identify those influences where possible.

IN THE BEGINNING . . .

The International Association for Suicide Prevention (IASP) holds biannual congresses in various parts of the world where information about activities in suicide and its prevention is exchanged. At the Sixth International Congress in Mexico City in December, 1971, one of the plenary sessions was devoted to a presentation of the cultural factors in suicide in nine countries: Argentina, Finland, India, Israel, Italy, Japan, Mexico, Holland, and the United States. The papers were short but stimulating, and their reception was enthusiastic. Requests for copies were so numerous that the members of the symposium agreed that the papers might be expanded and, with new ones added, a book prepared. Accordingly, each of the contributors was asked to develop his paper further to take advantage of the opportunity to provide more detail than had been possible in his oral presentation. In addition, experts from other countries were asked to prepare original contributions.

A tentative outline was given to each person who was invited to prepare a chapter of the book. Each contributor was specifically asked to avoid presenting the usual tables or rates and epidemiological or demographic distributions, unless he felt such presentations were necessary to illustrate or clarify his comments about the culture he was describing. Each contributor was asked to include in his discussion, insofar as possible, some material around the items in the outline, although he was not limited to them. The areas suggested were:

1. *What has been the historical cultural attitude toward suicide in your country?*

Cultural attitudes toward any phenomenon will vary depending upon the particular era in which that phenomenon is being examined. The contributor was asked to specify any changes in attitude toward suicide in his country as they occurred concomitantly with changes in cultural development.

2. *How has the cultural background of your country influenced the form and frequency of suicide?*

For example, guns and explosives are the most common methods for suicide in the United States. The traditions of privacy, property, and self-determination have played a prominent role in the right of a United States citizen to possess guns. As a result, guns are readily available in many households. On the other hand, self-burning or immolation is common for some Asian countries, especially for women. Each contributor was asked to delineate those influences in his culture which determined the methods used in self-destructive behavior in early times and today.

3. *What has been the influence of the country's geography and climate and of religion on the phenomenon?*

One reason frequently advanced for the high suicide rate in the Scandinavian countries has been the fact that they are so close to the Arctic Circle and thus spend many months of their year in nearly all-day darkness. This does not explain, however, why other countries in similar climatological conditions do not report comparably high rates. Similarly, Catholicism is said to be the reason for the low rate in many countries, such as Italy, Spain, and Ireland. Yet Austria is almost 95 percent Catholic and reports one of the highest rates of any country.

4. *Within the culture of your country, what is the general attitude toward the act today?*

Is suicide considered, for example, brave, courageous, crazy, cowardly, shameful, weak, etc.? This kind of question is of great interest, for example, in the United States where the cherished rights of each person to determine his own fate paradoxically conflict with feelings of shame, embarrassment, and guilt when suicide occurs.

5. *What is the general attitude toward the person who has committed or*

attempted suicide, viz., *sympathetic, understanding, condemnatory, laudatory, etc.?*
6. *What is the attitude toward the survivors,* viz., *embarrassed, ashamed, ignored, disparaged, etc.?*
7. *What are the burial and mourning practices for a committed suicide?*
8. *What reflections on suicide are found in the literature, folk songs, art, etc. of your country? Examples would be desirable.*

Readers will find few tables in the following chapters. The participants were asked to avoid extensive tables, where possible, and to present discussions or narrative accounts rather than compilations of figures and accumulated data. Those tables that do occur have been included because they are needed to illustrate a particular point or provide the data for the comments in the text.

ORGANIZATION OF THE BOOK

Not every country, of course, is represented. Selection of countries for inclusion was out of both choice and necessity. The latter depended on whether an expert in both suicide and culture resided in the country and was interested and available to write a chapter. Some effort was made to obtain representation among as many continents as possible.

The books opens with an overview of the history of suicide, a paper illustrating the variability in attitudes and feelings toward suicide over the past centuries in the different cultures of the world. Then, the Western hemisphere is dealt with first, with suicide in the United States described in several chapters. The first describes the special difficulties in understanding and interpreting the unique significance of suicide among several tribes of American Indians. In each, suicide has its own connotations so that it is inappropriate to generalize to all Indians from the study of one tribe. A second reports a study of cross-ethnic attitudes toward suicide among Caucasians, Blacks, Orientals, and Spanish-Americans, showing the different meanings and impacts of suicide within each subgroup. Two additional chapters (7 and 12) report cross-cultural research by comparing the findings of "psychological autopsies" of suicides in Los Angeles with those in Vienna and with those in Stockholm. Identical questions asked of survivors explored the facts of the death along with personality items, life style, communication, interpersonal, and other factors characterizing this kind of death.

South America is represented by one chapter in which suicide in Buenos Aires, Argentina, is examined, especially as it was influenced by waves of immigration and the forces of acculturation that occurred over several eras in the history of this thriving South American capitol city.

Suicide in the Scandinavian countries is described in reports from Norway by Professor Retterstøl and Finland by Professors Achté and Lönnqvist. Myths and folklore are evaluated for their contributions to today's attitudes. The lower rate in Norway is examined in detail and possible reasons found in the rural, religious and seafaring characteristics of the population. The chapter by Dr. Rudestam which compares suicides in Los Angeles with those in Stockholm by means of the "psychological autopsy," provides much information about the culture of Sweden with its emphasis on achievement and production and its relation to suicide.

Europe is represented by chapters on Britain, Netherlands, Italy, Austria and Bulgaria. Dr. Maxwell Atkinson, sociologist, examines suicide in British culture and emphasizes the problems in choosing between competing versions of cultural influence. The emergence of a strong suicide prevention movement and a marked increase in scientific interest in the problems are, he states, of themselves indications of crucial cultural significance. Two papers on the Netherlands appear. Professor N. Speijer, psychiatrist, in the paper originally presented at the I.A.S.P. plenary session in Mexico City, draws on the depths of his personal studies and work in the government's mental health departments to describe the personality characteristics and social traditions of the Dutch. It has been only since 1945 that suicide in Holland has been transformed from one of the worst "taboo topics" to a subject deserving discussion and social action. An opportunity arose through personal friendship with Pieter Noomen, a minister, to invite an additional chapter on the Netherlands which explores in detail the development of religious and legal viewpoints toward suicide and offers a sensitive evaluation of the church's current attitudes toward it. Suicide in Italy is presented by Dr. Maurice Farber, an American social-psychologist who had just completed a Fulbright Fellowship spent in the examination of psychocultural variables in Italian suicide. The material is related to Farber's previous book, *Theory of Suicide,* in which he expounds on the role of hope in suicidal persons. Another chapter by Drs. Farberow and Simon discusses suicide in Austria by comparing the data obtained through "psychological autopsies" in the suicide deaths in Vienna with those in Los Angeles. Suicide in Bulgaria is examined in a unique study by Schipkowensky, Milenkov, and Bogdanova which focuses on Bulgarian folksongs in which are embedded the various attitudes, myths, and traditions which have accumulated around suicide.

The Middle East is represented by a discussion of suicide in Israel by Dr. Lee Headley, who spent many years living in Israel examining its traditions and cultures. The diverse populations and their separate subcultures emphasize the difficulty in talking about suicide as if it had the same meaning for all Israeli inhabitants. Suicide in India, represented by one chapter, presents the same kind of problem. India has many diverse cultures within a vast country which, like the United States, contains wide variations from region to region and even greater variability in the culture of each region. We learn that *suttee*, the immolation of the widow on the funeral pyre of her husband, was actually an imported custom which became incorporated into the culture of India. Although it saw many abuses with women burned to death against their wishes, one Punjabi tribe saw the custom as a good means of preventing the wife from poisoning her husband. *Suttee* was finally legally banned in 1892, although rumor has it that it still occurs in isolated back regions of the country.

The Far East is represented by a chapter on suicide in Taiwan where the cultural history of suicide is traced in fascinating detail through myths and folklore to illustrate the origin of present day attitudes toward suicide. A second chapter on Oriental suicide examines the suicide of Japan's Nobel Prize winner in literature, Yukio Mishima, in order to illustrate the characteristics of and attitudes toward suicide in Japan. Mishima's death by *hara-kiri* was his expression of a desire to return to the feudal customs and values he prized so highly. Such attitudes valuing authoritarianism apparently still exist along with the strong feelings around love and obligation that have characterized Japanese culture then and now.

CONCLUDING REMARKS

The reader should not expect to find that each chapter will follow the outline suggested, nor will they read the same in style, expression, and grace. No edited book made up of papers from many contributors can ever read as smoothly as a book by one author. The editor of a collection of papers from within one country has a formidable task, but when the papers come from all parts of the world he faces an even more difficult task. The editor cannot help but be filled with admiration for those contributors writing in a language not their own and for their considerable linguistic skill as well as professional expertise. However, not everyone was equally facile in his translation and some of the contributions required considerable editing. Where any such rewriting has occurred, maximal effort was made to express what was felt to be the author's intent. If any inexactness has appeared, the editor assumes full responsibility.

The International Association for Suicide Prevention notes officially its pleasure in the preparation of this volume. The Association's primary objective is stimulating international study and exchange of information, and the book will serve to encourage others to explore, study, and research this pervasive social-psychological-cultural problem as it occurs throughout the world. Only by further study and increased understanding can we hope to improve efforts to control and prevent what is generally accepted as an unnecessary, premature, and often tragic loss of life.

one

CULTURAL HISTORY OF SUICIDE

NORMAN L. FARBEROW, PH.D.

Suicide has been known to man as long as recorded history. However, the word *suicide* is of relatively recent vintage. It does not appear in the Bible nor in the famous pamphlet by John Donne (1644) on self-homicide. One possible derivation is the word "suist," meaning a selfish man, and "suicism," meaning selfishness. In 1671, the third edition of Phillips' *New World of Words* protested against the word "suicide." The index to Jackson's *Works*, published 2 years later in 1673, used the word "suicidium." However, the *Oxford Dictionary* states that suicide was first used in English in 1651, just 6 years after Donne's *Biathanatos*, and is derived from the modern Latin "suicidium," which in turn stems from the Latin pronoun for "self" and verb "to kill."

Viewing suicide from the perspective of its sociocultural history allows a more comprehensive understanding of the phenomenon. Two main threads of self-destruction appear, each present in varying proportions depending on the era. These threads are: 1) social or institutional suicide and 2) individual or personal suicide. The relative degree and importance of each vary in the successive epochs, but both are always present in some degree.

Institutional suicide is self-destruction that society demands of the individual as part of his identification with the group. Institutional suicide has taken many forms, with some existing to this day. Thus, a general

This chapter is reprinted with permission from the Nordiska Bokhandelns. It appeared as a chapter in the book *Suicide and Attempted Suicide* (1972), J. Waldenstrøm, T. Larsson, and N. Ljungstedt, (eds.), a collection of papers originally presented at the Skandia International Symposia, September 29–30, 1971, Stockholm.

attitude of approval arises when the act conforms to the ideals of the society, for example, sacrificing one's life for another. Those institutional suicides that have disappeared did so because they were specific for the age and were felt no longer to serve any good purpose. Not only did institutional suicide prescribe the *occasion* in which the self-destruction was to occur but frequently the *form* it was to take. There were, for example, sacrifices of widows and servants of a great lord or king, or even the sacrifice of the king himself after a prescribed period. One form of institutional suicide was practiced in a country where there were food shortages, and the old and the sick were expected to sacrifice themselves for the good of their group. Among some primitive cultures, suicide was a way of expressing anger and revenge, highly personal motives, but for which the form for expression was nevertheless rigidly prescribed. Thus, in a primitive tribe described by Malinowski (1908), when an individual was accused of having transgressed one of the taboos of the tribe, he climbed to the top of a palm tree, declared his hurt at having been so charged, named who it was that had insulted him, and then plunged head first to his death.

On the other hand, personal suicide was an individual act of protest or declaration against either interpersonal hurts or transgressions against society. The motives were preservation of honor and dignity, expiation of pusillanimity or cowardice, avoidance of pain and ignominy by old age and/or disease, preservation of chastity, escape from personal disgrace by falling into the hands of the enemy, unwillingness to bear the hurt of separation or loss of love, and others.

The overview of suicide also makes it clear that the rate of suicide has been high or low in particular eras in direct relationship with variations in social controls and different emphases on the value of the individual in comparison with the state, such as idealization of reason, rationality, individuality, and democratic processes. Where the controls were greatest the rate was lower; where the individual was more free, the rate was higher. In those eras of greatest social control, the attitudes toward suicide were usually lodged in the emotional, nonrational aspects. For example, in primitive and precivilized areas characterized by a highly structured society, the attitudes could be found in the beliefs of magic and superstitions developed to control social behavior. In more civilized cultures the attitudes became lodged in the beliefs and faith of religion, often incorporating the magical elements from the primitive heritage into the canonical regulations. In the society led by the dictator the attitudes were integrated into the tightly organized, strictly controlled political ideology needed to develop the required loss of self and overidentification with the state. The concepts are similar to those of Bayet (1922), who posited two kinds of morality. The first, *morale simple*, was a primitive morality for the common people developed from religion and superstition; the second, *morale nuancée,* was the morality of the intellectual and had its roots in reason and awareness of the complexities of any human act.

Most of the early writers on suicide were concerned with the rightness or wrongness of the act. Although our interest is divorced from such moralistic evaluations, the early writers reflected the psychocultural history of suicide, providing insights into its extent, form, and characteristics over time. On the one hand, suicide has been strongly condemned. As mentioned above, one has to go back to the early magic of the primitive in order to determine the source of the irrational attitude toward the suicide (Fedden, 1938). It is this irrational attitude that has surrounded the act with horror and antagonism. In primitive societies death has always been a highly tabooed subject; taboos were accumulated around suicide by its very nature, many to ward off the possible evil from a self-inflicted death. Thus, Baganda women were especially fearful of ghosts of suicides who might possibly "impregnate" them, and they threw grass or sticks on the place where the suicide had been buried. The later English custom of burial at a crossroads was directly linked to the primitive custom of burying at a crossroads a child who had been born feet first and so was considered unclean. The taboos later became rituals, practiced for the purpose of purification; the original act became a moral and religious sin.

There were two other reasons for the growth of the strong feeling of revulsion around suicide. First, the fact that a man was rejecting all of the things he prized showed a contempt for society, compelling society to question everything it valued. The second reason was an economic one, for a suicide deprived the tribe of a useful warrior or a potential mother.

Among the earliest of the great cultures, Oriental sacred writings contained many contradictions about suicide. Although it was encouraged in some parts, it was vigorously condemned in others. Brahmanism institutionalized and sanctioned suttee, a ceremonial sacrifice of widows that was as common in China as in India. The Brahman doctrine was sympathetic to suicide, for it was consonant with denial of the flesh, a common objective in philosophies of the Orient. One goal in Oriental mysticism was to divorce the body from the soul so that the soul might occupy itself only with supersensual realities. Buddhism emphasized that through extinction of craving or passion life's chief purpose of acquisition of knowledge could be achieved. Both Brahmanism and Buddhism are religions of resignation and despair. In Japan, suicide became embedded in the national tradition and eventually developed the highly traditionalized rituals of *seppuku* and *hara-kiri*. On the other hand, Mohammedanism always condemned suicide with the utmost severity, for one of the cardinal teachings of Mohammed was that the Divine Will was expressed in different ways and man must submit himself at all times.

Suicide among the Jews was generally rare. The Old Testament expressed the value of life for the Jew. A Jew was permitted to transgress every religious commandment to save his life with the exception of three things: murder, the denial of God, and incest. Suicide in Jewish law was wrong. As a result, when the act did occur, the victim and his family were punished by denial of a regular burial and the customary rituals of mourning. However, suicide was acceptable under extreme conditions, such as apostasy, ignominy, disgrace of capture, or torture. At least four instances of suicide appear in the Old Testament, those of Samson, Saul, Abimelech, and Ahitophael. Samson (Judges 16:28–31) killed himself and the Philistines by pulling the pillars of the temple down; Saul (Samuel 31:1–6) slew himself after defeat in battle to avoid the ignominy of capture; Abimelech (Judges 9:54) killed himself after being mortally wounded by a woman so that it could not be said he had been killed by a woman; and Ahitophael (Samuel 17:1) hanged himself when his betrayal of David to Absalom failed. Talmudic times (200 to 500 A.D.) reported an increasing number of suicides, with a condemnatory tone appearing for the first time.

The most notable instance of mass suicide in Jewish history is probably that of the Zealots who took refuge in Masada on the western shore of the Dead Sea. When capture was inevitable, Eleaszar Ben Jair, the leader, urged his followers to kill themselves rather than to fall in the hands of the enemy. Several versions of the story then occur: one is that each committed suicide; the other, that a plan was drawn to determine for each person to kill one other person, which they all did, including the women and children. There were additional outbursts of suicide among Jews when persecution became intense during the Middle Ages and the early Renaissance. Suicides were also noted in more recent periods of persecution, such as in Nazi Germany, although the records are unclear about this.

In the Greek and Roman periods, the primitive and religious forces weakened. While the attitudes of horror and condemnation for suicide were preserved in the lower classes, the upper classes seemed to develop a different religion and different morals, expressing tolerance and acceptance. Contributing to the latter were the international philosophies that appeared with the establishment of the Roman Empire. This replaced the old city states of Athens and Sparta with their stricter, more localized codes of mores and ethics. The number of suicides grew throughout these periods, mainly from four motivations: 1) to preserve honor, 2) to avoid pain and ignominy, 3) to express bereavement from loss of a loved one, and 4) suicide for the state or for a patriotic cause.

Examples of bereavement suicide are Dido, who preferred to stab herself on her husband's funeral pyre rather than to marry again; Portia, who swallowed red hot coals when she learned of Brutus' death at Philippi; and Paulina, who tried to follow Seneca in death after he had killed himself on Nero's order.

Patriotic suicide is exemplified by Decius Mus, a consul of Rome, who learned that an oracle had proclaimed the battle could be won only by the sacrifice of a Roman noble, and who met certain death by dashing into the ranks of the enemy far ahead of his own troops.

Suicide to avoid pain of sickness or old age was considered quite acceptable. Pliny the Elder considered the existence of poisonous herbs as proof of a kindly Providence because it allowed man to die painlessly and quickly. Seneca says: "I will not relinquish old age if it leaves my better parts intact, but if it begins to shake my mind, if it destroys its faculties one by one, if it leaves me not life but breath, I will depart from the putrid or tottering edifice. I will not escape by death from disease so long as it may be healed and leaves my mind unimpaired. I will not raise my hand against myself on account of pain, for so to die is to be conquered. But if I know that I must suffer without hope of relief, I will depart, not through fear of pain itself, but because it prevents all for which I would live." Zeno, the founder of Stoic philosophy, preached the above doctrine all the way to age 98, apparently without meeting a situation serious enough to warrant his taking his life. At 98, however, he fell down and put a toe out of joint and he was disgusted enough to go home and hang himself.

The death of Cato of Utica was an example of a cool, reasoned death to preserve honor and express patriotism. Cato killed himself out of a concern for his country and for his own principles. When he tried to rally the Republican party at Utica in Libya, he might have been successful except for Scipio's defeat. As Caesar, defeat, and certain slavery approached, he felt he had no other recourse except to kill himself.

The Cynic, Stoic, and Epicurean philosophies of this world fostered an acceptance of suicide while two main lines of thought were in opposition. One was from Pythagoras, who viewed life as a discipline imposed by the gods to which man must submit himself. His theory of numbers lent itself to his position, for he hypothesized there were just so many souls available for use in the world in any given moment. With a suicide the spiritual mathematics were upset, for it might well be that no other soul was ready to fill the gap in the world caused by the sudden exit. The Aristotelians considered suicide an act against the best aims of the state and therefore an act that must be punished. Plato's position was in the middle. In the *Phaedo*, he has Socrates state his position on suicide. Because man is God's child, he is not merely the property but also the soldier of the gods. Suicide is therefore tantamount to desertion. However, in certain cases, such as incurable illness or when God had summoned the soul, suicide is acceptable.

The laws formulated about suicide in this period, primarily among the Romans, became more and more economically oriented. The suicide of a slave or a soldier represented a considerable financial loss to the master or a weakening of the effective force of the Roman armies. Punishments began to be named in the laws, detailing terms of forfeiture and confiscation of estates. A suicide when under arrest robbed the treasury of goods it might have been able to obtain. This loss in revenues was stopped by decreeing that those who killed themselves to escape conviction were without legal successors and their goods were to go to the state.

The advent of Christianity about this time brought with it, at the beginning, a marked indifference to martyrdom. There was pessimism, longing for a better life, a struggle for redemption, and a desire to come before God and live there forever. As a result, suicides occurred in great numbers. A quick halt was brought about by St. Augustine's "City of God" in the 4th century A.D. in which the first codification of the Church's official disapproval of suicide spread. In all of the Middle Ages from about the 4th century to the 12th or 13th, while the Catholic Church held great sway in Europe, suicide became practically unknown.

Until 250 A.D., the attitude toward suicide was the same as before the birth of Christ. Suicide was common, especially among the early Christians. The courage of these martyrs and their disregard of pain was amazing and at times frightening. It was as if nothing could deter them in their active seeking out of death. As the 4th century began, changes appeared, with the Church adopting a hostile attitude that progressed from tentative disapproval to severe denunciation and punishment. Antagonism toward suicide developed. Suicide became proof that the individual had despaired of God's grace, or that he lacked faith and was rejecting God by rejecting life, God's gift to man. As Rome's civilization and influence declined, starting about the 3rd century, the intellectual aspects and characteristics of society also began to dissipate and suicide again became a social crime. These attitudes were not, however, incorporated into the Church from its authorities and intellectuals and then handed down to the people; they were, instead, morals that came from below—a transference of the popular pagan idea into the semi-Christianized world.

St. Augustine produced four arguments to justify the Church's anti-suicide stance: 1) no private individual may assume the right to kill a guilty person; 2) the suicide who takes his own life has killed a man; 3) the truly noble soul will bear all suffering from which the effort to escape is an admission of weakness; and 4) the suicide dies the worst of sinners because he is not only running away from the fear of temptation but also any possibility of absolution. The Council of Arles in 452 A.D. repeated Rome's legislation against suicide by exercising forfeiture of estate, and the Council of Braga in 563 A.D. ordered no religious rites for the suicide.

Three kinds of suicide continued to be accepted: voluntary martyrdom, self-inflicted death of the ascetic, and death of the virgin or married woman to preserve chastity. The Circumcelliones in North Africa almost seemed to enjoy killing themselves (they did in great numbers) when threatened with persecution. Some of the young monastics who chose celibacy and solitary seclusion killed themselves by extreme privation or by a starvation diet. St. Augustine's arguments were used to prevent the rush of women to kill themselves to preserve their chastity by arguing that no woman can lose her chastity by violation, since real virginity was an attribute of the soul and not of the body.

The Antisidor Council of 590 A.D. added for the first time a system of penalties to the condemnation of suicide, and in 1284 the Synod of Nimes invoked the Church's final weapon for prevention, denial of Christian burial. Suicides were buried outside of the church or close beneath the wall. Desecration of the corpse occurred as the body was dragged through the streets and buried at the crossroads, often with a stake through the heart. Odd customs appeared, such as in Danzig when the body of a suicide was not permitted to go out through the door but rather had to be taken out through a window. Sometimes a hole had to be knocked in the wall when there was no window.

There was only one period in the Middle Ages when there was a change from the suicide-horror attitudes that characterized this time. This was the brief era of Charlemagne's rule (768 to 814 A.D.) when intellectual aristocracy and respect for learning and reason flowered. This period saw the first occasion for the use of "suicide because of insanity" as an excuse, an explanation that continues to be used even today as subterfuge to evade antisuicide legislation without an open breach with popular prejudice. After Charlemagne's premature civilization broke up, the old attitudes of absolute condemnation returned.

Outside of the framework provided by the Church during the Middle Ages, there were two main groups where suicide was common: 1) the heretics and 2) the Jews. The most famous suicide martyrs of the Middle Ages were the Albigenses in Southern France. In 1218, some 5,000 were put to death as heretics. There were also many pogroms against the Jews in England, especially in the early years of Richard the Lion-Hearted. On more than one occasion there were mass suicides, such as at York in 1190 when 600 died to escape oppression.

There were still people, however, who attempted suicide out of personal and individualistic motives. One, for example, was Joan of Arc, who attempted suicide while in prison at Beaurevoir. In her trial the bishops used this suicide attempt against her, finding in it one more proof of her susceptibility to the Spirit of Evil.

In the 13th century, Thomas Aquinas in his *Summa Theologiae* formulated the authoritative Church position on suicide for that time. Suicide was absolutely wrong for these reasons: 1) it was unnatural, 2) every man was a member of some community and suicide was therefore antisocial, and 3) life was a gift of God and was not at the disposal of man. About this time the *Inferno* appeared, in which Dante illustrated the current attitudes toward the suicide by condemning him to eternal unrest in the woods of self-destruction.

The Renaissance and the Reformation that followed, however, facilitated a shift in the attitudes toward suicide. The individual began to emerge and values in religion began to change. Luther became the representative of orthodox Protestantism. His ideas caused a shift from absolutism and obedience to personal inquiry and a sense of personal responsibility. The contrast with the rigidified framework of the Middle Ages led man to questions, doubts, and challenges of what had formerly been taken for granted. Along with these, however, came a sense of isolation and self-consciousness. Luther at first fostered reason as a challenge to the principles of the Catholic Church but later became distrustful of the rapidity with which reason spread and he began to condemn it.

Calvinism also appeared about this time, starting first in Switzerland and sweeping across France (Huguenots) to England, while Lutheranism in general became firmly entrenched in Scandinavia. Calvin's opposite approach exalted God and tended to remove Him to a plane of inaccessible superiority. In this way, he tended to minimize and humble man even more and thus raise indirectly the question of the value of the individual human soul. Italy saw a revival of learning and resurrection of ideas that began to diminish the strong feeling of suicide-horror. In France, where Montaigne's writings appeared about this time, the absolute condemnation of suicide disappeared from the enlightened classes but not from among the common people. In England, Sir Thomas More displayed a reasonable attitude toward suicide in his *Utopia,* writing in an unemotional way about euthanasia and certain types of suicide.

As the Renaissance spread and man began to find life more and more intolerable because of his awareness of poverty and lack of a future, he also became more melancholy. Although Death had been an important figure in the concern of the Catholic Church during the Middle Ages, the Renaissance saw a marked intensification of preoccupation with death, with many editions of the *Danse Macabre*, or scenes illustrated by the presence of a skeleton. Literature also began to reflect the melancholy of the time and to show an increasing awareness of psychological complexity. In this period we find Shakespeare producing in-depth psychological studies with such characters as Hamlet, Lear, and Prospero. In his eight tragedies may be found no less than 14 suicides. Two other important literary figures—Burton in 1621 and Donne in 1644—wrote on melancholy and suicide. Burton's *Anatomy of Melancholy* broke sharply with church dogma of the time and questioned the eternal damnation of suicide. Donne's *Biathanatos* dealt with suicide from a practical angle and stated openly that because circumstances alter the cases of suicide, each must be judged individually. Donne's work is the first defense of suicide in English.

Although suicide was now readily tolerated by the educated group, among the lower classes the powerful Church was still staunchly against suicide. Its influence was strong enough to produce reactionary secular legislation in 1670, in which suicide was not merely murder but high treason and heresy. One additional important cultural element appeared about this period, the stigma associated with poverty. In medieval times being poor had not been associated with any moral position; indeed poverty in some groups had acquired a certain mystical importance, mostly from religious association. However, with the rise of commercialism and the advent of Protestantism, there was a drastic change in the attitude of society toward the poor. Social relationships were evaluated from purely economic standards. Puritans talked about rewarding good with prosperity and meting out poverty to evil. Economic failure became a mark of sin. The poor now became both social and moral outcasts and as a result suffered as never before. It was, however, more the change of fortune, a decline from prosperity to poverty, rather than the fact of poverty itself, that accounted for most suicides at that time. The man who was impoverished suddenly found added to his sad lot contempt and damnation.

The 18th century saw further changes in suicide with opposition arising to the prejudice and penalties against suicide. Most activity appeared in France where the liberal currents of criticism and skepticism were expressed by such men as Voltaire (1766), who brought a reasonable approach toward suicide, Rousseau (1761), a romanticized approach, and Montesquieu (1721), for the first time, a criticism of suicide from the point of view of the survivors. Rousseau's work was incorporated into the *Declaration of the Rights of Man*, which inaugurated the French Revolution in 1789.

England developed attitudes of greater tolerance somewhat more slowly than France. The most significant publication at this time was David Hume's *Essay on Suicide* (1783) in which he argued that suicide, if it were to be abhorred, had to be proved a crime against God, neighbor, or self. He pointed out that first it was not a crime against God because He gave man the power to act and therefore death at one's own hands was as much under the control of the deity as if it had proceeded from any other source. Second, suicide was not a breach against neighbor and society, "For a man who retires from life does no harm to society, he only ceases to do good and which, if it is an injury, is of the lowest kind." Third, Hume stated that suicide cannot be a crime against self because he believed that no man ever threw away a life while it was still worth keeping. Poverty continued to be a significant cause of suicide. In 1732, Richard Smith and his wife killed their infant daughter, hanged themselves, and left a long letter addressed to the public describing the hopelessness of poverty and complaining that life was not worth living.

Of those who continued to write against suicide, an important new argument offered by Merian (1763) became equivalent to the first medical theory and separated the arguments from moral theory. Merian stated that suicide was not a crime but an emotional illness. All suicides were therefore in some degree deranged and so did not run counter to the law of nature, a rationalization that led to the Church's use of "suicide while of unsound mind" in later years as a way of skirting Church laws against suicide.

Madame de Staël (1814), writing against suicide in France, argued that living through pain and crisis makes a person a better man so that it was folly to commit suicide. The opinion that crisis may be a turning point in life with positive potentialities is used by some writers today (Morley, 1965). She stated that since God never deserted man, the individual need never feel he was completely alone. Finally, she offered the interesting argument that suicide was against the moral dignity of man, an argument that placed suicide in the opposite camp of the Stoics and Epicureans who felt that suicide helped preserve man's dignity and self-concept.

In England, Bishop Charles Moore (1790) continued the criticism of suicide but was much more lenient, stating that each case of suicide had to be judged on its own merit. In Germany, Immanuel Kant (1797) wrote about the sacredness of human life which therefore must be preserved at all costs. On the opposite side, Goethe's *Sorrows of Werther* (1774) swept across Europe at this time and precipitated an epidemic of suicide. Goethe himself, however, weathered his own emotional traumas and later wrote about the value of work as the one great means toward grace and health.

The 19th century saw Schopenhauer (1851) giving explicit expression to the pessimism characteristic of so much of this era. He has often erroneously been considered an advocate of suicide but actually he ruled against it. His theory is that moral freedom, the highest ethical ideal, can be obtained only by the denial of the will to live. Suicide is not such a denial, for the essence of negation lies in shunning the joys, not the sorrows, of life. The suicide is willing to live but is dissatisfied with the conditions under which life is offered to him.

The greatest change brought about by the 19th century was the introduction and emphasis of the word "disgrace," a social value. This contrasted markedly with the principal words associated with suicide heard in the century preceding, "crime" and "sin." Disgrace was now associated with the feelings of the survivors, the status of the family, friends, and neighbors who remained. This theme was related to an emerging characteristic of this century, *i.e.*, the development of a strong family and middle class status in society. Because it was essential for the family to maintain status within the community, suicide became secretive and hidden, especially for the upper class, as it grew more and more to be associated with insanity.

Another reflection on the social versus the individual aspects of suicide was voiced by Bonser in 1885, who came out strongly against any kind of state interference with suicide. For him these are rights which the individual does not give to society and therefore cannot be taken away from him. Life has been given value primarily by society; actually, in nature it is valueless. Society has no right to demand that others should suffer because it considers life sacred.

During the 19th century the old religious and social groupings, which were the strongest bulwarks against suicide, began to lose effectiveness. Capitalism with its insistence on purely material values added to the difficulties of the suicide, as it exerted a disintegrating force on social life. Capitalism made people more interdependent economically but isolated them socially; cities grew larger and individuals grew more solitary.

Scientific writing on suicide began to appear. Medical theories of the time attempted to fit suicide into the current theories of physiological medicine. For example, it was hypothesized that the act of suicide occurred in people with thick craniums or that it resulted from excess phosphorus in the brain. Esquirol (1838) claimed all suicides were insane, although later Kraepelin (1917) stated that only 30 percent showed symptoms of insanity. Statisticians gathered factual data and investigated quantitative and medical aspects. Writers of this period, such as Lisle (1856), Bertrand (1857), and Brierre de Boismont (1865), felt that suicides had to be judged on their own merits. The last quarter of the century saw researches by Morselli in Italy (1882), O'Dea in America (1882), Legoyt in France (1881), and Strahan in England (1893).

Durkheim's *Le Suicide* in 1897 was one of the most important books to appear with the viewpoint that suicide as a collective phenomenon was influenced by specific factors characterizing the society in which it appeared. Essentially, the theme was that where social solidarity was strong there would be little suicide, where it was weak there would be more.

Legal changes saw abolishment of the laws prescribing desecration of the corpse and forfeitures for penal offenses. In 1882, the maximal sentence for attempted suicide was reduced to 2 years. By the end of the century the law punished only attempted suicide and aiding and abetting suicide. In France, the attitude toward suicide followed the fluctuations of French politics. When the liberal legislation of the Code Napoleon was overthrown, suicides and their survivors were punished; when liberty and democratic government re-appeared, the rights of the suicides were respected.

In 1897, William James wrote his famous essay, "Is Life Worth Living?", in which he concluded that man did not commit suicide primarily because of his religious faith. For James, religion was belief in the existence of an unseen order in which one believed only because of faith, not our incomplete knowledge based on science. It was faith that helped man to believe, even in deep depression, that life was still worth living.

The attitudes toward suicide today are reflected in the laws of the various countries of the world. Suicide continues to be a sin in canonical law, especially of the Catholic Church. However, the practical attitude is one of leniency and frequent use of the terminology, "suicide while of an unsound mind." A study of Roman and Greek priests in their parishes in Los Angeles, dealing with suicides and their survivors, indicated that rarely was burial denied or opprobrium attached to the family (Demopolous, 1968). To some degree, the attitude toward suicide of predominantly Catholic countries is reflected in their unusually low rates, such as in Italy, Spain, and Ireland. However, studies have shown that in many instances suicides are certified under another mode, such as "accident" or "natural." Paradoxically, in some Catholic countries, such as Austria, the opprobrium does not exist and the rate of suicide is high. Personal communications with investigators from Austria have indicated that Catholicism as practiced in Austria today is considered neither strict nor intense.

In many of the Middle European countries, secular law continues to hold attempted suicide a crime. Usually this results in registration of suicide attempts, probably permitting better statistics; Austria, the Soviet Union, and Hungary are examples. England abolished the statute against attempted suicide in 1961. American law retains a statute against attempted suicide in 7 of its 50 states but considers aiding and abetting suicide a crime in 18 of them. Likewise, abetting suicide is still punishable in Germany, Hungary, Russia, Holland, Japan, and Italy. In most laws today the presumption is almost always against suicide and in favor of death from natural causes. Suicide is not generally found unless the evidence excludes every other reasonable hypothesis.

In the past, accusations have been made that the extensive social welfare programs in Scandinavian countries have contributed to the higher suicide rates. Social welfare is an important characteristic of Scandinavian culture. These countries in comparison with others represent probably the most advanced level of concern of a state for its citizens through all aspects of their lives. Dr. Ruth Ettlinger, a prominent investigator of suicides in Sweden, found in her 1964 follow-up of attempted suicides a significant excess of social-minus factors among people who later committed suicide versus those who died a natural death or who were still alive. Suicide was found, in other words, to be related to people whose social contacts were characterized more by "incomplete welfare" than by loss of contact or interest in society.

Ruth Link (1969) in a popular article in *Sweden Now* explained Sweden's higher suicide rate by pointing out that Sweden has the world's most reliable statistics, that autopsies are performed routinely, that there are fewer moral and religious taboos against suicide, that Sweden has a very low birth rate and a predominance of older people, and that if unpredicted deaths are viewed as a whole (including accidents and homicides), Sweden's figures are similar to those of most other Western countries.

The above comments on Sweden illustrate the value of knowing the cultural background in which suicide appears. Cultural history provides a perspective for viewing suicide as it has been influenced by religion, law, philosophies, and thought. Deeper understanding permits more reasonable reactions and, especially, improvement in treatment approaches.

REFERENCES

Aquinas, T. 1947. *Summa Theologiae*, reprint of the first edition. Benziger Brothers, New York.

Augustinus, A. 1950. *De Civitate Dei* (The City of God, Books I–VII), reprint, Vol. 8. Fathers of the Church, New York.

Bayet, A. 1922. *Le Suicide et La Morale.* Librairie Felix Alcan, Paris.

Bohannan, P. *et al.* 1960. *African Homicide and Suicide.* Princeton University Press, Princeton, N.J.

Bertrand, L. 1857. *Traite du Suicide, Considere dans ses Rapports avec la Philosophie, la Theologie, la Medecine et la Jurisprudence*. J. B. Bailliere, Paris.

Bonser, T. O. 1885. *The Right to Die*. A paper read before the Dialectical Society of London, the Richmond Athenaeum and the Deptford Branch of the NSS. Freethought Publishing Company, London.

Brierre de Boismont, J. F. 1865. *Du Suicide et de le Folie Suicide*. Librairie Germer Bailliere, Paris.

Burton, R. 1621. *The Anatomy of Melancholy*, reprint of the first edition, 1881. Chatto and Windus, London.

Demopolous, H. 1968. *Suicide and Church Canon Law*. Unpublished doctoral dissertation, Claremont School of Theology, California.

De Staël (Staël von Holstein), G. S. 1814. *Reflexions sur le Suicide*. H. Nicolle, Paris.

Devereux, G. *Mohave Ethnopsychiatry and Suicide. The Psychiatric Knowledge and the Psychic Disturbances of an Indian Tribe*. Smithsonian Institution, Bureau of American Ethnology, Bulletin 175, U.S. Government Printing Office, Washington D.C.

Donne, J. 1930. *Biathanatos*, reprint of the first edition, 1644. Facsimile Text Society, New York.

Durkheim, E. 1897. *Le Suicide*. Librairie Felix Alcan, Paris. (Reprint 1912, J. S. Spaulding and G. Simpson, Translators. The Free Press of Glencoe, New York, 1951).

Esquirol, J. E. D. 1838. *Mental Maladies: A Treatise on Insanity* (Translated by E. K. Hunt) Lea and Blanchard, Philadelphia 1845; Hefner, New York, 1965.

Ettlinger, R. 1964. Suicides in a group of patients who had previously attempted suicide. *Acta Psychiatrica Scandinavica*, 40:363, 378.

Fedden, R. 1938. *Suicide: A Social and Historical Study*. Peter Davies, London.

Goethe, J. W. von. 1774. *Die Leiden des Jungen Werther*. In the Weggandschen Bookstore, Leipzig.

Hume, D. 1929. *An Essay on Suicide*, reprint of the first edition, 1783. Kahoe and Company, Yellow Springs, Ohio.

James, W. 1927 Is life worth living? In: *The Will to Believe*, p. 27, reprint of the first edition, 1897. Longmans, Green & Company, New York.

Kant, W. 1971. *The Metaphysic of Ethics* (Translators J. W. Semple, T. & T., Clark, Edinburgh, 1797).

Kraeplin, E. 1917. *Lectures on Clinical Psychiatry* (Authorized translation from the 2nd German edition, revised and edited by Thomas Johnstone, 3rd English edition, Wood, New York).

Kraus, H. H. 1970. A cross-cultural study of suicide. *Journal of Cross-Cultural Psychology*, 1, No. 2: 159, 167.

Legoyt, A. 1881. *Le Suicide Ancien et Moderne. Etude Historique, Philosophique, Morale et Statistique*. A Drouin, Paris.

Link, R. 1969. Suicide: The deadly game. *Sweden Now*, 12: 40–46.

Lisle, P-E. 1856. *Du Suicide: Statistique, Medecine, Historie et Legislation*, J. B. Bailliere, Paris.

Malinowski, B. 1908. Suicide: A chapter in comparative ethics. *Sociology Review* 1: 14.

Merian, 1763. *Sur la Crainte de la Mort, Sur le Mepris de la Mort, Sur le Suicide, Memoire*. In volume (tome) XIX of the Histoire de l'Academie Royale des Sciences et Belles-Lettres de Berlin, pp. 385, 392, and 403.

Montesquieu, C. L. 1721. *Persian Lettres (Letter LXXVI)*. John Davidson, Paris (Trans. George Routledge and Sons, Ltd, London).

Moore, C. 1790. *A Full Enquiry into the Subject of Suicide*. Rivington, London.

Morley, W. E. 1965. Treatment of the patient in crisis. *Western Medicine,* 3: 77.

Morselli, E. A. 1892. *Suicide: An Essay on Comparative Moral Statistics*. D. Appleton and Company, New York.

Noyes, R., Jr. 1968. The Taboo of Suicide. *Psychiatry*, 31 No. 2: 173–183.

O'Dea, J. J. 1882. *Suicide: Studies on its Philosophy, Causes and Prevention*. G. P. Putnam's Sons, New York.

Pretzel, P. W. 1968. Philosophical and ethical considerations of suicide prevention. *Bulletin Suicidology*, July.

Rousseau, J. J. 1761. *La Nouvelle Heloise*: Lettres 21 et 22, Paris.

Schopenhauer, A. 1851. On suicide. In: *Complete Essays of Schopenhauer*. T. B. Saunders, Wiley, New York.

Strahan, S. A. K. 1893. *Suicide and Insanity*. S. Sonnenschein & Company, London.

Voltaire, F. M. A. 1766. *De Caton, du Suicide, et du Livre de l'Abbe de Saint-Cyran qui Legitime le Suicide*.

Westermarck, E. 1908. *Origin and Development of the Moral Ideas,* Vol. II, pp. 229–264. Macmillan & Company, London.

two

SIX AMERICAN INDIAN PATTERNS OF SUICIDE

JOHN P. WEBB, M.A., and WILLIAM WILLARD, PH.D.

Suicide is believed to occur at a higher rate among the American Indians than in any other subgroup of the American population. A close examination of the research on American Indian self-destructive behavior throws doubt on this belief for two reasons: 1) the difficulty in discerning any one common American Indian suicide pattern, and 2) the absence of any reports of suicide in many studies of American Indian groups. The too ready acceptance of statistical surveys without some knowledge of the cultures of the American Indian groups leads to the continuation of these questionable assumptions. Spradley (1973) has made this point in the support of ethnographic studies that reveal the culture of disparate groups within the American society. Spradley (1973) cited Baratz in "Writing about Black Americans." "We have not seen Afro-American culture as a distinct culture. We have treated it as a disturbed form of Western culture" (p. 32).

It is our contention that many of the current studies of American Indian suicide are examples of the mistake of viewing American Indian cultures as disturbed forms of Euro-American culture, and therefore to be treated within the same framework as that used for disturbed Euro-Americans. This "disturbed framework" is readily identified in those studies that have made observations on specific local groups and generalized them to all American Indians. It is our thesis that this ethnocentrism is misleading and does not help in understanding the multicultural nature of American Indian society.

It is curious that the pronouncement of a high suicide incidence among all American Indians has been so uncritically accepted. From the "disturbed framework" viewpoint, conventional suicide prevention programs, designed for and by Euro-Americans, have been applied with only the most minimal adjustments to a variety of conditions, such as areas without telephones, and Indians reluctant to talk to nongroup members about suicidal feelings. It almost seems that no one has really asked the question, "Does a hot-line telephone service have much relevance either to urban Indians or to reservation Indians?"

An anecdote from a recent conversation with a colleague who is employed by a large mental health service will illustrate our point. During 1972, representatives of the mental health service program met with the members of a tribal council of the local Indian group to discuss priorities in the delivery of mental health services. The tribal councilmen identified a suicide prevention program as their top priority. The people from the mental health program were intrigued by this priority because, to their knowledge, suicide almost never occurred in the area among either the Indians or non-Indians. Further discussion turned up two interesting items of information. First, the councilmen, when pressed, could recall just two suicides of tribal members over the past 25 years. Both men had been prisoners-of-war in Asian prison camps, one in World War II and the other during the Korean War. However, the tribal councilmen had attended a series of mental health workshops, each of which had identified suicide as the number one American Indian mental health problem. Therefore, despite evidence to the contrary, they accepted what they had been told.

The literature on American Indian suicide includes six cultural divisions: Navajo, Shoshone, Papago, Dakota, Cheyenne, and Apache. Among each of these groups are discernible differences in the patterns of self-destructive behavior. These differences reflect very diverse cultures interacting with the dominant Euro-American culture. In some cases an acculturation process seems to be generating suicides; in other cases the discussion of acculturation in relation to suicide is not relevant. Nor are these six Indian groups representative of all American Indian suicide or even of all the research done on Indian suicide. However, they do illustrate some of the variation. For example, suicides among Alaskan natives have not been included in this paper because a very comprehensive study is being conducted by Dr. Robert Krause at the present time. Any discussion on Alaskan natives' suicides at this time would be based only on supposition. Most of the research on American Indian suicide has been done either to rationalize the establishment of a suicide prevention program or to evaluate the results of one. In this paper we suggest patterns of suicide based on previous research, independent of programmatic consideration.

STATISTICS AND AMERICAN INDIAN SUICIDES

In order to understand American Indian suicides, one must understand how statistics have been used in determining suicide rates, where they are of value and where they are misleading. In mental health, suicide statistics have generally been used to identify groups in need of mental health services. For example, rising rates among adolescent and youth groups have indicated the need for more prevention activities directed toward them. Suicide statistics have also been used to justify both local and national mental health programs for American Indian groups. Suicide statistics for American Indians have been quoted extensively in the popular media, such as the statement that some reservations have a suicide rate 10 times the national average.

Reporting and certifying American Indian suicide statistics causes further overemphasis in comparison with Anglo suicides because the latter are usually under-reported as a result of cultural values, insurance claims, denial by the attending physician, or the wish by the physician to protect the surviving family and friends of the suicide. In two examples in Anglo culture, attitudes toward reporting of suicides have been hypothesized as the basis for seemingly high rates. Thus, Sweden (Rudestam, 1970) and San Francisco (Donovan and Nash, 1962) are reputed to have exceptionally good suicide reporting systems and fewer inhibitions in accepting suicides. This has resulted in higher rates of reported suicide than in other populations with less efficient reporting systems.

The problem of reporting American Indian suicide is acute. Prior to Anglo contact, none of the Indian groups within the United States had a written language. They had very well developed oral traditions, but no written records. Thus, the possibility of having written reports of Indian suicides could not begin until Anglo contacts first occurred. However, these early colonists, missionaries, trappers, and conquistadores were not interested in making detailed written observations. The first systematic reporting of native American Indian behavior did not begin until reservations were established and the take-over of the American Indians by Federal bureaucracy was initiated. On the reservations, the early reporting systems depended on the disposition of the man in charge. Although volumes of annual reports are available from the reservations, they have never been systematically examined to establish the incidence of suicide during the formative periods of the reservations. As a result, the suicide rates on the early reservations are unknown. The American Indians have run the gamut from having no recorded history to becoming one of the most highly documented collection of peoples in the world. For example, when American Indian reservations became a part of the Public Health

System, every clinic contact was recorded. Presently, this information is stored in computers.

Although the reporting system used on the reservations casts doubt on any use of American Indian suicide statistics in comparison to the country as a whole, there are still other factors. The population of the American Indians is very small in relation to that of the nation as a whole. The total population is usually around 600,000 but this varies between 455,000 and 650,000, depending on the means used to classify American Indians (Ogden, Spector, and Hill, 1970). With such a small population base, localized occurrences and conditions can have a marked effect on the national statistics; for example, a sudden spate of just nine suicides among the Dakotas would raise the rate for the American Indians nationally by 1.5 (using 600,000 as the population base).

The demographic characteristics of the American Indian population are different from that of the nation. It is, first of all, a younger age group, with over 50 percent under 20 years of age. It is also a highly mobile population with much movement between reservation and cities. There are also special features, such as a trend for the more successful Indian to no longer rely on medical service from the Indian Health Agency, and thus drop out of the Native American statistics, and to repudiate his "Indianness." (With the rise of pan-Indianism, this trend has reversed.)

In summary, the statistics about Indian suicides that have been gathered in many studies in the past are of little value. The character of the population, the nature of the reporting system, and the movement of the population between reservations and cities all combine to make Indian suicide statistics a very complicated set of data and to make any comparison with the nation as a whole meaningless as an aid to understanding Indian suicide.

The wide-ranging differences in the specific characteristics of six of the American Indian subcultures will illustrate our thesis.

THE SHOSHONE INDIANS

The Shoshone Indians are important in the study of American Indian suicide (despite the fact that they are small in number, less than 5,000), because of the quality of the research on them. They have been studied frequently, and it is these investigations that are most often quoted when American Indian suicides are referred to by both the American public and the mental health professionals.

Before the white man came, the Shoshone roamed the Great Basin desert of Nevada, Idaho, and Utah in extended-family size bands, mostly living off plants and small animals. They adopted some of the Plains culture but never had access to the large buffalo herds to provide abundance. Some large game hunting did occur (the killing of a deer had ceremonial significance in becoming a man), but basically life consisted of using all that was available to live a very marginal existence in one of this continent's harshest environments (hot and dry in the summer and cold and windblown in the winter). Now, the Shoshone are found on small reservations in Idaho, Wyoming, and Nevada. These reservations lack employment opportunities, and the Shoshone are still living a marginal existence. The difference is that they are surrounded by the abundance of others.

The Indian suicide rate of 100 per 100,000, or 10 times the national average, was derived on a Shoshone reservation. There have been studies from two Shoshone reservations indicating a very similar suicide pattern (Shore et al., 1972; Reznik and Dizmang, 1970). This pattern is characterized by an extremely high rate of suicide among adolescent males who have been found to have many problems in school, have often dropped out of school, have experienced difficulties with the law, and have records of abusing alcohol and sniffing solvent. A high level of family disorganization with deaths of significant members appears frequently. Unemployment and other economic problems are also found in association with these suicides. One member of the Shoshone tribe (Crum, 1972), commenting on the relationship between suicide and economic conditions, stated that most of the traditional Shoshone culture is still present, but he did not discuss how this relates to youth suicides. Some of the other very important questions for understanding suicide in the Shoshone tribe, such as their conception of death and postdeath and the presence or absence of an institutionalized pattern of suicide in the indigenous culture, were not explored.

Although the picture of suicides among Shoshone youth is tragic, its use in generalizing to all American Indians and in setting national policy based on it is dangerous. The Shoshone pattern is, at this point, only a Shoshone pattern. There is need for further study even to understand that pattern better.

THE PUEBLO INDIANS

The Pueblo Indians have varied so much, depending on time and place, that the suicide patterns derived from available data either have created a picture of suicide that is so complicated as to be incomprehensible or have glossed over the variations so completely that validity is questionable. The

Pueblo Indians represent peoples with at least eight different language stocks who are commonly grouped together because they live in the same close communities and share a common culture and history. The Pueblo peoples have interacted intensely with European culture for the last 400 years yet have been able to maintain much of their precontact culture despite many attempts to eradicate it. Over these 400 years some Pueblo groups have acculturated to the dominant culture much more than have others. Levy (1965), in his article on Navajo suicide, pointed to the more traditional Pueblos as having lower suicide rates than the more acculturated Pueblos. However, this as yet has not been completely demonstrated.

The general pattern of suicide among the Pueblos has not been studied. Every indication is that the Pueblos do not represent a unified group for whom generalizations on suicidal behavior are meaningful. Among the eight Pueblo groups listed in Levy (1965) the range in suicide rates over a 10-year period was from zero to about three times the rate of the surrounding region. This pattern is not consistent with time. One Pueblo subgroup listed by Levy (1965) as having an extremely low suicide rate had four suicides in the year following his study. As a result this group would now have a high rate. The opportunities for research that lead to a better understanding of self-destructive behavior are great among the Pueblos. Some Pueblos have almost no suicides while others have suicides every year.

The Suicide Pattern of One Pueblo

One of the authors (Webb) studied the pattern of suicide in one of the more acculturated Pueblo groups. This group was selected 1) because it had a high suicide rate [second highest among the eight Pueblos with populations over 1,000 (Levy, 1965)], and 2) because the people would be more amenable to discussing suicides with a researcher. These data are representative only of the one Pueblo studied and were taken from statistics prepared by the state of New Mexico and from Public Health Service records. There were 15 suicides over an 11-year period. Fourteen of these suicides were male while 1 was female. There were two age clusters, one representing adolescents and young adults age 16 to 23, while the other grouped in the late twenties. The 11 recorded years, from 1960 to 1971, showed great variation. Six years had no suicides; 3 years had 1 suicide; 2 years had 3 suicides, and 1 year, 1970, had 6 suicides. There was also very wide variation among communities, with 8 of the 15 suicides belonging to one community, although that village contained only one-fifth of the population.

The suicide pattern from this one Western Pueblo shows great diversity. The authors feel that the two age clusters may represent two separate suicide patterns functioning simultaneously. The five suicides clustered in the late twenties might represent an old pattern reflective of the difficulties of males adjusting to a matri-local society (Levy and Kunitz, 1971). The six suicides grouped in the late teens and early twenties (the one female was age 16) reflect the acute acculturation pressures experienced by adolescents (Allen, 1972).

An interesting observation by one of the Pueblo informants was the statement that suicides, excessive drinking, and other antisocial experiences were expected in some families. On the other hand, one suicide by the son of a man high in the ceremonial structure was looked upon as indicative of serious social problems.

THE DAKOTA AND CHEYENNE INDIANS

The study of American Indian suicides presents both difficulties and opportunities to understand how self-destructive behavior relates to adaptation. This is most apparent in the study of suicide among the Plains Indians. The difficulties they present include a marked reluctance to talk with nongroup members about death and a self-destructive pattern that does not show up as suicide on the mortality records. The opportunities lie in understanding how institutionalized patterns of suicide can be reapplied to deal with the stresses of acculturation.

The Dakota and Cheyenne are members of the Plains tribes that feasted on buffalo and fought the cavalry. Their gallant struggle for survival created the great American Indian myth; their warriors staffed the Wild West shows at the turn of the century.

There have been more studies of suicidal behavior among the Plains groups than there have been of any other peoples except the Navajo. Unfortunately, they have generated much smoke and little light. For example, none of the four articles written on Plains Indian suicide (Dizmang, 1967; Mendell and Stuart, 1968; Curlee, 1969; Maynard and Twiss, 1969) documented a suicide. Each report identified patterns in the suicide attempts they studied, but then generalized these to Indian (completed) suicide. One report (Dizmang, 1968) did not even discuss completed suicides. All the papers, on the other hand, did raise a significant alternative question, *i.e.*, why do the Plains Indians groups, who have suffered such great acculturation stress, manifest so few or no suicides?

We feel that in reality the Plains Indians groups do have a high prevalence of suicide, but that this suicide rate is masked by an institutionalized pattern of suicide through extreme risk taking. Mendell and Stuart (1968) pointed to this possibility but did not document it. During the early Anglo-contact period a pattern of institutionalized suicide seemed to emerge among the Plains groups, a pattern described by Wissler (1916) as "Crazy-Dog-Wishing-To-Die." This is a role or status assumed by a member of the tribe because of mourning or because of an affront. Once a man has declared himself a Crazy-Dog, he is obligated to do everything backwards; that is, he must say the opposite of what he means and must attack the enemy until he or they are killed. An account of one such incident in Wissler (p. 197) tells the story of a Crow Crazy-Dog who attacked a group of Dakotas:

> Spotted-Rabbit (a Crow Crazy-Dog) mounted and rode through the camp singing, followed by his mother. The Crows went towards the hills where the Dakotas were. They espied a humpback Dakota Crazy-Dog and stopped, but Spotted-Rabbit went straight on towards the Dakota, who was waiting for him. The Dakota shot Spotted-Rabbit in the chest and killed him.

Compare this report with the account of an automobile accident of Melvin One Crow as described in the more modern study of Maynard and Twiss (1969, p. 167):

> Twice during the final week of Melvin One Crow's life he dreamed of a man 'all black' . . . The afternoon of October 14 was spent drinking in White Clay with his friends and glasses were raised to 'happy growing to your child.' It was still daylight when Melvin walked out of the bar alone, got into his car and started toward Pine Ridge village. He weaved back and forth across the road and turned around, driving back on the wrong side of the road. Near Moccasin Park a head-on collision occurred with a car filled with passengers. (Melvin One Crow was killed.)

Both of these deaths seem very similar in form. Both were declared in advance, in the first case by wearing the sash of a Crazy-Dog, in the second case by the discussion of the dream. Both cases represent a deliberate seeking of a headlong rush into death. Of course, an explanation of a cultural pattern cannot be based on one case. The Sioux (Maynard and Twiss, 1969) have a high death rate from accidents (second highest cause of death), while they report no deaths from suicide. Again this is not proof, but the continuation of the Crazy-Dog pattern certainly seems worthy of investigation. Personal communication with an anthropologist who has spent years researching the Sioux (although never directly dealing with suicide) indicates that the "Crazy-Dog" pattern of suicide, where death comes from another's hand, continues. Men walk across freeways and barroom brawls are fought to lose; both point to homicide or accident as a form of self-initiated deaths.

THE UTO-AZTECAN SPEAKERS OF THE SOUTHWESTERN DESERT

Much of the discussion in this paper emphasizes the importance of the Indian group's pre-Anglo culture in explaining suicidal behavior. Among the Uto-Aztecan speakers of the Southwest suicide is a new phenomenon. In some communities suicide is considered a major indication of the breakdown of the "old ways;" in other communities, although suicides are beginning to appear, they are still officially denied (Conrad, 1972). In still other communities self-destructive behavior through drug and alcohol abuse and victim-precipitated homicide are beginning to concern community leaders.

The Pima, Papago, and Yaquis, all speakers of dialects of the Uto-Aztecan language and predominantly farmers in the Sonoran Desert, are being considered together because of insufficient research on suicide patterns among the separate groups. Much of our information was collected from conversation with members of these tribes and lacks the validity of a well controlled study.

Suicide is believed to be a new phenomenon among these groups. A family that has been traditionally the keeper of one community's cemetery reports that suicide was virtually unknown until about 10 years ago. Now almost all burials are the result of a violent death, with suicides occuring two or three times a year. (The population of the community is less than 1,000). The one formal study of suicide among the Papago (Conrad, 1972) lists 10 suicides over a 3-year period. These suicides were predominantly male (9 to 1), the methods chosen being firearms (6), hanging (3), and drug overdose (1). Eight of the nine male suicides were between the ages of 20 and 29 years. Alcohol consumption was involved in eight of the 10 suicides.

One of the Indian communities on the edge of a metropolitan area reported only one suicide in a 20-year period. However, there is concern that the danger of suicide is growing. Recently there has been an increase in suicide attempts and other self-destructive behavior among the youth. At least one homicide showed signs of being victim-precipitated.

A poem in a reservation newspaper, *Red Giant*, begins "Indian mother attempts suicide . . . (but the party goes on)." Groups that had adopted many of the Catholic values concerning suicide are alarmed by this increase. The problem appears to occur primarily among men in their twenties. There is evidence of an increase in self-destructive behavior, expressed by victim-precipitated homicide, alcohol abuse, and drug abuse. The rise in suicidal behavior is seen by the community leaders, as well as by the village members, as an indication of serious community breakdown.

THE WHITE MOUNTAIN APACHE INDIANS

Suicide and homicide among the White Mountain Apaches are very closely related. This relationship, as described by Apache informants, occurs in particular situations in which the only options available to an individual seem to be either to kill oneself or to kill another. The rise in female suicides among the Apaches over the last 10 years is a part of this suicide-homicide system.

The White Mountain Apaches live in a portion of the same area in which they were living at the time of Euro-American conquest. Their reservation is located in the central mountain region of Arizona. The early patterns for subsistence, consisting of farming, hunting and gathering, and raiding have been replaced by a welfare and tribal industry economy. Generally, the industries are managed by non-Apaches. The Apaches have a reputation for wild drinking sprees, but a relatively low rate of death from cirrhosis of the liver (Levy and Kunitz, 1969).

Apaches are popularly thought to be highly aggressive. This reputation, at least in American myths, is supported by tales of homicides, clan feuds, and spectacular suicides through self-immolation. The reports on Apache suicide and homicide provide some support to these myths. Levy and Kunitz (1969) reported a homicide rate of 133 per 100,000 population during the early reservation period. Reports are contradictory on the pattern and rate of suicide. Levy and Kunitz (1969) stated that White Mountain Apache suicides have been fairly constant since the 1880's, while Everett (1972) reported a very low suicide rate before 1930, and a much higher rate following 1930. Only two suicides were reported from 1880 to 1930, while 56 confirmed suicides were reported from 1930 to 1970. The greatest increase in the occurrence of suicide was from 1930 to 1950. The rate seemed to level off in the 1950's and 1960's at a fairly high level, 50 per 100,000 (Everett, 1972; Levy and Kunitz, 1969). One of the clinically interesting features of the increase in suicide over the 40-year period between 1930 and 1970 has been the increase in female suicides. During the 1930's the male to female rate was four to one, but by the 1960's it had developed to 0.06 male suicides to every one female suicide. Whatever the increase in the total White Mountain suicides, much of it can be attributed to an increase in female suicides.

Everett (1972) presented a description of the interpersonal dynamics surrounding White Mountain Apache suicides. He researched the 56 suicides that occurred since 1930 and found that 32 of the suicides followed arguments with a spouse or kinsman. The other main categories of events preceding a suicide were either a homicide (four cases) or an assault (four cases). A characteristic of Apache suicide is the use of highly lethal methods. Thirty-two out of the 35 male suicides used a gun while 16 of the 21 female suicides used burning. Everett's informants talked of the relationship between aggression and suicide. As one man expressed it (p. 40): "In the old days, a person could murder someone he was mad at. But now he will be arrested and punished. Now the only way to show a person how much he has hurt you is to go kill yourself. That will show him."

The White Mountain Apaches include in their subculture examples of several of the forces that have been significant in shaping Indian suicide. All of the Apache groups in prereservation days expressed much outer group aggression; their raids and their vendettas usually followed the killing of a clan member. With the advent of the reservation system the raiding and the warfare decreased, and the punishment of murders and assaults was the obligation first of the Army managing the reservation and then of the tribal courts and the police. The adjustment to the reservation system can be seen in the reduction of homicides. The question whether the suicides represent a turning inward of aggression, which in prereservation times would have been expressed outwardly, is one which may be applied to the understanding of Apache suicide. The precipitating event in 43 out of the 56 suicides researched by Everett (1972) was verbal fighting, or "bad-words" as the Apaches call it, usually with a kinsman or spouse. In eight cases an aggressive act of either homicide or assault occurred prior to suicide. Everett's informants, in explaining the meaning of suicide, said that if you really want to hurt someone you kill yourself rather than him, leaving him to deal with the grief and the community's accusations. Thus there is a very aggressive element to suicide. But aggression toward kinsmen, even during prereservation times, was unacceptable in the Apache culture. It would appear that the White Mountain Apache suicide pattern is basically aboriginal, a means of expressing unacceptable aggression toward a spouse or kinsman, or the result of actually expressing the unacceptable aggression. In the last 10 years there has been a rise in female suicides through burning with kerosene (Everett, 1972). They appear to be primarily expressions of aggression toward a spouse or kinsman, reflecting the combination of a prereservation pattern with a new institutionalized method.

THE NAVAJO INDIANS

One of the greatest problems in studying the suicide pattern of any American Indian group is the lack of research. With the Navajo this problem is not present. There have been extensive ethnographic studies of the Navajo, and a comprehensive picture of Navajo suicide can be drawn.

This picture contradicts sharply the belief that American Indian suicides result from the pressures of acculturation and from the stressful environment of the Indian reservations. The Navajos are a branch of the Athabascan speaking people who had moved into the Southwest in the two or three centuries preceding the Spanish conquest. They occupied the open desert regions while the Pueblo Indians farmed the river valleys. The arrival of the Spanish provided the Navajos with villages to raid, with sheep to herd, and with silver to work into jewelry, an art learned from the Spanish. The famed Navajo rugs represent weaving learned from the Pueblos. The Navajo culture is thus one based on the incorporation of new ideas and the utilization of new economic resources. The implication that the Navajo culture has remained static and has resisted acculturation changes ignores the ethno-history of the Navajo people. Presently, they are a most important tribal group for several reasons. First, with over 100,000 members, they are numerically the largest Indian group in the country. Secondly, the large Navajo reservation with its picturesque canyons and rugged monoliths represents the "ideal" setting for American Indians; it has been used in numerous movies for this reason.

The Navajo believe that any death which is not the result of old age is unnatural. they believe that any contact with the dead is dangerous and that contact with a violent death is almost certain to cause some sickness or bad luck. Kluckhohn and Leighton (1946, pp. 184–185) have written:

> The intense and morbid avoidance of the dead and of everything connected with them rests upon the fear of ghosts. . . . A ghost is the malignant part of a dead person. It returns to avenge some neglect or offense. . . . Ghosts may chase people, jump upon them, tug their clothes, or throw dirt upon them. Not only are their actions frightening in themselves but they are omens of disaster to come.

This belief in ghosts is still an important force on the Navajo reservation. A program administrator reports that most nighttime activities are curtailed in order to avoid ghosts.

"The act of suicide is universally condemned by the Navaho, not because it is inherently bad but because it has an adverse effect on the living" (Levy and Kunitz, 1971). There are several characteristics of Navajo suicide that become significant when examined in the light of Navajo beliefs about death. The first is that Navajo suicide rates have remained fairly constant since 1900. The second is that the usual precipitating event is strife with a kinsman or spouse. Third, the suicides usually occur near the residence of the suicide. Other characteristics of Navajo suicides are: 1) they are usually male (a ratio of 13 to 1), and 2) they are clustered in the age range of 25 to 39 years. The Navajo's fear of the dead combined with the usual cause of suicide, family strife, points to suicide as an act of outward aggression. Any Navajo finding the body of a suicide is likely to suffer some misfortune, and if the suicide is a family member this danger is compounded.

The rate of suicide among the Navajos is not high. Levy and Kunitz (1971) placed it at 8 per 100,000, or considerably less than the states that the reservations are in (Arizona 14 per 100,000; New Mexico 12 per 100,000). The possibility that this reported rate is low as the result of accidents and victim-precipitated homicides has been investigated by several researchers. One study (reported in Ungar, 1972) did not show conclusively that fatal accidents had self-destructive motives. Males from 35 to 39 were reported to have suffered fatal accidents, usually with alcohol present. Homicides among the Navajos occurred about as frequently as in the surrounding areas. The homicide was commonly committed by a man (8.2 to 1) while the victim was most often a woman (0.6 to 1). Over 50 percent of the victims were family members and 30 percent were wives. In 10 cases, or 22 percent of the total sample, the homicide was followed by a suicide.

Suicide attempts were found to fit the pattern of the dominant Anglo culture, with the attempter usually a female. The method of choice was the ingestion of drugs. The expressed reason for the suicide attempt was to influence the behavior of some other member of the family.

The pattern of Navajo suicide seems to fit very well into the indigenous beliefs about death. The act of suicide does not cause an individual to leave an untenable situation (the acculturation explanation), but rather causes the individual to stay in the situation in a new status, as a ghost. The most commonly found cause for suicide, family fighting, and the place where suicides most frequently occur, near the residence, support this explanation. The homicides also seem to be the result of family difficulties, and they also show many of the same revenge dynamics. The homicide victim is usually female and is most often killed by a spouse or family member. With homicide, as with suicide, the family members are exposed to death and the dangers it brings. Accidents well might have a strong self-destructive component for the Navajo, but it does not represent an institutionalized substitute for suicide as found among the Plains Indians.

Navajo suicide has been examined by Levy and Kunitz (1971) to determine whether it is a by-product of acculturation to the dominant Anglo culture or a carryover from the old beliefs. Their findings indicate that the suicide and homicide rates found in regions of the reservation that vary greatly in the amount of contact with the peoples and institutions of the dominant Euro-American cultures do not differ significantly. An examination of the belief about death and ghosts and the danger that a suicide creates for the survivors point to the possibility that suicide is deeply rooted in Navajo culture.

Adjusting to new cultures is not just a modern phenomenon for the Navajo. In the last 500 years they have adjusted to the Pueblo, the Spanish, and now the Anglo culture. In each case many aspects were "incorporated" (Vogt, 1961), but always in an uniquely Navajo way. The hypothesis that suicide resulted from the breakdown of Navajo culture is not consistent with their history. Rather, it seems to be more related to family difficulties, events that are not unique to their contact with the Anglo.

SUMMARY

The available literature supports the basic fact of cultural differentiation among American Indian tribal groups. The different patterns of suicide among the six tribal groups in this paper point to the error of attributing one suicide pattern to all American Indians. Statistics derived from the Shoshone pattern, although only superficially reported, have been transposed onto all American Indian groups. The Dakota and Cheyenne do not seem to have suicides as such, but they do place themselves in high risk situations in a pattern closely paralleling the "Crazy-Dogs" of the pre-reservation Plains culture. A perilous charge into the midst of an armed and ready enemy group and the modern example of a man driving his car on the wrong side of a highway are certainly similar in outcome. Navajo and Apache suicide patterns seem relatively unchanged over the years, according to available data. Self-inflicted death is, and always has been, intended to influence the behavior of someone in a close kinship of marital relationship.

The various Pueblo groups, on the other hand, seem to represent a case of incomplete reporting, with indications that undifferentiated acculturational stress may be contributing to some deaths, while in others "pathological families" are the source of most suicides. Among the former desert farmers, the Pima, Papago, and Yaqui, there has been an increase in attempted suicides and, in some communities, completed suicides. Acculturational stresses seem to be involved in these groups where suicide until recently was a rarity.

Most works on suicide have pointed to American Indians as having a noble past, a dismal present, and no future. These observations cannot help but shape public policy and, more importantly, the beliefs of Indians concerning their self-value. We have attempted to show that there is no one pattern of American Indian suicide and that the cultures of American

Indian groups are not necessarily disturbed forms of the Euro-American pattern.

So much of the literature on American Indians has dwelt upon pathological behavior in the forms of alcoholism and suicide. It seems far more significant that they have survived at all. In our viewpoint it would be much more instructive to study the creative adaptations of the American Indians that have allowed them to continue to exist as culturally distinctive groups.

REFERENCES

Allen, J. R. 1972. The Indian adolescent: Psycho-social tasks of the Plains Indian of Western Oklahoma. Paper presented at the American Orthopsychiatric Association Meeting.

Baratz, S. S. 1970. Social science's conceptualization of the Afro-American. In: J. Szwed (Ed.), *Black America,* pp. 55–66. Basic Books. New York.

Biernoff, M. 1970. A survey of Pueblo Indian suicides. Unpublished manuscript.

Blanchard, J. E., and E. L. Blanchard. 1972. Postmortem of an Indian adolescent suicide. Psychological Autopsy Community Services Recommendation. Unpublished manuscript.

Brown, R. B. Burunanjappa, R. Hawk, and D. Bitsuie. 1970. The epidemiology of accidents among the Navajo Indians. *Public Health Reports*, 85: 881–888.

Conrad, R. D. 1972. Suicide among the Papago Indians. Unpublished master's thesis, University of Arizona, Department of Psychology.

Crum, B. 1972. Young Indian male suicides. Elko Community College, Unpublished manuscript.

Curlee, W. V. 1969. Suicide and self-destructive behavior on the Cheyenne River Reservation. In: *Suicide among the American Indians*. pp. 34–37. Public Health Service Publication No. 1903.

Devereux, G. 1942. Primitive psychiatry, funeral suicide and the Mojave social structure. *Bulletin of History of Medicine*, 11: 522–542.

Devereux, G. 1961. *Mojave Ethno-Psychiatry and Suicide: The Psychiatric Knowledge and the Psychic Disturbances of an Indian Tribe*, Smithsonian Institution Bureau of American Ethnology Bulletin No. 175.

Dizmang, L. H. 1967. Suicide among the Cheyenne Indians. *Bulletin of Suicidology*, July, pp. 8–11.

Dizmang, L. H. 1968. Observations on suicidal behavior among the Shoshone-Bannock Indians. Paper presented at the First Annual National Conference on Suicidology, Chicago.

Donovan, W. B., and Nash, G. 1962. Suicide rate, a problem of validity and comparability. *Marquette Medical Review*, 27:150–157.

Everett, M. W. 1970. Pathology in White Mountain Apache's culture: A preliminary analysis. *Western Canadian Journal of Anthropology,* 2, No. 1:180–203.

Everett, M. W. 1972. Conflict, Adversaries, and Retaliation: Suicide Among the White Mountain Apache, Unpublished manuscript, University of Kentucky, Department of Anthropology.

Fenton, W. W. 1941. *Iroquois Suicide: A Study in the Stability of a Culture Pattern.* Bureau of American Ethnology Bulletin No. 128, Anthropological Papers No. 14, pp. 79–136.

Halpern, K. 1971. Navajo accidents: An exploratory case study. Final Summary Report of NIMH Grant 2749 from the Center for the Study of Suicide Prevention.

Havinghurst, R. S. 1971. The extent and significance of suicide among American Indians today. *Mental Hygiene*, 55:174–177.

Kenmitzer, L. S. 1970. Country drinking parties on Pine Ridge Reservation. Paper No. 21 presented at Southwestern Anthropological Association Meeting, Asilomar, Calif.

Kluckhohn, C., and D. Leighton. 1946. *The Navajo*. Harvard University Press, Cambridge.

Leighton, A. H., and C. Hughes. 1955. Notes on Eskimo patterns of suicide. *Southwestern Journal of Anthropology*, 11:327–338.

Levy, J. E. 1965. Navajo suicide. *Human Organization*, 24, No. 4:308–318.

Levy, J. E., and S. Kunitz. 1969. *Notes on Some White Mountain Apache Social Pathologies. Plateau*, 42:11–19.

Levy, J. E., and S. Kunitz. 1971. Indian reservations, anomie, and social pathologies. *Southwestern Journal of Anthropology*, 27, No. 2:997–128.

Maynard, E., and G. Twiss. 1969. *"That These People May Live"– Conditions among the Oglala Sioux of the Pine Ridge Service Unit*, pp. 147–148. Aberdeen Area Indian Health Service, Pine Ridge, S. D.

Miller, S. I., and L. S. Schoenfeld. 1971. Suicide attempt patterns among the Navajo Indians. *Mental Hygiene*, 55:174–177.

Mendell, C., and P. Stuart. 1968. *Suicide and Self-Destructive Behavior in the Oglala Sioux*. Pine Ridge Research Bulletin No. 1, pp. 14–23.

Mendell, C., and P. Stuart. 1969. Suicide and self-destructive behavior in the Oglala Sioux: Some clinical aspects and community approaches. In: *Suicide among the American Indians*, pp. 25–33. Public Health Service Publication No. 1903.

Ogden, M., M. I. Spector, and C. A. Hill. 1970. *Suicides and Homicides among Indians*, Public Health Report No. 85, pp. 75–80.

Pamburn, A. 1970. Suicide among the Blackfeet Indians. *Bulletin of Suicidology*, 7:42–43.

Resnik, H. L. P., and L. H. Dizmang. 1970. Suicide behavior among American Indians. *Sandoz Psychiatric Spectator*, 6:9:7.

Resnik, H. L. P., and L. H. Dizmang, 1971. Observations on suicidal behavior among American Indians. *American Journal of Psychiatry*, 127:882–887.

Rudestam, K. J. 1972. Demographic factors in suicide in Sweden and The United States. *International Journal of Social Psychiatry*, 18, No. 2: 79–90.

Shore, J. H. 1972. Suicide and suicide attempts among American Indians of the Pacific Northwest. *International Journal of Social Psychiatry*, 18:91–96.

Shore, J. H., J. F. Bopp, T. R. Walter, and J. W. Dowes. 1972. A suicide prevention center on an Indian reservation. *American Journal of Psychiatry*, 128:1086–1091.

Spradley, J. P. 1973. The ethnography of crime in American society. In: L. Nader and T. W. Maretzki (Eds.), *Culture Illness and Health*, Anthropological Studies No. 9, pp. 23–34. American Anthropological Association, Washington, D.C.

Ungar, B. L. P. 1972. Dying the Navajo way. Unpublished master's thesis, Department of Community Health, Federal City College, Washington, D.C.

Voegelin, E. W. 1937. Suicide in Northeastern California. *American Anthropologist*, 39:445–456.

Vogt, E. 1961. The Navajo. In: E. Spicer (Ed.), *Perspectives in Culture Change*. University of Chicago Press, Chicago.

Westermeyer, J. 1971. Disorganization: Its role in Indian suicide rates. *American Journal of Psychiatry*, 128:123–124.

Wissler, C. 1916. Societies of the Plains Indians. In: *Anthropological Papers of the American Museum of Natural History*, Vol. XI, New York.

Wymann, L. C., and B. Throne. 1945. Notes on Navajo suicide. *American Anthropologist*, 47:278–288.

three

A CROSS-ETHNIC STUDY OF SUICIDE ATTITUDES AND EXPECTATIONS IN THE UNITED STATES

DAVID K. REYNOLDS, PH.D., RICHARD A. KALISH, PH.D., and NORMAN L. FARBEROW, PH.D.

Suicide is strongly influenced in form, meaning, and frequency by the culture in which it occurs. In order fully to understand the self-destruction of any individual, it is necessary to know the cultural matrix within which it occurs. For some parts of the world, where the population unit is small and relatively cohesive, this background is not difficult to learn. For other parts, where the population is large and diffuse, the number and kind of influences upon the event of suicide are much more difficult to encompass. It is surprising, nevertheless, that these sociocultural factors continue to be ignored, perhaps because for the most part a member of the same culture conducts the study and takes for granted the subtle contributions with which he is familiar. It is only when he attempts to examine the phenomenon in another culture that he becomes aware of the diverse and ramified network with which he is dealing.

As is more or less true for every other country, it is very difficult to interpret suicide as it occurs in the cultural context of the United States. The United States has a long tradition of extensive mixture of ethnic and

---

This research was funded by Grant 7ROI M420822, from the Center for Studies of Suicide Prevention, National Institute of Mental Health.

racial groups from many parts of the world. In varying degrees, these groups retain their native land characteristics into their residence in the United States, some for many generations, while others are integrated quickly.

The predominant ethnic subculture in the United States is the WASP, the white Anglo-Saxon Protestant. A picture of the most common suicide in the United States as obtained from the modal demographic characteristics reported to the National Bureau of Vital Statistics follows a recognizable pattern. Thus, the person who most frequently commits suicide in the United States is a white Protestant male in his 40's or 50's on a downwardly mobile social course, who has suffered a severe interpersonal loss in a relationship with wife or girl friend, and who has used a gun to kill himself.

Although it is possible to infer some things about the culture from these facts (*i.e.*, cultural concern about masculine role; feelings about dependency relationships; investment in masculine, aggressive activities; significance placed by the culture on achievement; etc.), these are general influences and do not provide us with any information about the specific subgroups making up the population. More appropriate would be sensitive examinations of identified subgroups, both predominant and minority, in the population.

BACKGROUND INFORMATION

No study has effectively investigated the impact and influence of culture on suicide in the United States, although both discursive and epidemiological reports on suicide and ethnicity have been published, *e.g.*, on native Americans (Dizmang, 1967; Havighurst, 1971), on Black Americans (Hendin, 1969); on Asian-Americans (Kalish, 1968); and on Eskimos (Parker, 1962). However, to our knowledge, no research has focused attention on more than one American ethnic group at a time, except for the usual epidemiological compilations.

The opportunity to initiate some data gathering related to this concern was provided by an on-going study of death and bereavement among four major American ethnic groups in the Greater Los Angeles area: Black, Japanese, Mexican, and Anglo-Americans (*i.e.*, persons of European-Caucasion origin). The collection of data offered the chance not only to make comparisons between ethnic groups with fairly adequate controls built in for social class differences, but also included comparisons by age, sex, educational level, and self-evaluated religiosity within the ethnic groups. It is too often the case that persons studying cross-cultural and cross-ethnic matters lose sight of intragroup differences while concentrating on intergroup differences.

Two cautions are required, however. The degree to which Blacks, Japanese, Mexican, and Anglo-Americans in Los Angeles represent those ethnicities elsewhere in the United States is uncertain. That many similarities can be found among, for example, male Japanese between 20 and 39 years of age in Los Angeles, Honolulu, Boston, and Chinook, Washington is undoubtedly true, but we are insufficiently sensitive to the differences that will be found. In like fashion, the threads that bind elderly Mexican-American women in Los Angeles to those in Chicago, New Mexico, or rural east Texas are numerous, but major differences in past history and present circumstances require careful consideration. Comparable examples for Black Americans and for Anglo-Americans are readily developed. Thus we hope that our data will be interpreted contextually and generalized cautiously. Another necessary warning also refers to any research involving ethnicity. Although great care was taken to include numerous knowledgeable persons of the various ethnic groups in the planning and conducting of every step of the research to be described, the present article was authored by Anglos. Readers will need to make their own judgment regarding the adequacy of this circumstance.

METHODOLOGY

One segment of the study of death and bereavement in a cross-ethnic context consisted of 1-hour interviews with over 400 adult residents in the Los Angeles area, asking them to respond to moderately structured and highly structured questionnaire items. We incorporated into the survey a number of questions about suicide.

Our sample included 434 respondents, divided approximately equally among Black Americans, Mexican-Americans, Japanese-Americans, and Americans of European descent. Equal representation was also given to men and women. Since our quota sampling aimed at equal thirds in 20 to 39, 40 to 59, and 60 years and older age groups, the over 60-year-olds were slightly over-represented proportionate to their numbers in the general population. To reduce contamination of ethnicity by social class, all interviewers were visibly members of the ethnic community in which they were to do their work. Interviewers for the Japanese and Mexican communities were bilingual.

All questions under discussion were asked in open-ended fashion, with the interviewer coding most responses during the discussion. Coding categories were established only after extensive pretesting.

RESULTS AND DISCUSSION

When asked the *main reasons for a person killing himself*, all four ethnic groups attributed suicide mostly either to psychological stress or to mental illness (see Table 1). The over-all χ^2 was significant ($p < 0.001$), and when each ethnic group was paired with each other all resulting χ^2s were significant except that between Japanese and Caucasian Americans (see Table 2). Although discussing suicide as the outcome of personality problems and emotional illness, rather than money, health, or work problems does require a reasonable sophistication, some interesting differences appeared. When the four ethnic groups were ranked by the proportion attributing suicide to psychological stress (Japanese, Anglo, Black, and Mexican, in that order), the ranking coincided exactly with the rank order of median education among the groups; the rank order attributing suicide to mental illness was directly related to education also, but in an inverse fashion.

Of course, the fact that Mexican-Americans were most likely to label suicidal persons as mentally ill and least likely to consider them as under psychological stress may just be the result of differential education, rather than differences in ethnicity *per se*. For the pooled data, educational level is directly related to frequency of "psychological stress" responses. Regardless of its basis, however, the fact that Mexican-Americans and Black Americans are more likely than Japanese-Americans or Anglo-Americans to consider suicidal persons as mentally ill and less likely to see them as responding to psychological stress has ramifications for suicide prevention agencies and other community groups. Contemplate, for a moment, how you—whether or not you are a professional in the field—would respond to someone you saw as "crazy" as opposed to someone you saw as suffering a high degree of personal distress. Consider as well, the problem of self-esteem in the suicidal person himself. Is he to see his suicidal impulse as a response to a situational stress or as representative of some basic abnormality within himself? These disparate views carry implications as to the laws of necessary change—*i.e.*, in the individual himself (*e.g.*, cure) or in the social/personal situation in which he finds himself (*e.g.*, social/family action). Furthermore, there may be temporal implications, *i.e.*, one may more quickly change a situation than modify a person. Agencies serving primarily those subgroups would need to be prepared for those attitudes.

When asked *what kind of persons commit suicide*, we were again told by Black and Mexican-Americans that they were crazy or mentally ill, and by Anglos that they are emotionally disturbed (Table 1). The Mexican-Americans, however, were most likely to consider a suicide victim as cowardly, an attribution which was made second most often by the

Table 1. Percentages and Numbers of Ethnic Group Responses to Selected Items on Survey

Item no.	Item	Blacks, % (No.)	Japanese, % (No.)	Mexican, % (No.)	Caucasian, % (No.)	Significance level ($p <$)
54.	What do you think are the main reasons for a person killing himself?					
	Serious physical illness	2(2)	2(12)	9(9)	11(9)	
	Insanity/mental illness	42(43)	17(17)	50(56)	24(21)	
	Financial stress	5(5)	5(5)	6(7)	2(2)	0.001
	Psychological stress (guilt, frustration)	29(30)	33(33)	13(15)	30(29)	
	Troubles in love	5(5)	4(4)	8(9)	3(3)	
	Loss of occupation, home, other	18(18)	28(28)	14(15)	29(26)	
56.	What kind of individuals commit suicide?					
	Brave ones	4(4)	3(3)	7(8)	3(3)	
	Cowardly ones	7(7)	27(25)	31(35)	8(7)	
	Crazy ones/mentally ill ones	40(43)	16(15)	35(40)	25(22)	0.001
	Emotionally upset (guilt-frustration)	28(30)	22(20)	19(21)	40(35)	
	Inconsiderate, evil ones, other	22(24)	31(29)	8(9)	24(21)	

continued.

Table 1. *Continued*

Item no.	Item	Blacks, % (No.)	Japanese, % (No.)	Mexican, % (No.)	Caucasian, % (No.)	Significance level ($p<$)
58.	Some persons threaten to kill themselves, but don't seem to be serious. How do you feel about them?					
	Angry	5(5)	4(4)	10(11)	5(5)	
	They should be serious about it or not act that way	3(3)	9(10)	6(7)	2(2)	
	They need professional help	15(16)	9(10)	30(34)	14(14)	
	They need to be punished	1(1)	0(0)	0(0)	4(4)	0.001
	They only want attention	26(28)	19(21)	25(29)	32(32)	
	They are emotionally sick	19(21)	10(11)	15(17)	13(13)	
	Sympathy	18(20)	17(19)	10(11)	13(13)	
	Other	14(15)	32(35)	4(5)	18(18)	
60.	Has anyone you have known well ever committed suicide?					
	Yes	22(24)	25(27)	31(35)	29(29)	0.50
	No	78(85)	76(83)	69(79)	71(72)	
62.	(If yes) was/were this/these person(s) (a)					
	Friend(s)	63(15)	74(20)	40(14)	45(18)	

	Relative(s)	8(2)	15(4)	26(9)	38(11)	0.10
	Neighbor(s)	13(3)	4(1)	20(7)	7(2)	
	Someone else	17(4)	7(2)	14(5)	10(3)	
63.	Did you know someone who you think committed suicide, but it was concealed and reported as a natural of accidental death?					
	Yes	5(5)	20(22)	7(8)	5(5)	0.001
	No	95(104)	80(88)	93(106)	95(96)	
65.	If you knew someone who was seriously considering suicide whom would you contact for help?					
	Priest/minister	7(7)	20(21)	25(28)	20(19)	
	Physician/psychiatrist/Suicide Prevention Center	15(16)	19(20)	19(21)	27(26)	
	Friend	2(2)	11(12)	4(4)	3(3)	0.001
	Relative	26(28)	15(16)	15(17)	9(9)	
	Police	44(47)	21(22)	29(32)	29(28)	
	Other	7(6)	14(15)	8(9)	12(12)	
67.	Have you ever heard of the Suicide Prevention Center?					
	Yes	35(38)	39(42)	18(20)	48(48)	0.001
	No	65(71)	61(66)	83(94)	53(53)	

continued.

Table 1. *Continued*

Item no.	Item	Blacks, % (No.)	Japanese, % (No.)	Mexican, % (No.)	Caucasian, % (No.)	Significance level ($p \leq$)
75.	Which seems most tragic: natural death, accidental death, suicidal death, homicidal death, or death in war?					
	Natural	0(0)	1(1)	5(6)	1(1)	
	Accident	34(36)	32(34)	19(21)	16(16)	
	Suicidal	9(10)	10(11)	8(9)	12(12)	0.001
	Homicidal	21(22)	32(35)	33(37)	48(47)	
	War	36(39)	25(27)	35(40)	22(22)	
99.	Suicide is more common among Caucasians (Anglos) than among other races.					
	Agree	89(91)	34(25)	68(60)	43(23)	
	Disagree	11(11)	66(48)	32(28)	57(30)	0.001

Table 2. Chi Square Significance Levels between Pairs of Ethnic Groups on Selected Survey Items

	Significance levels, $p <$							
	Item no.[a]							
	54	56	58	63	65	67	75	99
Blacks vs.								
Japanese	0.01	0.001	0.02	0.01	0.001	0.70	0.20	0.001
Mexican	0.05	0.001	0.01	0.70	0.01	0.01	0.01	0.001
Caucasians	0.02	0.30	0.70	0.90	0.001	0.10	0.001	0.001
Japanese vs.								
Mexican	0.001	0.001	0.001	0.01	0.20	0.001	0.10	0.001
Caucasian	0.90	0.01	0.01	0.01	0.20	0.30	0.10	0.50
Mexican vs.								
Caucasians	0.001	0.001	0.001	0.80	0.70	0.001	0.05	0.01

[a]See Table 1 for description of each item.

Japanese-Americans also. At first blush these findings seem strange, especially in light of the long tradition within each culture of honored self-sacrifice. The overall χ^2 was again highly significant ($p < 0.001$) as were all pairs of ethnic groups except Blacks and Caucasians (Table 2).

Some responses occurred too infrequently to be classified but are certainly relevant to this discussion. Thus 8 Blacks, 2 Japanese, 9 Mexican-Americans, and 2 Caucasians mentioned lack of faith in God or some related consideration, in responding either to the main reasons a person commits suicide or the kind of person who commits suicide. Drugs were brought up by 4 Blacks, 4 Japanese, 2 Mexican-Americans, and 10 Anglos. Stupidity or ignorance was cited by 9 Blacks, 2 Japanese, 5 Mexican-Americans, and no Caucasians.

Perhaps one sort of useful understanding involves the distinction between collectivistic and individualistic cultures. The literature indicates that we can characterize Japanese-American (Kitano, 1969) and Mexican-American (Grebler *et al.*, 1970) subcultures and their parental cultures, Japan (Norbeck, 1965) and Mexico (Paz, 1961), as collectivistic in orientation. Such cultures are oriented strongly toward preserving in-group solidarity even at the expense of placing some limitations on individual expressiveness. Behaviors that threaten the integrity of the family or nation are strongly discouraged. In traditional Japan and Mexico institutionalized suicides, for the most part, took forms that reaffirmed the group's cohesiveness and the group's goals. For example, in Japan *hara-kiri* or *seppuku* generally involved a person's punishing himself for a socially recognized misdeed. Other suicide acts involved public displays in order to draw attention to some perceived deviance on the part of the government from national goals and interests. Similarly, in the case of voluntary sacrifice among the Aztecs of Mexico, the result was thought to be the sustenance of the gods so that the nation might prosper. In both cases suicide took the form of self-sacrifice for the group. These days, however, such self-sacrifice is possible only in a limited sense in war and revolutionary activity. Such situations are unlikely to be defined as purposive self-destruction, however, and we suspect that the image in the minds of our respondents when asked about suicide fits a much more self-centered, individualistic act. If this is indeed the case, then the socially disruptive consequences of suicide take precedence. Suicide disrupts families; it disrupts the community's solidarity in the eyes of the larger society. We would expect, then, for there to be some resentment and depreciation of suicidal individuals. And, as we shall see, the opprobrium attached to the suicide threatener is most apparent in these collectivistically oriented subcultures.

Conversely, Blacks and Whites appear more individualistic in their orientations. Elsewhere in their interview responses Blacks and Whites showed a tendency to rely less heavily on family resources than did Japanese-Americans and Mexican-Americans. Rather, they turned to personal and public sources of relief. The result may be that individual acts of suicide are less threatening and so less strongly deprecated in the more individualistically oriented subcultures.

Respondents were asked *how they felt about those persons who threaten to kill themselves, but do not seem serious* (Table 1). Except for Mexican-Americans, the most frequent response was that these persons were calling for help and wanted attention. The Mexican-Americans were most likely to state that they needed professional help (from interviewer notes, we gather that they were thinking of the priest, not a mental health professional), but considered calling for help and wanting attention as second most important. As before, the over-all χ^2 was significant, ($p < 0.001$) and all ethnic pairs were also significantly different except for Blacks and Anglos (Table 2).

We also found, although again with very small percentages, that the Mexican-Americans were more likely than the other groups to feel angry about such behavior (10 percent versus 5 percent for the other groups), while some of the Japanese-Americans either expressed a fish-or-cut-bait philosophy (9 percent of them suggesting resentment of what they perceived as a game or fraud) or felt indifference (15 percent replying that such persons should not be taken seriously and should be ignored). It may be a tribute to sophistication about the act that even in the case of a nonserious suicidal behavior, very few of the respondents in any subgroup felt that they should be punished.

We also wanted to know about the possibility of a respondent's *personal encounter with the suicide of close friends, relatives, and acquaintances* (Table 1). The Mexican-Americans were most likely to have known someone who had committed suicide, and the Blacks were least likely to have known such a person. About one out of four in all subgroups had known someone *well* who committed suicide, an impressively high proportion. The over-all χ^2 was not significant, however, ($p < 0.50$) and analyses between pairs were not performed. When asked who it was that had committed suicide, the most common answer was "friend," while the next most common (except for Blacks) was *relative*. Among Anglos, fully 38 percent had been relatives, while among Blacks it was only 8 percent. The validity of those results are somewhat in doubt because of the protectiveness (therefore under-reporting) of relatives, especially in collectivistically oriented subcultures, and the fear of hereditary conclusions being drawn from some suicide-insanity linkage. The over-all χ^2 was not significant ($p < 0.10$) and individual pairs were not tested for significance.

We also asked *whether Anglos were more likely to commit suicide than members of other ethnicities* (Table 1). Here the Blacks gave the most resounding affirmative (89 percent); only 6 percent did not respond. Nearly half the Anglos (48 percent) were unable to respond, 53 out of 101, and over half of those who did answered in the negative (57 percent). Interethnic differences are highly significant. According to statistics gathered for Los Angeles County by the coroner's office, the Anglos indeed do have the highest suicide rate, although evidence has accrued that suicides among Black Americans have increased substantially (Allen, 1973). Table 3 shows the number of suicides in Los Angeles County for each 100,000 members of the involved ethnic groups.

A careful content analysis of newspapers with the largest circulation in each ethnic community in Los Angeles showed that the paper serving the Black community was relatively more likely to print suicide articles (a significant difference appeared only between the Black press and White press) while the Japanese language paper played them down. But it was obvious from our data that the Blacks rejected the picture of themselves as strongly suicidal (Table 1). The Japanese-Americans recognized their newspaper's silence as an effort to protect the families involved. In fact, 20

Table 3. Reported Suicide Rates, Los Angeles County, 1970, by Ethnic Group and Sex[a]

		No. of suicides	Rate per 100,000 (approximately)
Black American	Male	48	13
	Female	40	10
	Total	88	12
Japanese-American	Male	7	14
	Female	6	10
	Total	13	12
Mexican-American	Male	30	5
	Female	19	3
	Total	49	4
Caucasian American	Male	655	29
	Female	433	18
	Total	1,088	23

[a]Los Angeles County Coroner's Office. Our thanks to Dr. Thomas Noguchi and Miss Emily Koshida.

percent of them reported having known of at least one occurrence where *a suicide was reported as a natural or accidental death*. This compared to between 5 and 7 percent for the other three ethnic groups. As the percentages indicate, differences between Japanese-Americans and each of the other groups are significant (Table 2).

One final question was, *whom would you contact if you knew someone who was seriously considering suicide?* (see Table 1). Here there is some doubt in interpretation, *i.e.*, did the respondent assume we were asking about someone who was on the window ledge, ready to jump? Or were they thinking of a depressed person talking about ending it all? In any event, all four ethnic groups would first turn to the police, an interesting answer in terms of obvious belligerence in many ethnic communities regarding law enforcement personnel. Clergymen were the favored second choice of Japanese, Mexican-Americans, and the Anglos; but were only fourth choice among Blacks, indicating that Blacks do not see the minister as functioning primarily in this particular area of social concern.

Blacks were more likely than any of the other groups to contact police and were also more likely to call a family member than any of the others, although all of the groups were more likely to see this situation as calling for professional help of some sort. Although all groups contained a moderate minority of persons who would first call a mental health professional (either a physician, a psychiatrist, or a telephone counselor at the Los Angeles Suicide Prevention Center), only Anglos ranked the mental health or health professional as second choice (27 percent versus 29 percent for the police). The over-all χ^2 is highly significant ($p < 0.001$), as are differences between Blacks and other ethnic groups.

These are the major results of our comparisons among the four subcultural groups. We also examined the data for patterns of response within each group and pooled the data from all the groups to see if such dimensions as sex, age, degree of religiosity, and education cross cut the ethnic groupings. We found no interview items that were answered differently by sex or age or education or religiosity within as many as three of the four groups. For example, among the Japanese-Americans, older people were significantly more likely to contact the police in response to a suicide threat than younger people, but there was no such significant difference between old and young Mexican-Americans or Blacks or Whites.

On the other hand, one fascinating finding was that the dimensions that were significantly distinguishing within each group also tended to be characteristic of that group and reflected the in-group differentiations on the total 180 items of our interview schedule (see Table 4). We found that among Caucasians the respondent's *sex* was relatively important in determining his response. For Japanese-Americans the key factor was the respondent's *age*.[1] The Mexican-Americans showed the most differentiation from the other groups, indicating that their *cultural background* dominated responses, thus showing much less of the sense of absorption into American life styles that is reflected in the differential responses by age among the Japanese-Americans. The Black Americans showed an outstanding intragroup differentiation but responded in ways relatively *similar* to those of Whites. It is not surprising to note this in the light of the culture-stripping experience of slavery and the relatively long period of adjustment to dominant Anglo cultural norms.

Despite the examples of survival of Africanisms that Herskovitz (1941) enumerated, the position that covers a broader range of cultural behavior is that, given the description of family and linguistic ties, the coercion to learn colonial religions and work patterns, and the dehumanizing conditions of slavery, much of the Black African cultural heritage was lost. Black Americans adopted many characteristics from the dominant White

[1] For additional material on intergenerational differences among Japanese Americans, see Kitano, 1969, Table 4, and Iga, 1966.

Table 4. Frequencies of Significant Differences within Each Ethnic Group on Suicide-Related and All Survey Items[a]

	Black American	Japanese-American	Mexican-American	Caucasian American
Age	3 (3)	*4[a] (49)*	0 (31)	1 (23)
Age by sex	2 (36)	3 (63)	2 (35)	1 (28)
Education	1 (09)	1 (16)	0 (07)	0 (10)
Ethnicity	3 (23)	3 (34)	*5 (37)*	0 (17)
Religiosity	1 (12)	0 (10)	0 (09)	0 (12)
Sex	1 (12)	1 (10)	1 (11)	*2 (30)*

[a]First number indicates frequency of significant differences (beyond 0.05 level by X^2) within each group for *suicide-related* items. Number in parentheses indicates frequency of significant differences within each group for *all* interview items. *Highest* relative frequency (both suicide-related and total) among the subcultural groups for a single dimension is italicized.

subculture but transformed them and added new elements grounded in the unique aspects of their experience (Blauner, 1970).

On the whole, our data indicate that, in this tabooed area at least, some of the current conflict areas in American life ("the battle of the sexes," "the generation gap," and the rejection of dominant cultural norms) may be felt more or less keenly, depending on one's subcultural background.

From the pooled data we found significant positive relationships between increasing age and 1) increased attribution of suicide to mental illness, 2) increased number of people known well who committed suicide, 3) increased tendency to call a clergyman or policeman rather than a relative in response to a suicide threat, and 4) lack of familiarity with the Los Angeles Suicide Prevention Center. With increased education (the most productive variable in the analysis of pooled data), was associated significantly 1) increased attribution of suicide to psychological stress and decreased attribution to financial trouble and to mental illness; 2) decreased description of suicidal character as cowardly or crazy; 3) increased awareness that the suicide threatener needs professional help and wants attention, along with decreased punitive responses, *e.g.*, anger, demand to kill themselves or stop pretending, and desire to punish; 4) increased occurrence of friend as known person who committed suicide and decrease in occurrence of relative or neighbor; 5) increased tendency to contact a relative or mental health professional when someone else is considering suicide; and 6) increased likelihood of having heard of the Suicide Prevention Center.

CONCLUSION

To extract one characteristic for each group, based upon our present understanding, we might line up the following. The Black Americans are likely to see the suicidal persons as crazy, and—in spite of the recently publicized increase in suicide among young and middle income Blacks—do not see suicide as being a major concern of their ethnic group. The Japanese-Americans, although very likely to see the suicidal person as functioning under extreme stress, have less patience with both the person who succeeds in killing himself and with the person whose attempts are apparently not serious, perhaps viewing him as demanding unreasonable amounts of attention and concern. The Mexican-Americans, who ranked lowest in median level of formal education, see the suicidal person as mentally ill; they feel that the potential suicide should receive professional help, perhaps the counsel of a priest. The Anglo-Americans perceive suicide as the outcome of extreme stress, and they respond to it by turning to mental health professionals rather than friends or relatives.

We are aware of many limitations in our study. We recognize the inadequacies of responding to a standardized interview questionnaire; we realize how many disparate subgroups we have lumped together in each of our ethnic categories; and we also know that Los Angeles Mexican-Americans or Black or Japanese or Anglo-Americans are not fully comparable to similar groups in El Paso or San Francisco or rural Illinois. It has been our hope to add an increment of knowledge about the different attitudes and concepts of suicide which may be related to subcultures in the United States and, hopefully, to provoke others into adding more.

REFERENCES

Blauner, R. 1970. Black culture: Myth or reality? In: E. Norman, Jr., J. F. Szwed, and Whitten (Eds.), *Afro-American Anthropology*. Free Press, New York.

Dizmang, L. H. 1967. Suicide among the Cheyenne Indians. *Bulletin of Suicidology*, July, 8–110.

Grebler, L., J. W. Moore, and R. C. Guzman. 1970. *The Mexican-American People*. Free Press, New York.

Havighurst, R. J. 1971. The extent and significance of suicide among the American Indians. *Mental Hygiene*, 55, No. 2:174–177.

Hendin, H. 1969. *Black Suicide*. Basic Books, New York.

Herskovits, M. J. 1941. *The Myth of the Negro Past*. Harper, New York.

Iga, M. 1966. Changes in value-orientation of Japanese Americans. Paper presented at the Western Psychological Association Meetings, Long Beach Calif.

Kalish, R. A. 1968. Suicide: An ethnic comparison in Hawaii. *Bulletin of Suicidology*. December, 37–43.

Kitano, H. H. 1969. *Japanese Americans.* Prentice Hall, New York.

Norbeck, E. 1965. *Changing Japan*. Holt, Rinehart and Winston, New York.

Parker, S. 1962. Eskimo psychopathology. *American Anthropologist*, 64:76–76.

Paz, O. 1961. *The Labyrinth of Solitude*. Grove Press, New York.

Seiden, R. H. 1970. We're driving young Blacks to suicide. *Psychology Today*. 4 No. 3:24–28.

four

SUICIDE IN BUENOS AIRES: SOCIAL AND CULTURAL INFLUENCES

NASIM YAMPEY, M.D.

Psychiatrists in Argentina have become interested in the problem of suicide from both the epidemiological and therapeutic points of view mostly within the past 20 years. The data they have used have come from the Federal Police files and from the Buenos Aires Department of Statistics. There were, of course, earlier researchers from the late 19th and early 20th centuries who were interested in the subject. We find reports from Gache (1884), Ramos Mejia (1896), Rodriguez (1903), Arreguine (1905), Bosch (1920), Belbey (1928), and Tubio Ovide (1945), among others. Suicide has been studied more recently from a psychological viewpoint by Garma (1940), Abadi (1959), and Rolla (1970). The decade of 1960 to 1970 has seen various hospitals and mental health centers set up to provide treatment for suicidal patients, and the last 5 years have seen an increase in interest among both specialists and the general public in the problem of suicide.

Geographically, the city of Buenos Aires is divided in two parts, one represented by the city itself (Federal District), bounded on the north and east by the River Plata and to the west and south by General Pan Avenue. It contains an area of 196 square kilometers and a population of three million people. Tied to it, more politically than geographically, is the second part, Greater Buenos Aires, which belongs to the Province of Buenos Aires whose capitol is La Plata. Greater Buenos Aires keeps growing in population, but the number of inhabitants living in the metropolis remains practically unchanged.

Suicide has fluctuated widely in Buenos Aires over the years. There was a high incidence of suicide in Buenos Aires at the end of the 19th century, where it reached an annual rate of 33 in the years 1895 and 1896. After that the rate decreased to 14 per 100,000 in 1910, a decline which may, however, have been due more to registry deficiency than a real drop. Between 1910 and 1914, the rate went back up to 21. Then the curve fluctuated until, coinciding with the depression in the 1930's, it reached its highest point in 1932, a rate of 27. From then on, the rate gradually decreased until it reached 7.6 in the period 1960 to 1964.

When suicides are grouped on the basis of nationality and sex, we find that from 1915 to 1940 there was a clear predominance of masculine, foreign-born over native-born (about one-and-a-half to one). Only since 1950 have the native-born suicides been more frequent. Since 1930 suicide has been more frequent among native-born than among foreign-born women.

THE INFLUENCES OF THE TRANSCULTURAL PROCESS IN THE ARGENTINE REPUBLIC

In order to understand the relationship between suicide and the culture of Argentina, one must know both the history of suicide and the sociocultural processes that have taken place in Argentina in the last hundred years. European immigration and, more recently, Latin American migrations have played an important role in the development of the country. In order to sketch their impact on the structure and development of the country, the works of Germani (1962*a,b*), Di Tella *et al.* (1965), de Imas (1969), and others have been consulted.

The Argentine Republic, during this period of transition, went through a series of transformations which began in the 19th century. Modernization developed quickly and reflected the significant influence of large scale immigration. About this, Germani (1962*a*) said:

> Contemporary Argentina cannot be understood without a detailed analysis of its massive immigration. First of all, this immigration was an integrating and fundamental feature of the process which transformed the Argentine society in the middle of the 19th century from a structure still tied to the traditional frame into a modern nation. In the second place, the intensity and volume of its immigration in relation to the resident native population was so great that, in a non-metaphorical way, it is possible to speak about a substantial renewal of the country's population, particularly in the areas with greatest economic, social and political significance (p. 179).

After independence, leaders in charge of the "national organization" had as an objective the transformation of the country by means of: 1) massive immigration, 2) compulsory education, 3) importation of capital, 4) development of modern forms of production (agriculture, cattle raising, industry), and 5) establishment of a transportation network. The effect has been "a substantial modification in the population composition." To illustrate, annual immigration, which had scarcely reached 10,000 in the period 1875 to 1880, increased in the 80's to an annual average of 64,000 under the incentive of grants of lands confiscated from the Indians. It reached its maximum in 1889 with 200,000 immigrants. It was considerable during the 1st decade of the 20th century (annual average: 112,000) and during the years previous to World War I. Despite fluctuations in the interim, the annual average stabilized around 100,000 immigrants between 1947 and 1951. Also, from 1940 onwards immigration from the neighboring countries such as Paraguay, Bolivia, and Chile intensified. This movement coincided with internal migrations and forms part of the recent process of urbanization and industrial development. Practically half of the immigrants who came from overseas were Italians while a third were Spanish. The rest were Polish, Russian, French, German, and Arabs.

The impact on demography of the immigration can be better understood when we note that the Argentine Republic had 1,700,000 inhabitants in 1869 and that in 1959 it had increased to 20 million inhabitants. For comparison, the United States increased about four times in 80 years (1870 to 1950), Brazil six times in 90 years, Chile four times in 110 years, and Peru less than four times in the same period. The consequences of the immigration in Argentina were even greater because most of the immigrants concentrated in a few areas of the country, mostly in the cities. For example, more than 50 percent of the foreign population settled in Greater Buenos Aires. From the middle 1930's onwards, the process of urbanization was due mostly to internal migrations of neighboring countries. The majority of the immigrants belonged to lower socioeconomic groups and in their own native country had worked at agricultural and pastoral tasks. In spite of their rural background, about half of them stayed in metropolitan Buenos Aires. For most of them, it meant not only a change from the country to the city, but also a change of work. The others stayed in rural areas, especially in agricultural colonies. In the most important provinces the adult population consisted primarily of foreigners with a predominance of adult males. Before 1914, a certain number of families with their children had immigrated; from 1930 onwards, the foreign population entered an "aging" phase.

When an industrial society appeared, replacing the traditional one, the foreigners were found even more often in areas reflecting the new structure. Although they participated in essential areas of community activity, they did not, however, displace the leading group or "high class," which for a long time guarded jealously their sources of power. The "high class" increased its power and wealth by adding new land to its patrimony, which became even more valuable. Beyhaut *et al.* (1965), in their analysis of "The Immigrants in the Argentina Occupational System," said that "the immigration provided handwork, qualified personnel and a certain number of business men," but that this expansion, "under British dependency and with rigid controls that prevented changes in the local economic structures, was limited to industrial and business activities" (p. 85).

Meanwhile, with the strong stimulation toward commercial and speculative activities, there was a quick urbanization, resulting in a distortion of the social structure. The continuation of the land-owning oligarchy in control of the power and the wish for social promotion on the part of the newcomers created an artificial third sector that contained a great number of nonproductive activities. The processes of adaptation and integration were not done without conflicts, tensions, and problems, nor without sufferings, which sometimes reached the point of self-elimination. There was personal adaptation, but it was established at considerable cost. Regarding the immigrant's participation in the different social structures: it actually made for more efficiency in the economy of the country, since it represented an important element in the organization of the family and in the transition from agriculture to industry; it promoted culture; but it was practically of no importance as far as politics was concerned. With the internalization of the values of the native society, some identification with the new country as well as the loss of previous identity seems to have taken place. New cultural forms were the result. When integration was inadequate, a cultural juxtaposition resulted "which has a hybrid characteristic, formed by a mixture of foreigners and natives, neither of them being predominant in one sense or other" (Romero, 1956). This syncretic culture has been gaining more and more acculturation and identification within the new country.

The Argentine Republic led the other countries in changing from a traditional Hispanic-colonial society into an urban-industrial society, but it contained many irregularities along the way. For example, family structure suffered considerably. In 1869, the average size of a family was 6.0 people; in 1895, it went down to 5.5, and in 1947 it was 4.3. The isolated nuclear family is prevalent today throughout the entire country, but in some marginal provinces there are still families that include three generations. Germani (1962*a*) hypothesized that the Argentinian family, under the impact of urbanization and industrialization, underwent three stages of change: 1) starting point: "traditional family" (authoritative father as the center or internal relationship, numerous families of three generations); 2) transition: "lack of stability and crisis" (low birth rate, divorce, intergenerational conflicts); and, 3) "modern urban family" (planned increase of the birth rate, democratic relationships, stability based on love and interpersonal adjustment).

THEORY OF THE HISTORIC EVOLUTION AND THE CAUSES OF SUICIDE

How should the relationship between the culture of Argentina and the high prevalence of suicide at the turn of the century in Buenos Aires and its gradual decrease be interpreted? The factors of massive immigration, quick urbanization and industrialization, and social disorganization must have caused many crises. The long stage of disorganization and reorganization must have especially affected the foreigners, with the double pressures of first, the need for adaptation in the horizontal sense, *i.e.*, a change from rural to urban life; and second, the need to adapt in the vertical sense, *i.e.*, change in activity, status, etc. However, this second point is not clear unless we examine the actual composition of the population in those days. From 1869 through 1914 the number of foreign adult males in Buenos Aires City outnumbered the native born males by a ratio of 4 to 1. It was not until 1947 that the ratio was reversed and the native-born males again exceeded the foreign born by 1.5 to 1. This disorganization affected the native population as well as the foreign born, but perhaps the former was the most affected. There was a greater frequency of young suicides and a greater number of women suicides between the ages of 16 and 25, data that are inversely related to the adult foreign composition. These data may be interpreted as a failure of the young people in the transcultural process. Also, most of the foreign suicides were Italians or Spaniards, which is not surprising considering the population of Buenos Aires. Even more important is that suicide in both Italy and Spain was not so common.

The high rate of suicide during the early period of this century may be explained by the conflict between wishes and the means of fulfilling them, by the change of values and patterns of behavior, by the loss of collective and personal identity, and finally, by failure in the social management of aggressiveness (increased by the frustration in the process of adaptation to a society in rapid change). Another important factor was the frustration in the efforts to own land by those people who sought higher social status and who had a high degree of initiative. They were instead confined to urban life and commercial activities, resulting in an artificial growth of this third sector. This produced an unstable base and an unharmonious urban growth and promoted a speculative greediness. The immigration actually produced much of the middle class, with children who had different levels of aspirations such as "prestige" and participation in power. The limited possibilities were also responsible for the "humanistic" education of the masses, a factor which brought about both frustrations and radicalization of the student population. Arrivals from overseas came under much different circumstances than those who came from Latin America. The arrivals from distant lands were liked by the natives and were provided the protection of the law and other institutions. However, even here there was still ample evidence of the effort of adaptation and its cost in terms of mental disturbances.

In two earlier works (Yampey, 1964, 1966), the conflicts and mental disturbances in migrating families who, during the last 3 decades, moved from one country to another or from the country to the city, were studied. There are a total of two million South American, non-Argentine inhabitants in this country with about 300,000 to 500,000 from Paraguay. The observations probably apply to other social settlements within the same country or in the neighboring ones (Rivarola and Margullis, 1967). Lack of political stability, economic problems, and social and cultural deprivation were responsible for their emigration. These factors also affected the middle class and the rural classes, the more active and dynamic people. They were attracted to the opportunities for progress in the great cities. The movement was not a planned one. The idea of permanent emigration was not explicit either. Most of them left their country or village with the idea of returning to it. The family group did not emigrate as a whole but rather in parts and in successive stages; nor was this migration in any way organized even though there was a collective purpose that united them. They came as a scattered collection with no protective organizations to help them face the first obstables of adaptation. The cooperation of a fellow countryman or relation was always implicit. Only in the neighborhood-type groups ("shanty towns") were there more or less dependable organizations of cooperation and mutual help. For them the apparent lack of adaptation conflicts was a result of factors: 1) ethnic identity, 2) good psychological environment, and 3) gratifying working conditions. These three factors are much different today than they were 50 years ago, and close examination reveals that the anxieties produced by this change took their toll.

Lack of systematic planning and the feeling of impermanence may help the new emigree to settle down more quickly, but in the long run they do not permit the necessary integration into society within a reasonable period of time. The manifestations of the conflict are transferred to areas other than mental and are not identified with the event that provoked them. The psychological regression is exemplified by the child who leaves his home and starts having a stomach ache. Somatization, with many hypochondriacal aspects of long duration, appears frequently. At first there may be euphoria and activity, with a search for collective expressions of the feeling of exaltation, or there may be paranoid or depressive reactions. Once settled in the new environment, the immigrant adapts in what has been called a horizontal sense; *i.e.*, he accepts the cultural habits, the economic activity, and interpersonal relations that do not imply a substantial modification in his personality patterns. Still, this coincides with his feeling of impermanence, the feeling of not having primary roots which tie him to his homeland. He notices the change, but he protects himself on the one hand by denying the present reality. The Oblisco, the skyscrapers, Florida Street, the people lack any reality for him, while, on the other hand, he idealizes his own native country, its geography, its history, its people. He also projects onto his surroundings the reason for his pain and aggression. Meanwhile he cannot establish anything permanent and lasting, anything that gives meaning to his transitory existence. Political organizations assume the role of creating an *esprit de corps* and channeling aggressiveness. Living with hopes for returning to their native country prevents a more active and creative adaptation. The marginal condition in which thousands of Paraguayans live in Buenos Aires illustrates the difficulty in passing from one scale of values to another. Critical attitudes against the associations that heretofore helped to control their anxieties and wishes, intragroup or extragroup projection of the aggression, all show the insecurity and hostility brought on by this situation.

Suicides, however, were very rare. Between 1964 and 1968 there were in Buenos Aires (Federal District) 10 suicides, 8 women and 2 men. On the other hand, the incidence of homicides doubled, and there were 20 deaths from accidents between 1965 and 1969. Alcoholism is not frequent either, although there are episodes of inebriety and aggressiveness. Drunkenness is resorted to as a way of counterbalancing various crises; big parties or social meetings become the most common resort against loneliness and hopelessness. They get excited dancing the "polka" and cry when listening to a "guarania." A collective demonstration, socially and culturally acceptable, represents the deep meaning of a sacred and revitalizing reunion with the (mother) homeland.

Those who, in the end, decide to stay in Argentina undergo another critical period, which has the significance of an affective mourning that relates to the process of adaptation in the vertical sense. This kind of a crisis is more likely to lead to suicide. It implies setting aside certain deep internal values and acquiring new ones. They must accept the fact of a struggle for status within an urban, dynamic, and competitive society. They must not only keep up but must also transcend. The social, economic, and cultural demands affect their working style, their habits, and their new goals and may arouse the opposition of the members of the family. The family, individually or as a whole, is urged, by the standards and values of the new society, to adapt to the aspirations and communicative interrelations of the modern habitat.

The disturbances can be expressed through the whole group or through one or more of its members. It may adopt the characteristics of a conflict with the extra group, between fathers and sons, or individual clinical forms. This process of transculturation means, in its external aspect, completely accepting the new affective and emotional structure and being accepted by it. Internally, it means getting rid of the mother country, just as it is for the child leaving aside his paternal figures (with the consequent feelings of fear, hostility, and guilt) and their reunion in a more free, wide, and operative level. This process ends either with a creative outcome or with failure and sterility on an individual and/or social level. The middle class dramatizes most clearly this internal mourning, which is generally seen in its negative aspects in psychophysiological symptoms, such as hypochondria, depression, and, sometimes, suicide. In its positive aspects, it increases family harmony, personality expansion, and objective attainment. On the social level, this stage represents the beginning of stability and permanence.

My own analysis of several cases has led me to believe that the integration of a person into a new cultural environment may depend essentially on the vicissitudes of his early development, above all in the identification with his parents. For example, in the rural Paraguayan family the mother represents a strong and protective figure who creates firm ties with her child. She accepts maternity, nurses her offspring for a long time, and gives him her care without making great demands from him. On the other hand, the figure of the father appears more remote and unavailable than in other social groups. His image for the child is a rough and dramatic character who practically never represents an element that protects, guides, and comforts. The parents as a couple are not completely integrated either, especially because of the tendency to exclude the paternal figure. How are these basic sentiments related to the adaptative processes? The horizontal adaptation of the rural Paraguayans is remarkably fast. This implies adjusting to different conditions and new events, which gives the impression of an extraordinary flexibility and adaptative talent. I feel that it is primarily the influence of the mother's rearing with its psychological factors of idealization and negation which is responsible for the easy adaptation one finds.

The vertical adaptation acquires intensely dramatic profiles. It represents in the psychosocial level the integration of the third person into the deep layers of the mind. It is exemplified by the docile worker who adapts himself to all kinds of jobs without great problems for a long period of time but suddenly one day, when facing something unacceptable, becomes completely irrational. It is the family head who, after constant efforts, is able to buy his own house and to reach a solid and stable occupational position and suddenly begins to feel ill. It is the technician who climbs his way to a point of success at which point a single wrong detail occurs and spoils the whole thing. This scheme helps us to understand some very general aspects of the problem, but I consider it important in the therapeutic or educational aspect that the conscience of a community is necessary to produce an active and healthy integration. In any case, it is a suitable hypothesis for wider and more systematic investigations.

The transcultural process just described had its origins in the transoceanic migrations, but the cultural process which originated in the clash between the Spanish and Indian cultures took place earlier. Before that, violent encounters occurred between the middle and the most primitive cultures existing in America before Columbus's arrival (Yampey, 1963, 1969).

CURRENT SUICIDE DATA

In the period 1964 to 1968 (Municipalidad de Buenos Aires, 1970*a*), the suicide rate was a little over 10 per 100,000, determined from the death certificates by the Department of Statistics of the City Government. However, many cases, especially poisoning, are grouped under other diagnoses (accidents, intoxications, etc.). The figure of 10 expresses, then, an approximate total, which can be used as a guide but by no means accounts for the full number of cases. There are no available means yet to calculate more exactly the real frequency of suicide in Buenos Aires.

The rate of 10 for the Federal District is also very close to the official rates of other provinces. In 1965 the rate of suicides in the Argentine Republic was 9.1; it was 9.4 in 1966 and 9.6 in 1967. Of the total suicides, 66 percent were Argentines and 34 percent foreigners. According to the census of the year 1970, there was a proportion of 82 percent natives and 18 percent foreigners (Municipalidad de Buenos Aires, 1970*b*). It is important to keep in mind the fact that the foreigners were much older.

Regarding *sex*, the distribution of committed suicide is 70 percent men and 30 percent women. The process of secularization and modernization has influenced women's decisions to commit suicide. The past records show that in 1915 the proportion was four male suicides to each female suicide; in 1930, three men to one woman; and from 1930 it was a bit more than two men to each woman. As far as suicide attempts are concerned, the proportion was the following: in 1915 twice as many women as men; in 1930 and 1940, a third more were women. Nowadays, the number of women who attempt suicide is only slightly higher than that of men. Obviously, I am referring here to the official registers. Perhaps in reality there is one suicide for every 10 attempts.

In all countries of the world one finds an increasing rate of suicides among old people. However, in Argentina between 1915 and 1920 there was a high incidence of suicide among those in the 16- to 25-year age group, especially for females, a situation which remains unchanged up to the present. The distribution according to age groups has changed little by little toward a predominance of older ages. About 1930, it was highest in the 23- to 30-year-old age group; in 1940 and 1950, between the 30- and 50-year olds; while in the 60's, old age suicides were predominant, especially for the age group between 60 and 70.

Referring to the suicide's occupational situation may give an idea of their status or social condition. The greatest number of suicides is registered among housewives, pensioners, students, and bond holders, that is to say, those who economically represent the least productive part of the population. In 1968 there were 149 cases, consisting of 82 pensioners, 60 housewives, and 7 students. The pensioners constitute a special group. They number about 25 percent of the total of suicides, although they are only 10 percent of the city's population. Males are in the majority in this group. The professional group has the same number every year. While the City Government records about 22 professionals annually, the police record 18. This is because the total registration by the police is always about 15 percent below the City Government's registration.

From police files I have obtained the following data for the period 1960 to 1965: upper class, 144 cases; middle class, 1,130 cases; lower class, 2,848 cases. The fact that the upper class accounts for so few suicides may be attributable to the methods normally employed by such people of high social and cultural status, barbiturates and psychodrugs. In general, the methods employed to commit suicide indicate that guns rank highest and are responsible for 41 percent of the suicide deaths. Over the years it has always occupied first place, especially for males (1915 to 1920); but in 1930 and 1940, poisoning was used just as often. Since 1950 guns again have been used most often by males. In 1940, jumping off buildings was in fourth place but this method increased, especially for females, so that it occupied first place for them between 1950 and 1965. In third place appears hanging and strangulation, 12 percent. In fourth place is poisoning (analgesics and sleeping pills, 6 percent; solids and liquids, 4 percent). It is probably among these latter methods that the diagnosis has become changed or has been omitted most often, explaining why they do not appear among the higher rankings. There is frequent use of potassium cyanide, considered a traditional element by certain people. It is a very toxic product, used in galvanoplasty and easily obtained. Mercuric chlorine was also very popular in the past (Belbey, 1928). Drowning is used by only 1 percent of the suicides, but it is probable that some cases are taken for accidents. Information from the National Coast Guard (jurisdiction including the New Port, Puerto Madero, Boca, and Hiachuele) lists the following deaths between the years 1950 and 1960: 119 suicides, 73 men and 46 women; 367 accidents, 349 men and 18 women. Under the category "others and nonspecific," one finds throwing oneself under a train or subway, burning to death, etc. As seen, the principal methods used to commit suicide are violent.

The causes leading to suicide are generally so multiple and complex that only a deep psychoanalysis can elicit the basic motivations and intrinsic mechanism. It is important to distinguish between the determining and precipitating causes. The act of suicide implies a psychotic phenomenon. The most apparent reasons, according to the police files, are: 1) weariness of life, 2) physical sufferings. In much smaller frequencies are: 3) mental alienation, 4) family disgust, 5) lack of resources, and 6) love contradictions. On the other hand, in past historical overviews, "physical sufferings" occupied first place, followed by "business troubles" and "other causes" ("drunkenness" and "lack of resources" mostly). The expressions "weariness of life," "physical suffering," and "alienation" together with the currently greater frequency of suicides among older people (60 to 70 years), reveal the social isolation and hopelessness of certain social groups. I have mentioned the pensioners and housewives, but it is necessary to consider all those who are over 50 years old. I do not attribute the high rate to age alone, but rather to the psychosocial factors associated with it in the socio-dynamic context of this cosmopolitan metropolis.

What can be said about the prevalence of suicide in older ages? Many decades ago young people were the ones who killed themselves, and now the older people predominate. I consider this a result of the greater freedom and possibilities to externalize aggressiveness that the adolescent and young people have today. Either at work or at leisure, study or recreation, sports or sexual relations, be it psychopathic or sociopathic, they have means and resources that were and still are denied to older people. The contemporary young people are more free, spontaneous, or mad, but they commit less suicide than before. Many of them even have access to the resources of psychotherapy. It is obvious, of course, that this "freedom" or "liberation" does not imply "maturity" or insurance against suicide. But it is the older people who must make efforts to adapt in order to gain an adequate integration into the new and constantly changing way of life, created in a way by the young people. This need occurs at a time in which the individual stereotype has become rigid. The socioeconomic and cultural conditions isolate them socially. They are excluded and lonely, which is why they constitute a group vulnerable to self-destruction. The family in this city is becoming more and more nuclear and isolated. The masculine members–if they do not have an occupation within the family–frequently represent a burden. When illnesses and other stressing factors are added, the situation becomes critical.

RELATIONSHIP BETWEEN SUICIDES AND SUICIDE ATTEMPTS

If we compare the group of committed suicides with the attempt group, those identified by the police files, certain differences can be found. For example, fewer suicide attempts are registered than committed suicides. Insofar as the method employed is concerned, in both groups firearms, jumping from buildings, and poisoning are used most often. However, in the attempts, cutting and poison are most common among females; in committed suicides, hanging and throwing oneself under a train are most common.

The precipitating causes have the same order of priority in both groups. Suicide attempts are most frequent among young people, especially those 18 to 30 years old, and less frequent among the 40- to 50-year age group. After this age, the committed suicides are definitely greater. In the epidemiological researches by Tolchinsky at the J. M. Penna Hospital (including the period 1964–1967, and the period from January, 1967 to April 10, 1968), it was learned that the suicide profile was similar to those observed at other hospitals in Buenos Aires. During the first period 150 cases were registered, of which 106 were women and 44 men; in the second period, there were 68 cases, 46 women and 22 men. Of these 218 cases, 4 were younger than 14 years, 93 were 15 to 24 years old, and 99 were 25 to 49 years old. One hundred twenty-seven cases took place during the summertime and 97 during the winter time. In the first group of 150 suicides the methods employed were: barbiturates, 48; psychodrugs, 43; other poisons, 8; and cutting, 12. Tolchinsky said that the psychodrugs as a suicide element have definitely displaced barbiturates. He emphasized the necessity of detecting depressions and particularly severe reactive depressions for quick medical psychiatric treatment.

In a study done at the Araoz Alfaro Clinic on a sample of 40 cases and 30 controls, Fernandez Moujan (1969) stressed the importance of management of anxieties in adolescents. Failure, he felt, produces isolation and increases hostility, which the adolescent relieves by either suicide or delinquency. His observations covered a period of 2 years on individuals 12 to 21 years old, of whom about 77 percent were females. Among the external causes are lack of family or social help; the internal cause is primarily identity crisis. He postulated the existence of two different groups—benign and malignant. The first group he characterized as a "feminine" way of dealing with aggressiveness; *i.e.*, the suicide attempt is an expression of a social and personal identity crisis in which masochism is important and the predominant structure is neurotic. The suicidal behavior is reactive, not a characteristic pattern. The other group is characterized by an indiscriminate way of dealing with aggressiveness and object relationships; confusion prevails and there is difficulty in symbolizing. The suicide attempts reflect the tone of the individual's self; he is trying to release his infantile traumatic experience. The understructure is predominantly psychotic, and suicidal conduct can be considered characteristic of this personality type. He postulated phobias as an antisuicide index, and, to a lesser degree, obsessions and other character symptoms.

In another investigation Fernandez Moujan (1970) studied intensively 20 of 70 families of adolescents who attempted to commit suicide and reached the following conclusions. Sixty-nine percent of the suicides came from "agglutinate" families, which are characterized by "deficiencies in the elaboration of aggression." The latter is defined as an incapacity to respond to natural or circumstantial sources of hostility, its verbalization or implementation. They were also unable to learn how to diminish its intensity or to modify its quality. On the other hand, 80 percent of the control families could be considered "integrated" in expressing aggression.

SUBSTITUTIVE FORMS OF DESTRUCTIVE BEHAVIOR IN BUENOS AIRES

Many authors have pointed out the close relationship between suicide and homicide, some even proposing that an inverse proportional relation exists between them. However, no such relationship can be demonstrated in Buenos Aires. Homicide has always been less frequent than suicide, and its curve in Buenos Aires is neither parallel to nor inverse to the suicide curve. Its rate had been higher than 10 for each 100,000 population from the end of the 19th century until 1925. Since than it has decreased steadily and has varied around 3 per 100,000. Thus, in Buenos Aires people kill themselves more than they kill other people in a proportion of nearly 3 to 1. However, if we add the figures of nonintended killings (unpremeditated manslaughter) to those of premeditated homicides, the number would equal or even surpass the total of suicides.

The common base lies in the handling of aggression. The changes that have occurred in Buenos Aires in methods for channelizing aggression are most clearly seen in adolescents. At the beginning of the century, young people were more rigid and had more dramatic conflicts which resulted in a greater tendency to kill themselves when facing great difficulties. Nowadays, society is more accepting and requires less from them, permitting them more spontaneous outlets for their aggressive impulses whether the impulses are psychopathic or not. In addition, the methods used in self-aggression are much more innocuous, and they also have psychotherapy more readily available.

Accidents are also closely related to this subject. In Buenos Aires, during the period 1965 to 1969, there were 1,519 deaths from accidents, of which 1,151 were males and 368 females. A few years ago, the Argentine Institute for the Prevention of Accidents was formed. Its purpose is to determine the origins of citizen tensions and to prevent accidents. Its integral objectives are the promotion of conditions that will offer the citizen good jobs and sufficient food and rest.

A special sector is represented by those who commit suicide in indirect ways, *e.g.*, diabetics who "manage" to enter a state of nonreversible metabolic imbalance; the cancer patient who is in the early stages of the disease but ignores his affliction until it is too late; those who do not want to live after surgery; and many other subtle cases. If we were to include all the different levels of suicide we would have to add "altruistic" or "martyr" suicides, as well as the different degrees of "psychic" suicides. We also have "mini-suicides" and "suicide equivalents." I have had the opportunity of studying many serious children's accidents and infantile deaths. In them, the suicide intent was expressed at different levels. The same would apply to delinquency and to other risky activities undertaken by adolescents.

ALCOHOLISM AND DRUG ADDICTION AS CORRELATIVE FACTORS

Argentina is one of the greatest producers and consumers of wine in the world. Among the hybrid population of the Northeast, Northwest, and Southwest there is a great tolerance for excessive ingestion of alcohol, but in the Federal District there is strong rejection of alcoholism. An investigation completed by Goldenberg and his collaborators (1965) revealed that 90 percent of the population drinks wine. Theoretically the "ideal" ingestion is ¼ to 1 liter daily, and the average person consumes almost that amount. People begin drinking wine at a very young age. The image of the alcoholic is an undesirable one and alcoholism is regarded as a vice. More than half of the people consider alcoholism an important problem of the country.

At the Araoz Alfaro Psychopathological Clinic, 4 to 8 percent of those admitted are alcoholics. In Buenos Aires, Federal Police files indicated that of the 559 homicides committed between 1960 and 1965, 39 were associated with alcoholic intoxication. Alcoholism was more of a problem at the beginning of the century. The first professional person to address himself to this problem was Juan B. Justo, in 1896. The psychiatrist, Domingo Cabred, in 1890, built the Alcoholic Hospital and in 1904 created the League Against Alcoholism. Nowadays, two institutions undertake this task: the Division for the Fight against Alcoholism (of the Mental Health Institute), and the Department for the Study and Treatment of Alcoholic Intoxication (Buenos Aires).

Vidal (1967) described the Buenos Aires alcoholic as a solitary patient whose addiction starts as a consequence of personal problems. The subculture expresses itself through certain occupational groups (as the harbor stevedores) or migrational ones (from Corrientes and Tucuman). The alcoholic reveals a great affective dependence on the mother or a subculture that replaces her.

The use and abuse of drugs has become an observable fact in the city of Buenos Aires these days. Ten years ago those who experimented with drugs were from certain artistic or intellectual circles. The present situation is very different and it has alarmed health authorities as well as the daily press. A recent report from the Mental Health Institute (1971) concluded that the increase in the number of young people who go to hospitals (30 percent higher in the last 4 years) is due to an excessive use of drugs. The use of common drugs (amphetamines, benzedrines and their derivatives, and other psychodrugs) now also includes lysergic acid diethylamide (LSD), marihuana, and heroin. This prompted the ministry to regulate the dispensing and consumption of drugs, including specifically hallucinogenics and depersonalizing substances.

Youthful restlessness is expressed not only in progressive and constructive ways but also in violent and destructive ways. The immediate causes are curiosity and imitation, but at the bottom lies the wish to reinforce a personality in crisis. The consequences have not been evaluated yet, but the problem has attracted public attention. A vast field has opened involving repression of traffickers, medical-psychiatric treatment for addicts, and the dissemination of information of the harmful effects of drugs (Eiman, 1970). Investigating addiction to drugs in general and psychodrugs in particular among university students on a sample of 200 people, Imas (1969) reached the following preliminary conclusions. Twenty-five percent of the students take drugs or psychodrugs habitually. Some of them use a variety of drugs and/or psychodrugs simultaneously in different situations: a) 18 percent use stimulants during exam periods; b) 8 percent use tranquilizers or stimulants in order to perform their daily activities; and c) 4.5 percent use LSD, heroin, marihuana, or other similar drugs in different activities.

Rosenfeld (1970) concluded that drug addiction in this city does not have epidemiological characteristics. It is endemic in regions. There is no large organization controlling the distribution of morphine, heroin, marihuana, amphetamines, sedatives, and other psychodrugs. In two recent works, Rosenfeld (1970, 1971) has analogized the stages of the psychotherapeutic process in the analytical situation and the origin of drug addiction. In the first one, characterized by the indiscriminate use of drugs, there is a terrific struggle in the patient's internal world and total confusion as regards the therapist; in the second and third stages, the patient uses only one drug. In the fourth stage the possibility of recovering lost objects appears. For example, he may play with a puppy and be its companion day or night, with the feeling that he may attack it without killing it, and at the same time take care and pet it. In the fifth he comes closer to the therapist as a live object. In the first and fourth stages there is greater danger of suicide. In the first stage the patient is disorganized; the fourth stage is the most dangerous because there are no prodromal clues. Behavior is strongly narcissistic and split, with an affirmation of omnipotence as an answer to the greater awareness of object loss and feeling of abandonment. The theory considers addiction as an intent to recover, through the primitive corporal sensations provided by the drug, concrete aspects of maternal love (skin to skin contact, warmth by means of cutaneous contact). Such individuals have difficulty incorporating a good object because of their sadism and maternal-self difficulties. They are always trying to recover the infrequent contacts with her.

Liberman (1959) said that all toxicomanias usually evolve from a problem of human relations, a conflict between man and culture. The addict has infantile, unresolved conflicts that are exacerbated by biological, social, cultural, and economic factors. The addict reveals global conduct disorder, resorting to drugs in order to avert abulia, insensibility, and sadness. What the addict is trying to avoid is depression and guilt feelings by blocking chemically the reign the superego has over some parts of the ego. He experiences a constant struggle between his tendencies toward violence and submission. The unconscious fantasies brought about by drugs may signify taking the body to remote places, taking possession of something very valuable, doing in secret something forbidden, all of which would satisfy desires of masturbation. Drugs may also be used to stimulate creative activities at times of personality conflicts.

ATTITUDES AND FEELINGS TOWARD SUICIDAL BEHAVIOR

On the superficial level the population's attitude toward suicide seems to be, in general, tolerant. A condemning attitude is not adopted even from a religious or moral point of view, although this may not exclude opinions which are disapproving or rejecting of it. The Buenos Aires citizen tends to attribute suicide to a mental disturbance as a result of an unsolvable conflict or a desperate situation. There are also attitudes of disapproval and appeasement, disapproval in view of the terrible impact of suicide, and appeasement of the feelings of guilt which derive from a perception of the hostile or homicidal impulses produced in the other.

The articles published in magazines on suicide present it as an emotional disturbance. They stress the social and economic factors that influence it. A public opinion poll on attitudes toward mental illness taken in an urban community by Bermann *et al.* (1964) indicated that most people attributed the cause of mental illness to psychological factors rather than organic or hereditary ones. They felt that the possibilities of cure were high. Those polled seemed to have a fairly good knowledge of the psychiatrist's role, even if the methods used by them were not well known. The majority interviewed preferred cancer to mental illness, indicating that mental illness may be intellectually recognized but, in general, not emotionally accepted. Since mental illness on an emotional level means loss of rationality and free will, it becomes menacing and causes fright. The possibility of change in these attitudes seems high because of the growing knowledge about mental illness and the impact of the newer information which is already beginning to be reflected in the people's attitudes.

In a subsequent study which examined the public's conceptions of the patient's role, Colombo (1967) reached the following conclusions. There is greater rejection of the person if the word madness is used instead of mental illness. With the latter, affect was reduced and emotional maladjustment was not attributed even when really pathological attitudes were observed. However, once the state of mental illness is established, rejection of the individual is great and practically excommunicates him. This act of segregation is reinforced by the imputation of dangerousness.

We need to take into consideration the role of scientific, medical, and technical opinion about suicide during the period comprised by this investigation, because all such published information has contributed to knowledge about suicide in the world today. Samuel Gache in 1884 stated that suicide conduct was always the product of a "neurosis." He said, "We think that the suicide act is based on a passion that bewilders and defeats him." He spoke about "neuropsychic impressions," which are influences of an indefinite nature exercising their effects in an imitative sense, or "contagion" neurosis. He referred to Esquirol in maintaining that, even if there are no manifest signs of madness, suicide was always produced by a highly emotional state, a state of brief alienation. Among other determining social factors of suicide, he mentioned the increase of population, the extraordinary intellectual and commercial activity, the fierce struggle, the search for more profits, alcohol abuse, and the pernicious influence of a certain type of press.

Arreguine, in an epidemiological study in 1905, pointed out that 1) the progression of suicide was a reflection of the deficiencies and imperfections of civilization and was not caused by progress of civilization itself; 2) mental and moral suggestions were the strongest factors leading to voluntary death; 3) alcoholism in itself did not explain suicide; 4) lack of social homogeneity in Buenos Aires or in any other country contributed to increased suicide in general and particularly among immigrants; and 5) maternity was what most preserved women from committing suicide. Ramos Mejia (1896), Rodriguez (1903), and others supported the idea that suicide was not always pathological, but the majority believed in the opposite viewpoint. Bosch (1920) affirmed that the problems began in the intrauterine period (direct tensions on the mothers and indirect ones on the child), in childhood (due to his malleability and suggestible condition), and in adolescence (necessity of a strong sexual morality). Adulthood was influenced by the lack of love between husband and wife, which brought about feelings of incompleteness and overwhelming anxieties. To counteract all this required great social changes, but meanwhile, religion must be fortified as a moral practice, and the negative effects of vice, alcoholism, games of chance, great emotions, etc., had to be suppressed.

The Argentina Red Cross, in one of its bulletins in 1938, considered fear and anger as fundamental causes of suicide in children. In 96 cases, 78 were committed in the country by rural males, a fact that was attributed to the difficulty of rural life.

Garma (1940) referred to the role played by auto-aggression in the genesis of suicide, a difficulty of the individual in handling aggression. The determining factors included both heredity and environment. On the one hand, there was the individual's constitution to which harmful childhood experiences were added, resulting in a masochistic distortion of the personality. On the other hand, there was the unfavorable environment, causing aggression against the ego which generated a counteraggressive feeling of the ego against the environment. Another element was the loss of an object, along with desire to get it back. But the impossibility of recovering the lost object led to an identification of the ego with that object, and the impossibility of expressing aggression toward the environment led to the channelization of aggression against the ego.

Licurgi (1942), in his book on suicide, stated that killing oneself was always a way of escape, defense, or attack, and in every suicide there was always a variable degree of psychic illness. Delma (1952) and other authors have studied the mental contagion phenomenon in suicide. He proposed mental health education for the general public, as well as the promotion of general education and financial security, especially in old age. He advocated preventing suicide with psychotherapy (in and out of the hospital), as well as moral education and work as preventive factors.

Cesio (1960) related a certain identification with a "lethargic object," as a result of which the death instinct might become dangerous and cause the loss of a person's life. Identification with a psychotic nucleus, frequently somatized, was expressed during psychoanalysis by a negative therapeutic reaction. Such identification with the "corpse" appeared in some of the most depressive suicides. Abadi (1959) stated that suicide was a psychotic attitude resulting from certain mechanisms of defense the ego used in confronting certain dangers it tried to avoid, such as intense paranoid anxieties and persecution feelings. The suicide interposed between himself and the persecuted the unpassable chasm of death. But it is a magical death, from which he felt his survival was possible, far from the persecutor's reach. Compulsion to suicide supposed a regression to the schizo-paranoid position and exacerbation of the masochistic mechanisms.

Rolla (1970) insisted on the importance of the internal handling of anxieties and stated that auto-aggression was not due to a supposed death instinct but rather derived from the fear of living. The individual tried to control his anxieties by acting aggressively with his objects and his self because of his inability to use them in creative activities.

I consider that the character-bound dispositions, structured during childhood as patterns of autoaggressive or self-destructive behavior, are restimulated in critical transcultural situations, *i.e.*, when the individual finds obstacles in the social or non-conflict-laden channelization of aggression. This aggressiveness cannot be counteracted by the individual's love capacity. Even being totally nonpragmatic, self-elimination is a magical solution to a dilemma. The pathological identification with one of the parents (with their ideologies or even with certain behavior features) and the prior experiences of certain never understood losses and departures play a prominent role in the regressive conduct revealed in the suicide act. The changing of early habitat is important to the individual because of the incorporation of space and the accumulated projection of the parental figures within the space contours. The metaphoric model would be self-elimination (in a moment of complete confusion) as a violent rejection of present life in order to go back to the previous one.

In 1971 Rolla proposed his theory on suicide. I will summarize it using the author's own words, because they include and clarify many points already expressed.

> For psychoanalysis, suicide does not mean the act of killing one's self (or a homicide against oneself), but a homicide committed against an internalized object. This internal object has become very persecutory and exacting, threatening the individual with abandonment or lack of love, so that he is forced to attack it, repelling its aggression. Suicide is, then, at the time of the act, a seriously disturbed judgment. Probably what has been called the death instinct is really those suicide fantasies, dramatized by the individual, which are present from the first moment of life. From a clinical point of view they are objectified as fantasies or self elimination attempts.
>
> The clarifying hypothesis is found in the primitive relationship between mother and child. The natural symbiosis does not develop because the child has a special significance for the mother. The mother, due to circumstances during conception, pregnancy, childbirth and a few days after childbirth, suffers a disorganization of her own self-identification, increased by the natural influence of pregnancy and childbirth. She cannot find objects for projection which might have absorbed her anxiety and destructive aggressiveness. The key is a tie consisting predominantly of hate and rage toward the child's father, stemming from the problem of exogamy, or the requirement to marry outside of the family. "When a woman gets married in order to leave her original family, she must undergo the difficult task of assisting her husband in forming a new family, which includes establishing him as the head of the new family and creating a new succession. Marriage then may result in a pseudo-exogen, or a false growth from the outside in, as a result of bonds formerly tied to internal objects now directed toward interpersonal ones.

The author analyzed in detail the Oedipus myth as a model to illustrate this thesis.

The situation is further confused when there is no interpersonal object on whom the projections can be imposed, for then identity superposition results and suicide appears as a symbolic equation of matricide. Matricide is the substratum of the suicide fantasy at a psychotic level. It consists of a situation in which the self-identity of the suicide is disorganized and confused. It is identified with the mother's image whom the suicide attacks, kills, or tries to kill. So, the act of suicide is one kind of epileptiform projection, a condition which generally finds expression in a destructive action, such as homicide or suicide.

Suicide, according to Rolla, is a result of a predominant and persistent situation in which the individual functions on an ideational level of integration. At this level he cannot reestablish his projective functioning and so cannot produce any creative expressions, not even any psychopathological ones, that is, not even a manic expression, a paranoid explosion, an hallucination, or a delirium.

TREATMENT AND PREVENTION PROBLEMS IN MENTAL HEALTH SERVICES

Very little has been done on an institutional level regarding treatment and prevention of the problem of suicide in Buenos Aires. Those who attempt suicide may go to a psychotherapist. The great majority of people who attempt suicide undergo psychotherapeutic treatment privately or in institutions. Those who receive emergency treatment receive medical care and are released without seeing a psychiatrist or a psychologist. Some are sent to psychiatric departments and may undergo a sort of psychotherapy. Although combinations of psychotherapy have been tried on an experimental level, no lasting systematic treatment has been achieved.

Psychiatric services and psychotherapy are now available in the general hospitals. They have demonstrated their usefulness and accumulated sufficient experience to be incorporated into the hospital system. However, in many hospitals they are not included as a regular department and do not have the level of organization they deserve. Some years ago, short term psychotherapy was initiated in some Health Centers for people who attempted suicide. This is still an experimental program and needs to be incorporated into the regular routine of the Centers. In individual or group psychotherapy, suicides present special difficulties because of the high risk of death which creates great anxiety and problems of professional responsibility to the therapist, different from other psychopathological cases. The suicide attempts or the repetition of suicide acts by patients under treatment and direct aggressive threats toward the therapist create disintegrating tensions. Such a situation emphasizes that institutions should plan for maximum security and treat all the cases that have no access to private psychotherapy.

The problem of suicide presents great tasks. First, we need an intensive epidemiological study with an analysis of its social implications. Latin America provides optimal conditions for the development of transcultural studies. With an interdisciplinary focus, these studies would be useful in promoting necessary changes in the mental health field of our countries.

The interdisciplinary studies could identify sociocultural factors affecting the family structure and its function as a group in the social problems of displacement and readaptation. Determining the motivations leading to suicide in its individual, familial, and social aspects should provide a clearer basis for outlining the tasks of prevention.

The second task is a preventive one, concentrating not only on social groups, such as pensioners and housewives, for example, but also on all cases of suicide attempts where there is a possibility of preventing new attempts. Suicide is an eloquent index of familial and social pathology and, apart from being a significant cause of human loss, it directly or indirectly affects the people who surround the suicide. This is a task that must be undertaken from an institutional point of view as soon as possible in all general hospitals and similar institutions. In Buenos Aires there are nearly 400 psychoanalysts, 300 psychotherapists, and more than 2,500 psychologists (a great number of them doing psychotherapy). The public is informed about psychotherapy and its possibilities.

The third task consists of mental health education to teach the population that suicide is a problem which can be helped by specialized treatment and to realize that the family and society are most important in helping the suicide. It is this area that university groups as well as the community of Buenos Aires have emphasized and are working on.

In legislation, the Argentine penal code does not consider suicide a legal matter. It states in its 83rd Article: "There will be imprisonment of one to four years for one who instigates another to commit suicide or helps him to commit it, if suicide has been attempted or consummated." The criminal or medical-legal problems that may originate in a suicide case or suicide attempt are multiple and sometimes complex. The death certificate may be signed by any doctor. He may give an incorrect certification, and if it is not questioned, there is no investigation. Police investigation occurs only with questionable cases. An autopsy is routinely done except when there is very clear evidence or a judge's order to desist. If the forensic doctor's report questions the death as either suicide or homicide, the Personal Security Department (of the investigation division) is asked for cooperation. Within the Police Legal Medicine Corps there are psychiatrists who, working together with social workers, investigate the psychological state and the habits of the individuals. Urine, blood, and residuum examinations are made, and levels of barbiturates, alcohol, etc., are recorded. In cases of suicide attempts, immediate emergency treatment in hospitals is given to the patient. There is an Artificial Breathing Institute for cases of respiratory insufficiency, etc., and a Childhood Toxicological Center for cases of poisoning in children. As I have already pointed out, in general, the suicide attempts do not receive extensive psychotherapeutic help.

The Suicide Help Center, founded in 1967, is a private institution, autonomous and nonprofit, possibly the institution that has been of most help in the popularization of suicide prevention possibilities in this city. Phone assistance is available 24 hours a day. It is the only establishment where a person in crisis and with suicide fantasies may be immediately helped. The telephone system allows immediate action during the vital crisis by helping the patient to overcome it and later guiding him to more specific help.

FUTURE DEVELOPMENTS

An Association or Society of Suicidology (presently being organized) will promote the dissemination of information and make data retrieval an easy task. The establishment of such an organization is most important in order to face the problem realistically and to interest the mental health authorities in concrete and solid programs.

The individual psychotherapy treatments allow the elaboration of theoretical and technical concepts of interest. The study of the family also has supplied ideas. The studies will be continued by various groups of investigators. In an interdisciplinary group, we are working on an investigation of social factors, the family, personality, and suicide.

In regard to treatment, experience seems to show that group psychotherapy may be carried out with the inclusion of two or three persons who made suicide attempts, if they are adequately selected. Its development depends on the elaboration of a model of brief psychotherapy, and the formation of a group of psychotherapists to deal with the task. Treatment in individual psychotherapy in health centers, barely begun at present, also depends on the elaboration of brief and dynamic methods.

REFERENCES

Abadi, M. 1959. Suicide: Psychoanalytic approach. *Psychiatric Act of Latin America*, 5:336.

Arreguine, V. 1905. Suicide: Psychiatry and Criminology Files, Year IV, School of Medicine.

Belbey, J. C. 1928. Increase of suicide due to potassium cyanide in Buenos Aires. *Medical Week*, 25(2):286.

Bermann, S., Colombo, E., and Torrents, A. 1964. *Attitude and Opinion towards Mental Illness: A Research on Public Opinion, and Its Analysis.* Argentine Congress of Psychiatry, Cordoba (Argentine Republic).

Beyhaut, G., Cortés C. M., Gorostegui, H., and Torrado, S. 1965. The immigrants in the Argentine occupational system. In *Argentina, Mass Society*, p. 85. Eudeba, Buenos Aires.

Bosch, R. 1920. Prophylaxis of suicide. School of Medicine, Buenos Aires.

Bulletin, Argentine Red Cross. 1939. Committee of the city of Rosario. Some of the causes of child suicide. School of Medicine, (2), 9.

Cesio, F. R. 1960. Contribution to the study of negative therapeutic reaction. *Review of Psychoanalysis*, 17:3.

Colombo, E. 1967. Sociostructural variables in mental illness. *Social Psychiatry*, 1.

Dalma, J. 1952. Suicide as a phenomenon of mental contagion. *Annals of Public Medicine.*

De Tella, T. S., Germani, G., Fraciarena, J., and collaborators. 1965. *Argentine, Society of Masses*. Eudeba, Buenos Aires.

Eiman, A. 1970. *The Path of Drugs*. Grassi, Cordoba.

Fernandez Moujan, O. 1969. *Suicide Attempts in Adolescence*. Argentine Congress on Infantile-Juvenile Psychopathology, Buenos Aires.

Fernandez Moujan, O. 1970. *The Family Group and Suicide Attempts in Adolescence*. Buenos Aires.

Gache, S. 1884. Pathogenia of suicide in Buenos Aires. Annals of the circle, T. 7, p. 548.

Garma, A. 1940. Psychology of suicide. *Review of Psychiatry and Criminology*, 279.

Germani, G. 1962*a*. *Politics and Society in a Period of Transition: From a Traditional Society to a Society of Masses*. Paidés, Buenos Aires.

Germani, G. 1962*b*. Urbanization, secularization and economic development. Doc. Sociol. Service, School of Philosophy, Buenos Aires.

Goldenberg, M., and coll. 1965. Attitudes toward alcohol, alcoholism, and the alcoholic. Buenos Aires, ES, 19–20.

Horwitz, J., Marconi, J., and Adis Castro, G. 1967. Epidemiology of alcoholism in Latin America. *Acts*.

de Imas, J. M. 1969. *The Ones in Power*. Eudeba, Buenos Aires.

Knobel, M. 1971. Drug addiction in general, with psychodrugs in particular, among university students. Buenos Aires (unpublished).

Liberman, D. 1959. Psychoanalysis of alcoholism and drug addiction. *Neuropsychiatric Argentine Act.*, 5:2.

Licurgi, A. 1942. *Suicide*. Ateneo, Buenos Aires.

Municipalidad de Buenos Aires. 1970*a*. Department of Statistics.

Municipalidad de Buenos Aires. 1970*b*. *Annual Report*.

Pichon Riviére, R. 1947. The sinister aspects in the Earl of Lautreamont's life and work. *Review of Psychoanalysis*, 4:41.

Ramos Mejia, J. M. 1896. The temptation of suicide. *Annals of the National Health Department*, XI Year, 23 and 24.

Rivarola, D., and Margullis, M. 1967. Migrations. Contributions. *Review of Social Sciences*, 3.

Rodriguez, F. 1903. A study of suicide in Buenos Aires. Logical determinants of suicide. *Criminology, Legal Medicine and Psychiatry*, T. 2, 257.

Rolla, E. H. 1962. *Individual and Group Psychotherapy*, Ed. 3.

Rolla, E. H. 1970. *Phobic personality*. Kargieman, Buenos Aires.
Rolla, E. H. 1971. A theory on suicide. Buenos Aires (unpublished).
Romero, J. L. 1956. *Argentina: Images and Perspectives*. Raigel, Buenos Aires.
Rosenfeld, D. 1970. Modifications in the object-relation in drug addiction. *International Congress on Adolescence*. Buenos Aires.
Rosenfeld, D. 1971. *Drug addiction. Revolutionary Stages in the Transference. New Approaches on Its Origin.* (To be published).
Tolchinsky, I. 1968. Suicides and psychodrugs. Penna Hospital, Buenos Aires.
Tubio Ovide, M. J. 1945. Suicide: Etiology, psychopathogenia, prophylaxis. Thesis for the Doctor of Medicine. Buenos Aires.
Vidal, G. 1967. Alcohol ingestion and psychopathologic factors. In *Epidemiology of Alcoholism in Latin America*. Acts, Buenos Aires.
Yampey, N. 1963. The myth of twins in the Indoamerican culture. *Latin American Psychiatric and Psychological Acts*, 9:3.
Yampey, N. 1964. Expatriation and mental health. *Latin American Psychiatric and Psychological Acts*, 13:3.
Yampey, N. 1966. Adaptation problem of the displaced family. *Paraguayan Review of Sociology*, 3rd Year, 7.
Yampey, N. 1967. Epidemiologic considerations on suicide in Buenos Aires. *Latin American Psychiatric and Psychological Acts*, 10:4.
Yampey, N., and Kielmaniwicz, R. 1968. Suicide. Panorama in Buenos Aires in search of its prevention. *Social Psychiatry*, 2.
Yampey, N. 1969. Analysis of two South American myths: Kurupi and Yay-yatare. *Anthropological Supplement of the Review of the Paraguayan Atheneum*, 4:1.

five

SUICIDE IN NORWAY

NILS RETTERSTØL, M.D.

Norway is the most western of the Scandinavian countries, has the smallest population, and is, no doubt, the country where nature has made living most difficult. Most of the country is a vast mountain massif with little cultivable soil, situated in the far north as the northernmost country in Europe, and with a very hard climate. It is surrounded by the open Atlantic Ocean and Arctic Ocean. Only in the southern eastern districts are there possibilities for agriculture and forestry, comparable to other European countries. The populations of few, if any, European countries experience this kind of continuous struggle against the powerful forces of nature and climate.

The country has existed as one kingdom from about 870 A.D., when the smaller local kingdoms were united by King Harald Härfagre (Harold the Fair Hair). The country was Christianized about the year 1000 A.D., in the Viking era (800 to 1100 A.D.), when the old Norse mythology was the religion. During the Viking era the Scandinavians were exploring and fighting in vast areas in Europe and were in turn gradually influenced by the common European culture. The Norwegians and Danes were especially influenced by England and France. In the 12th and 13th centuries the kingdom of Norway included Iceland, Greenland, the Faroe Islands, the Shetlands, Hebrides, Orkneys, and Man as well as parts of present Sweden.

When the country united with Denmark in 1380, it became a powerful kingdom. In this union, Denmark, as the central country, became the more powerful. In 1814 Norway was united with Sweden. The union provided only a common king and foreign policy and was dissolved in 1905, when Norway again became an independent kingdom.

Old customs and traditions have been well preserved in Norway. The Norwegian farmers have always owned their own land. This differed from most European countries, and in Sweden and Denmark as well, where most farmers were subjects on a nobleman's estate. As a result social class differences have probably been smaller in Norway than in any other country in Europe. The country has strong democratic traditions and the population is ethnically uniform. Slightly more than 95 percent belong to the State Church, which has been Protestant (Lutheran) since the 16th century.

Today Norway is a small country with a population of barely 4 million. The country has become increasingly industrialized during the last century essentially because of the extensive hydroelectric development of the many waterfalls in the country. Norway also has the largest quantity of electricity per inhabitant in the world. Today, industry provides a living for most people, but also important are trade, agriculture, forestry, fishing, and shipping. Calculated per inhabitant, the country's merchant fleet is the world's largest; in size it ranks number 4 in the world. These factors have made a vast expansion possible, so that the standard of living has risen markedly during the present century and it is now among the very highest in the world.

SUICIDE–HISTORICAL CULTURAL ATTITUDE

The old Norse mythology stressed the importance of being strong in every respect, physically and psychologically. The hard life in northern countries was not suited for weak persons. Battling against the forces of nature was paramount. Survival of the fittest was probably more pronounced here than in the southern countries. Culture came later to Scandinavia than to the southern European countries. The idealization of the physically strong person with a strong will and power was probably at its peak during the Viking time. The Sagas, our famous reports from these days, do not tell of suicide. Suicide was not heroic enough to be mentioned and was looked upon as a weak man's act. After the advent of Christianity the attitude changed somewhat to the more common view of suicide as a sin which is shameful for the committer and his family. Superstitions certainly covered the field of suicide. A common notion has been that the suicide never would find peace and was forced to remain on earth as a ghost.

In the older Norwegian laws suicide was classified under "the dishonorable homicides." The Norwegian Statute Book of 1687 stipulated: "Who takes his own life has forfeited his property to his employer and must not be buried in the church or the churchyard unless the act was undertaken in illness or rage." The same Act forbade clergymen to sprinkle earth on the coffin and to read the funeral sermon for a deceased who had committed suicide. Under the Act there however, was, no penalty for attempted suicide, remarkable in view of the Anglo-Saxon laws. However, in military legislation, attempted suicide for the purpose of avoiding bodily punishment carried the penalty of forced labor for life. The question of whether a suicidal attempt should be punishable was reviewed again by the Criminal Act Commission in 1828. A remarkably liberal view was supported. This body rejected punishment of suicidal attempters, arguing that threat of punishment "might easily cause the person not to stop at a mere attempt but to go the whole length in order to avoid the punishment involved in the attempted suicide." By the Criminal Act of 1842 (chapter 28, section 12), the stipulation of 1687, which stated that the person who committed suicide forfeited his property to his employer, was canceled, as was the stipulation that he could not be buried in the church or the churchyard. The prohibition of the funeral sermon was repealed in 1902. Since 1902, in Norway as in most other countries, *contribution* to a suicidal action has been the sole punishable offense in connection with suicide.

It would seem that the attitude toward suicide has changed from the Viking time up to now. Still, however, Norwegians like to see themselves as possessing strong will and physical health, as courageous, individualistic, and standing on their own. Suicidal acts are looked upon as signs of weakness. There are also strong religious traits in the average Norwegian, many of whom are a pietistic type. No doubt, many Norwegians would look upon a suicidal act as a sinful act against the will of God. Still, the general attitude toward the person who has committed or attempted suicide is most often that of understanding and a feeling of pity for the unhappy or sick fellow-being, who has done such a meaningless act. All would probably suggest medical treatment and an investigation of the life situation. Although the attitude toward suicide has changed a lot in our century, strong taboos still exist. This is reflected in the current attitude of the Norwegian Broadcasting Corporation, which allows no informative programs on suicide, on either radio or television, even if the program is staged exclusively by experts in suicidology.

Toward the survivors, the reaction of the environment encompasses a feeling of pity, but most people are unsure and insecure in their behavior. The survivors themselves are ashamed and never like to be reminded of the death. This phenomenon will be discussed later in this article. The burial and mourning practices are the same for those committing suicide as for others.

INCIDENCE OF SUICIDE IN NORWAY

Generally it is a well known fact that international suicide statistics are not very well suited for comparison between countries because of many sources of error. Registration, for example, is affected not only by differences in procedures, but also by the attitudes of the inhabitants and doctors toward suicide. These factors are in turn influenced by religious and moral traditions, laws, and social systems. However, within the same country comparisons may be acceptable.

It is hard to explain why the rate of suicide has remained so stable in Norway despite the immense development that has taken place with financial expansion and introduction of social security. The average rate of suicide from 1876 to 1900 was 6.6 per 100,000; from 1901 to 1925, it was 5.9; from 1926 to 1950, 6.6; and from 1951 to 1969, 7.4. Over the same period the rates for women averaged 2.6 per 100,000, ranging from a low of 1.9 in 1911 to 1915 to a high of 3.6 in 1966 to 1969. The men averaged 10.5 per 100,000 and ranged from 7.5 in 1916 to 1920 to 11.6 in 1961 to 1965.

In the latter part of the last and first part of this century the economic circumstances were generally pressing and the standard of living relatively low. During the 1930's there was a heavy unemployment period, while the years 1940 to 1945 brought terrible stresses to the population by the war and German occupation. Finally, the postwar period has brought a vast financial expansion with full employment and a large degree of financial security. Possible explanations may be that the most frequent causes of suicide are associated with conflicts with significant others or with mental disorders, factors that are not so prone to direct influence by external social conditions. It is also possible that concurrently with the rising standard of living and increased social security, life has become more complicated and stressful. It is also possible that these two presumably contrary social factors may have counterbalanced each other. The ratio of men to women has shifted somewhat, from 4 to 1 at the beginning of the century to about 3 to 1 at present. In most Western European countries the proportion is now 2 to 1. One explanation might be that the emancipation of women in Norway has been somewhat slower, which is also suggested by the fact that the percentage of housewives staying at home is somewhat higher in Norway than in the neighboring countries.

The suicidal rate for men and women alike always rose with increasing age, especially during the last century, but the suicidal peak is now in the age groups 50 to 59 years for both sexes. For men the rate rises from 2.9 per 100,000 in the age group 15 to 19 years to 22.6 in age group 50 to 59, and then levels to 20.9 and 19.2 for 60 to 69 and 70+ age groups, respectively (1961 to 1965). For women the rate goes from 0.7 at 15 to 19 years to 8.3 at 50 to 59, 5.8 at 60 to 69, and 4.5 at 70+. These shifts may be associated with improved conditions for the older generation through pensioning and the resulting financial security and also with the improved social care of the elderly and, not least, more efficient treatment of bodily diseases. It is probable that old people felt themselves more as a burden to their closest family in older days.

Suicide is rare in children younger than 15 years old in Norway. The incidence of suicide has remained fairly stable for the past 30 years for the youth group 15 to 19 years, a fact which may be confusing in our days, when adolescent problems are so to the fore.

SUICIDE IN DIFFERENT DISTRICTS

The suicide rate in Oslo is not much higher than the rate for the country, ranging from 9 to 13 compared to 7 to 8 for the years 1961 to 1968. The same applies to the second largest town, Bergen (200,000 inhabitants) (6 to 11). The distribution of men to women in Oslo is 2.4 to 1, a relatively greater share of women than in the other parts of the country (except for the Bergen district). The proportion for the country as a whole is 3 to 1. That Oslo does not differ markedly from the rest of the country as to suicidal patterns suggests that Oslo has assumed the stamp of a big city to a lesser extent than most other capitals. This is also true in other regards. About half of the inhabitants of Oslo have migrated from other parts of the country. Oslo has no slum areas and is a peaceful city with relatively equal socioeconomic conditions and a relatively low rate of criminality. Adolescent criminality and drug dependence is far less a problem in Oslo than in other Nordic capitals. The suicide rate in Oslo is about a third of that in the other Nordic capitals, as is also true for the rate of suicide for the entire country when compared with the other Nordic countries. It is interesting to note that the data for adolescent drug dependence in Oslo also is about one-third of that of Copenhagen and Stockholm.

For the period 1964 to 1967, which does not markedly differ from other periods, the incidence was 9.2 in Eastern Norway (Østlandet), which has the densest population and is the most industrialized part of the country, 4.5 in Southern Norway (Sørlandet), 5.5 in Western Norway (Vestlandet), 5.5 in the Trøndelag districts, and 5.8 in Northern Norway (Nord-Norge). There does not seem to be a big difference between the different years. In 1969 the suicide mortality was 10.4 in Eastern Norway, 8.0 in Southern, 5.8 in Western, 7 in Trøndelag, and 5 in Northern Norway. Thus, on the whole, the suicide rate seems to be highest in the most densely populated areas.

The above mentioned data give rise to several interesting reflections. *A priori*, one would have expected the rate of suicide to have been a lot higher in Eastern Norway and the Oslo area than in the rest of the country, in part because of the density of the population and the greater degree of centralization and industrialization, but also because of certain variations in cultural patterns. People in Southern and Western Norway are supposed to be of a more religious turn of mind than the rest of the population and their religion is also supposed to be of a more pietistic kind ("the dark coastline"). That the figures are so similar probably indicates the homogeneous character of the Norwegian population. As a matter of fact, the cultural traditions are very much alike despite the scattered population and difficulties of communication. As mentioned above, about 95 percent of the inhabitants belong to the State Church, which is Protestant, and this distribution is much the same in all parts of the country. No part of the country has larger minority groups apart from the northernmost county, Finnmark, whose population constitutes only 2.5 percent of the entire population. Here there is a considerable Lappish minority of some 20,000 to 30,000 people. However, the suicide rate is approximately the same (9) in this county as in the rest of the country. Unfortunately, there is no statistical material showing the incidence of suicide among Laplanders. According to Tom Andersen (personal communication, 1971), suicide appears to be more common among Laplanders than in the ordinary Norwegian population. If this is correct, it may reflect the problem of adaptation to the cultural and financial structure of the main society which represents a focal problem for the Laplanders in our days. Research on the psychiatric problems in Norwegian Lapps are going on from the new University of Tromsø, which is the world's northernmost university.

THE METHODS OF SUICIDE

The most frequent methods in the suicides registered in Norway are hanging and firearms for men and poisoning, submersion, and hanging for women. Suicide by firearms is seldom used by women, for example, only one person in the three years 1966 to 1968. The use of firearms is the preferred method of suicide in younger men up to the age group of about 50, and from then on hanging becomes the most frequent method. In the younger female groups poisoning is more common than in the older women, where submersion and hanging are the most frequent methods. Thus, there are distinct differences in preferred methods in the two sexes and in the different age groups. The patterns in suicidal methods in Norway are not very different from the patterns in the other Nordic countries and reflect tendencies similar to other Western European countries. Poisoning by analgesics and soporific substances are the only means of injury for which the female rates are much the same or even exceed the male rate in any part of the age scale. The frequency of submersion is for both sexes somewhat higher in Norway than in the other Scandinavian countries, probably because the concentration of the Norwegian population along the coastline is heavier than in the other countries. Submersion is also one of the suicide methods where it is most difficult to state whether the death was caused by suicide or accident. In the discussions about the lower suicidal rate in Norway compared with the other Scandinavian countries, the possibility of more hidden suicides in Norway in our submersion statistics is often mentioned, and probably correctly.

SUICIDE BY MONTH

For both sexes there is an excess of suicide in spring and early summer, May and June, a phenomenon seen in other comparable countries, and in all Scandinavian countries. If the frequency of suicide were related to variations in climate, one would have expected a higher rate in Norway during the hard winter months. However, the suicide rate is low throughout all the winter months. As demonstrated earlier, the suicide frequency is also very much the same in the different parts of the country, and not higher in the high north than in the rest of the country. The high rate in May and June possibly reflects that spring and early summer, with better possibilities of open air life, bring new contacts and new problems and constitute a critical time for human balance.

WHY THE SUICIDE RATE IS LOWER IN NORWAY THAN IN OTHER SCANDINAVIAN COUNTRIES

Few parts of national statistics should be questioned as much as suicide mortality, especially where they are compared with other countries. Even if the Nordic countries (Denmark, Sweden, Norway) are very much alike and might be considered an entity in regard to ethnic and cultural patterns (language, level of economic development, and social standard), there are factors that raise doubts about the statistics. The registered suicide rate in Norway has for years been about one-third that of Denmark and Sweden. This has been a fact through the hundred years over which comparison (with data from Denmark) has been possible. Many have tried to explain this phenomenon, and two books have been written on the topic (Hendin, 1964; Farber, 1968). Hendin, especially, accepted the Scandinavian suicide frequencies as reliable and did not even discuss the credibility of the statistics. Hendin's work has attracted much interest internationally. His study is based on a relatively short stay in the three countries, Denmark, Norway, and Sweden, and on a limited number of patients in the three capitals. Hendin interviewed various kinds of people in each of the three countries, people who had attempted suicide, nonsuicidal psychiatric patients, and nurses in hospitals. He also tried to get broad information about the literature and history of the countries. His conclusions depend upon his synthesis of this material. According to his view the differences in suicidal rate in some way are related to dissimilarities in child-rearing practices and aggression patterns. He feels that in Denmark the child is made too dependent on the mother and that suicide in this country is primarily associated with a loss of dependence. The prototype of a suicide in Denmark he calls the "dependency loss" type of suicide.

In Sweden most suicides can be traced back to a rigid and high ambition level and a morbid fear and guilty feeling about not being equal to the situation. This again is associated with an early mother-child separation (ambitious mothers who for lack of time or money do not stay home taking care of the child during the formative years). The prototype of a suicide in Sweden he calls the "performance" type of suicide.

The Norwegian manner of upbringing, according to Hendin, should give better possibilities of developing independence and of furthering the ability to bring aggressions and other emotions into the open. Hendin identified two types of suicide in Norway. Many Norwegians committed suicide in reaction to loss or threatened loss of a person on whom they were dependent. Norwegian men seemed to be overattached to their mothers, but their dependence was a kind of dissatisfied one, often colored with angry and tyrannical behavior. He found Norwegians much more able to express anger than Danes or Swedes. He also found that Norwegians committed a "moral" form of suicide, deriving primarily from rural areas. This suicidal pattern stemmed from aggressive antisocial behavior and then strong guilt feelings as a result of the behavior along with a background of puritanism and pietism. For these Norwegians suicide seemed to be a self-punishment they felt they deserved.

Farber is also of the opinion that there are differences in the child-rearing methods in Denmark and Norway, the two countries he studied. He is of the opinion that the Norwegian mothers concentrate more heavily than Danish mothers on the care of their babies and also that the Norwegian fathers are stronger and have a more central position in the family. He also suggested that the warmth of primary group succorance in Norway is a contributing factor to the lower suicidal rate in this country.

Rudestam (1970) has commented on some of the cultural determinants of suicide in Sweden. He felt that there were three qualities of

Swedish culture that were especially pertinent to suicide in Sweden: secularism, pacifism, and egalitarianism. He noted Sweden's heavy identification with the tradition of the Protestant ethic, its emphasis on hard work, thrift, individual responsibility, and a middle class, this-world value orientation. Materialism and secularism of the Church have coincided during the past years. He suggested that the secularism in Sweden also has led to more accurate suicide statistics in contrast to other countries where strong religious feelings may bring about the misclassification of suicide into accidental or natural certifications.

At any rate it does not seem accurate to conclude directly from the statistics without discussing thoroughly the comparability of the statistics, especially between the small and similar Scandinavian countries. There are, for example, some differences in the registration process. In Denmark it is clearly stipulated in which cases the doctor should report a death to the police. This includes suicide. In Norway the police are notified only if a crime is suspected. In Denmark the majority of suicides are submitted to a medicolegal examination; in Norway only 25 percent of the suicide cases during the period 1960 to 1964 were submitted to medicolegal examination (Gjertsen, 1970). This difference in procedure would, however, not make the suicidal rate artifically low in Norway. It might, on the contrary, reduce the number of registered cases in Denmark.

In all countries doctors sign a death certificate when called in, whether before or after the death. Whether a Norwegian doctor would hesitate more than a Danish or Swedish colleague to register a case as suicide remains to be proved. However, there is one factor that raises suspicion. The sum of deaths by accidents and suicide are about the same in Norway and Sweden, and only slightly higher in Denmark. This might indicate an underregistration of suicide in Norway. However, why this should be so remains to be explained. A Norwegian doctor traditionally might have a greater tendency to indicate other causes of death, so long as there is room for doubt. This might have something to do with suicide being more taboo in Norway as a result of stronger religious and "rural" traditions. Also, as mentioned before, accidental death by drowning might hide suicide to a greater extent in Norway than in the other Scandinavian countries, in that the bulk of the Norwegian population live along the coast and a higher proportion of this population have an occupational relationship with the sea (shipping, fishery). (In 1969, 347 deaths by drowning were registered, or more than the number of suicides). Link (1969) has explained Sweden's higher suicide rate by pointing out that Sweden has the world's most reliable statistics, that autopsies are performed routinely, that there are fewer moral and religious taboos against suicide, that Sweden has a very low birth rate and a predominance of older people, and that if unpredicted deaths are viewed as a whole (including accidents and homicides), Sweden's figures are similar to those of most other Western countries. Of all the factors mentioned the low birth rate and predominance of older people will also be found in Norway.

The comparability of the Nordic suicide statistics have been discussed by Bolander (1972). Her conclusions are: "Since Denmark, Finland, Norway and Sweden may be regarded as an entity in many respects—with great similarities in tradition, cultural standards, medical and social organization, climate etc.—they have often been thought of as a suitable sphere for epidemiological investigations. From the present report on suicides, on the other hand, one might suppose that Norway differs from the other three countries in physical health and well-being, unless other explanations can be found for the low rates. From many factors in Norwegian society one might in fact conclude that suicide rates are low but also that they are artificially reduced."

It thus seems to be a fact that Norwegian suicidal rates are distinctly lower than those in the other Scandinavian countries, but that the difference perhaps is not so marked as the statistics indicate. Perhaps the lower suicide rate in Norway compared with the other Scandinavian countries may reflect a lower level of criminal activity in Norway, especially an extremely low frequency of violent crime and murder, a lower adolescent crime rate, and a much lower frequency of adolescent drug dependence. Are there any explanations in common?

The lower suicide rate, the lower frequency of violent crime, the lower frequency of adolescent drug dependence might indicate that there are elements in the Norwegian society that, to a certain degree, promote emotional health in Norway. However, according to my own view it is very difficult to "analyze" the "national character" of a nation. One pertinent objection would be that there might be as much difference in "national character" and methods of child rearing between districts within the same country as between related countries. With reference to upbringing, there are more differences between Oslo and Finnmark than between Oslo and Copenhagen, and more differences between eastern and western districts than between an eastern district of Norway and a western district of Sweden.

Should one, nevertheless, accept that there are valid statistical differences, factors other than child-rearing procedures might enter the picture. Certain reflections seem natural, according to my view. One may be the geography, which makes Norway more of an outpost than Sweden and Denmark. With its scattered population the country has preserved more of its original "rural" character. The Norwegian pattern of living probably has not strayed as far from the original as in the other countries. More than any other Europeans, Norwegians spend their leisure time outdoors, summer and winter. This applies both to town and city population, and probably even more to the capital population. On winter Sundays, the town streets are practically deserted because all the inhabitants, young and old, are out skiing. A greater part of the town population have their own cottages in the woods or mountains or at the seaside where they spend most of their weekends and holidays. Norwegians enjoy the short summer to capacity at the seaside, boating and fishing, or in the mountains. And there is, up to now, more than enough space for everyone to enjoy the open air life he prefers, and many favor this in surroundings where they have unspoiled nature for themselves. It is probable that these traditions spring from a thousand-year struggle against a harsh and demanding climate. But these traditions may represent an elixir of life in today's industrialized society. It is a common experience among foreigners visiting Norway that people look more relaxed and less busy than people in most comparable countries, less harassed by the pressure of struggling for high standards. Probably this is only a superficial impression since the country least favored by nature still manages to keep up with the richer neighboring countries in the standard of living.

Among their northern brethren, Norwegians are counted as the most morally strict and the most religious. Religion, no doubt, still has a strong hold on the population, especially in the districts where people are fighting against the strongest forces of nature, in the west and north. This strong religious and moral attitude also is reflected in the Norwegian attitude toward phenomena such as pornography, which is permitted in the two other countries but highly disapproved of by a vast Norwegian majority. Norwegian politicians always have to bear in mind the strict religious and moral feelings in the population and are able to deviate even less when it comes to religion and sex. This general attitude toward life may be of significance in accounting for the low suicidal rate.

It may also be mentioned that in their sparsely populated country Norwegians possibly come closer to each other and form small societies in which people are more dependent on each other. The group fellowships probably have remained significant, so that there is a higher degree of status integration in Norway (Gibbs and Martin, 1964). This is also in accordance with Farber's view.

Finally, the Norwegian people have a harder battle to fight against the forces of nature, including the Atlantic Ocean, the Arctic Ocean, the high mountains, the long winters with masses of snow, the cold and partly wet climate. It could be that "the struggle for life preserves life."

The suggestions made here may actually supplement the theories of Hendin and Farber. While they have used a psychodynamic and psychological frame of reference, I have used a more demographic and sociological frame of reference. The theories need not necessarily be incompatible. The relationships in the primary family group are undoubtedly of some importance, and the demographic and sociological differences are also important. It is appropriate that in this field of suicidology, one must consider many hypotheses which can contribute to the solution of a problem which seems to exist as yet unsolved.

VULNERABLE GROUPS

Inasmuch as suicide in Norway is not registered in terms of social groups, statistical data are not available demonstrating possible relationships between social groups and suicide. However, Norway is a country where there is little difference between the social groups. Indeed, in no other country in Europe is there less difference in incomes between the social groups than in Norway. *A priori* one would therefore expect similar patterns in the incidence of suicide for various groups. Statistical material is available only for sailors, a relatively large group in this seafaring nation. According to Arner (1970) the rate of suicide of sailors is three times higher than the rate of a group of average population with a corresponding age and sex distribtuion. Suicide constitutes the second highest cause of mortality at sea in the Norwegian merchant fleet, 15 percent of the fatal accidents. Only death by accidental drowning ranges higher (28 percent), and it is likely that some of the drownings could also be suicides. It is notable that most suicides take place at sea, not in port. The absolute number of suicides registered in the Norwegian merchant fleet during the years 1957 to 1964 was 169. Especially vulnerable is the youngest age group, 15 to 29 years, and the first time at sea is particularly risky for very young people.

There are probably several explanations for the high risk in sailors. The lower grades in the seafaring profession traditionally have been filled with some youths having difficulties of adjustment at home, or backward at school and work. Some youths are sent to sea to improve or to be away from home. The special social situation of being at sea, where isolation from home, friends, and family all occur at the same time, certainly represents a stress for many. In addition, a sailor's work is hard, involving working irregular hours, little leisure time, and much alcohol. All these factors tend to make the group vulnerable to suicide.

Among other particularly vulnerable groups, patients in psychiatric hospitals have been especially studied (Ødegärd, 1952, 1967). During the period 1926 to 1941, there were 62 suicides registered in Norwegian psychiatric hospitals; during the period 1950 to 1962, 74. This represented a declining tendency relative to the patient population, from 91.7 percent in the first period to 67.6 in the second. However, within the last period, there was a distinct increase in the later years, suggesting a tendency toward increase following the introduction of ataractic drugs and a more liberal therapeutic pattern with "open door policy."

Patients with serious mental disorders, alcoholics, and drug addicts belong to the high risk groups with reference to later suicide, according to several follow-up investigations. The incidence of suicide in schizophrenia is about 1 percent (Dalgard, 1966), in paranoid psychoses 1.5 percent (Retterstøl, 1966), in manic-depressive psychoses 2 percent (Noreik, 1966), in alcoholism 3.8 percent (Sundby, 1967), and in drug dependence 5.3 percent (Retterstøl and Sund, 1965). In the last group the mortality of suicide is 60 to 80 times higher than in a corresponding group of the ordinary population. It is worthy of notice that the risk in drug dependence seems to be even higher than in suicide attempters. In suicide attempters Bratfos (1971) found that mortality from suicide was 2.5 percent (compared to 0.6 percent in ordinary psychiatric patients), Retterstøl (1970) found 1.4 to 2.8 percent, and Retterstøl and Strype (in preparation) found 5.6 percent. However, suicide attempters also are a very vulnerable group.

ATTEMPTED SUICIDE

It has been estimated that in Norway there are 7 or 8 suicidal attempts for every suicide. However, there is no official registration required for attempted suicides. In attempted suicide the most common method, intoxication by drugs, is used by more than 50 percent of those who are afterwards admitted to psychiatric departments (Retterstøl, 1970; Bratfos, 1971). Barbiturates have long been and are still the most commonly used intoxicants (Johnsen and Vogt, 1950; Lyngar, 1954; Omland, 1955; Käss *et al.*, 1959; Dale, 1969). The newer substances, minor and major tranquilizers and antidepressives, are steadily gaining ground among the intoxicants used. However, Dale (1969) demonstrated that barbiturates, alone or together with other drugs, were used in 63 percent of the cases as late as 1963 to 1965. After intoxication, wrist slashing appears to represent the second largest group in hospitalized cases (according to my own study 1970, 21 percent), whereas 14 percent used other violent methods or combination of methods. There is a strong relationship between suicidal attempt and abuse of drugs and alcohol, as demonstrated clearly by Käss *et al.* (1959), Retterstøl and Sund (1965), and Sundby (1967). The main precipitating factor for attempted suicides in Norway is sexual or marital conflicts. Johnsen and Vogt (1950) found such conflicts in 48 percent of their intoxication patients, Retterstøl (1970) found 48 percent in a study including all types of suicidal patients, and Bratfos (1971) found 45 percent. For the rest, more serious psychiatric disorders (psychoses) dominate. In the two latter studies the incidence of psychosis was 55 and 48 percent, respectively.

Finally, the follow-up studies of suicide attempters in Norway will be mentioned as these may also throw some light on the cultural aspects of suicide. Thanks to a sparse and relatively settled population and an advanced registration system, the Scandinavian countries are in a particularly favorable position for undertaking psychiatric epidemiological research and clinical research on the course of psychiatric disorders elucidated by personal follow-up investigations. I have personally undertaken a prospective personal follow-up examination of 71 suicide attempters, who were admitted consecutively to the University Psychiatric Clinic in Oslo after a suicidal attempt. I examined them during their stay and reexamined them myself, mainly in their homes after a 5- to 10-year period following their release, on an average of 8 years. Of the original group 1.4 to 2.8 percent had committed suicide during the observation period, 14 percent had repeated the attempt, and 81 percent were in full social function. Eighty percent were glad they had not succeeded in their attempt. According to my own, and also in the patients' evaluation, in about one-third the suicide attempt represented a turning point in their lives. The follow-up process was a more difficult task in suicide attempters than in other psychiatric patients. I have undertaken personal follow-up studies on two other categories of psychiatric patients, drug dependents and patients suffering from paranoid psychoses. It is far easier to get a previously psychotic patient to talk about his psychosis, or a former drug addict to talk about his drug abuse, than it is to get a patient who, many years ago, attempted suicide, to talk about the attempt. As a rule, the patient is most unhappy and tries to minimize the affair and switch to other subjects. Whether this is a phenomenon typical for Norwegians or more universal in our western culture is difficult to say. My own impression from psychiatric clinical work abroad (England) is that the situation would be about the same there.

Bratfos (1971) has followed up 316 patients, admitted to the Psychiatric Clinic, University of Oslo, during the years 1954 to 1966. However, the patients were not followed up personally. He had a matched group of hospitalized psychiatric patients as controls. Of the material 2.5 percent had committed suicide as against 0.6 percent of the controls.

Finally, Retterstøl and Strype (in preparation), in a personal follow-up study following the same design as in Retterstøl's 1970 study, were able to show that the rate of suicide is higher in patients who suffered from the more severe psychiatric disorders and had been admitted to a mental hospital. He found that 6.7 percent committed suicide in an observation period of 8 years on the average, and that 23 percent repeated the attempt. About one-third were functioning adequately socially, about one-third in reduced capacity, and about one-third were unable to function socially. Also, in this investigation it was clearly demonstrated how strong taboos continue pertaining to suicide, both in the suicidal patient himself and in his environment.

SUICIDE IN NORWEGIAN LITERATURE, FAMILIAR TO THE INTERNATIONAL READER

Suicide is hardly mentioned in the old Norse sagas, but Norwegian literature in the Middle Ages, especially the folklore, described cases of suicide in relation to loss of beloved persons. In modern literature, several authors, such as Hamsun, Duun, Garborg, and Skram referred to the problem of suicide. Internationally, the best known of the modern Norwegian writers is, no doubt, Henrik Ibsen. I will therefore concentrate upon the suicides in Ibsen's writing.

As is well known, Ibsen was very much occupied in describing and criticizing his countrymen. Peer Gynt was supposed to be the Norwegian as he is, Brand as Ibsen felt he should be. Suicide in Ibsen's plays has recently been examined by Lester (1972). Acording to him, there are seven suicidal deaths, five victim-precipitated homicides, and two equivocal deaths in Ibsen's plays. In *The Wild Duck*, Hedvig, strongly attached to her parents, commits suicide when her father verbally rejects her after he has realized that she is not his daughter. In *Rosmersholm*, Johannes' wife kills herself. The background is jealousy feelings, as she believes her husband to be having a love affair with Rebecca, with Rebecca becoming pregnant with Johannes' child. Johannes later commits suicide, overwhelmed by guilt feelings, when he realizes the part he has played in his wife's death. When saying good-bye to Rebecca, who is going to leave Rosmersholm, he persuades her to kill herself as his wife did. Rebecca is filled with guilt feelings and, although she loves Johannes, her conscience will not allow her to marry him or remain with him. Finally, she proves her love by killing herself for him. In *Brand* there is a description of a man who slew his child in the midst of a famine and after that committed suicide.

According to Lester, there are only two other unambiguous suicides in Ibsen's plays: Hjørdis in *The Vikings at Helgeland* and Hedda in *Hedda Gabler*. Hjørdis was frustrated in her marriage, having been given away to someone other than the man, Sigurd, who had won the right to marry her. She learns he really did love her so she decides to kill Sigurd and then herself in order that they could be together in death. Hjørdis: "Sigurd, now we belong to each other." Sigurd: "Now less than before. Here our ways separate, for I am a Christian." As Sigurd tells Hjørdis that he has become a Christian and so, after all, they will not be together after death, Hjørdis jumps over a cliff to her death hoping to find peace in the bottom of the sea.

Hedda Gabler's marriage to Jørgen was motivated by her ambitiousness. When there was a chance that Jørgen might not get the professorship he was expected to receive, she became very angry. By the time the suicidal act occurs she has lost all of her significant others, especially those over whom she had needed to have power. Her suicide by shooting herself in the head came unexpectedly in the presence of Tesman, Mrs. Elvsted, and Brack, who had power over her. Her suicide may be considered a dependency loss type of suicide in a socially isolated and frustrated woman but she also died to prevent her self-image from being tarnished.

Among the cases Lester registered as victim-precipitated suicides are Agathon, in *Emperor and Galilean*, who throws himself unarmed in the midst of a battle into the enemy ranks, and Earl Skule and his son who willingly meet the townspeople who are waiting to kill them. In addition, there are Oswald and Cataline in *Ghosts*.

Among the equivocal deaths are Løvborg's death in *Hedda Gabler*, the death of a man who is socially isolated from the people closest to him. Social isolation is also characteristic of Solness in *The Master Builder*.

Lester tried to discuss these suicides according to Hendin's theories on the different types of suicides in the three Scandinavian countries. In general, he found that the suicides had dependency loss characteristics. However, he is of the opinion that elements of suicide as a vehicle for preserving or restoring an ideal self-image were also present in many of the characters, suggesting that Hendin's conclusions about the Scandinavians may be oversimplifications. For a Scandinavian this conclusion seems correct.

Hendin has also suggested that John Gabriel Borkman committed suicide. I do not find evidence for a suicide in the play. He was quarreling with Ella Rentheim when he clutched his chest, evidently in pain, talking about an ice-hand which had caught his heart. His wife, who arrived shortly after, was suspicious and then much relieved when she learned that he did not die by his own hand. Suicide has also been suggested as the mode of death for Professor Rubek in *When the Dead Awake*, but as far as I can understand the text, Rubek and Irene were buried by accident in an avalanche of snow from the glacier, which they had, admittedly, taken a risk in approaching.

FINAL COMMENTS

Viewing suicide from the perspective of its sociocultural history allows a more comprehensive understanding of the phenomenon, as Farberow (1972) so clearly has demonstrated. A lot more could be said about suicide in Norway, *e.g.*, the results of follow-up investigations, the prophylactic measures and lack of such measures, the teaching of suicidology, the treatment measures, etc.; but I do not think these topics lie within the framework of this book.

However, I feel some words should be added to the accusations that have been made that the social welfare programs in the Scandinavian countries have contributed to their higher suicide rates. There is no doubt that social welfare is an important trait in the modern Scandinavian culture. As Farberow (1972) pointed out, these countries in comparison with others probably represent the most advanced level of concern of a state for its citizens through all aspects of their lives. Social welfare programs are almost identical in Sweden, Denmark, and Norway, giving a high degree of economic security to their citizens. The very fact that the suicide rate in one of the countries is lower than many in Europe, and that the incidence of suicide in the three countries has remained fairly stable through the last decennium, before and after the introduction of the modern welfare programs, gives little support to a theory of correlation between level of welfare state and suicide. The Scandinavians will continue to develop their welfare societies, well aware that it is important to give their fellow citizens economic and social security, but that this is only one of the factors which can help persons to find life worth living.

REFERENCES

Andersen, T. 1971. Personal communication.

Arner, O. 1970. Dødsulykker blant sjømenn. Universitetsforlaget, Oslo.

Bolander, A. M. 1972. Nordic suicide statistics. In J. Waldenstrøm, T. Larsson, and N. Lungstedt, *Suicide and Attempted Suicide*. Skandia International Symposia, pp. 57–88. Nordiska Bokhandeln, Stockholm.

Bratfos, O. 1971. Attempted suicide. A comparison of suicidal and non-suicidal psychiatric patients. *Acta Psychiatrica Scandinavica*, 47–48.

Dale, J. 1969. Akutte, selvpäførte intoksikasjoner i Bergensomrädet, Noen epidemiologiske, toksikologiske og psykiatriske aspekter. University, Bergen.

Dalgard, O. S. 1966. Mortalitet ved funksjonelle psykoser. *Nordisk Medicin*, 75:680–684.

Farber, M. L. 1968. *Theory of Suicide*. Funk & Wagnalls Co., New York.

Farberow, N. L. 1972. Cultural history of suicide. In J. Waldenstrøm, T. Larsson, and N. Ljungstedt, *Suicide and Attempted Suicide*. Skandia

International Symposia, pp. 30–44. Nordiska Bokhandeln, Stockholm.

Gibbs, J. P., and Martin, W. T. 1964. *Status Integration and Suicide*. University of Oregon Books, Oregon.

Gjertsen, J. C. 1970. Rettsmedisinsk undersøkte selvmord (Forensic investigated suicides). *T. Norske Laegeforen*, 90: 1859–1861.

Hendin, H. 1964. *Suicide in Scandinavia*. Grune & Stratton, New York.

Ibsen, H. 1954. *Samlede verker (Collected papers)*. Gyldendal, Oslo.

Johnsen, G., and Vogt, E. 1950. Selvmordsforsøk ved gift. 306 tilfelle hos 278 pasienter. *Nordisk Medicin*, 43:1013–1017.

Käss, E., Retterstøl, N., and Sirnes, T. 1959. Barbiturate intoxication as public health problem in Oslo. *Bulletin on Narcotics*, 11:15–28.

Lester, D. 1972. Suicide in Ibsen's plays. *Life-Threatening Behavior*, 2:35–41.

Link, R. 1969. Suicide: The deadly game. *Sweden Now*, 12:40–46.

Lyngar, E. 1954. Akutte intoksikasjoner. *Tidsskrift for den Norske Laegeforening*, 74:351–354.

Noreik, K. 1966. Suicid ved funksjonelle psykoser. *Nordisk Medicin*, 75:158–161.

Omland, G. 1955. Akutte intoksikasjoner. *Nordisk Medicin*, 53:153–157.

Retterstøl, N. 1966. *Paranoid and Paranoiac Psychoses*. Charles C Thomas, Springfield, Ill., and Universitetsforlaget, Oslo.

Retterstøl, N. 1970. *Long-term Prognosis after Attempted Suicide*. Charles C Thomas, Springfield, Ill.

Retterstøl, N., and Strype, B. Suicide attempters. A personal follow-up examination. (In preparation).

Retterstøl, N., and Sund, A. 1965. *Drug addiction and habituation*. Universitetsforlaget, Oslo.

Rudestam, K. 1970. Some cultural determinants of suicide in Sweden. *Journal of Social Psychology*, 80: 225–227.

Strype, B. 1972. Suicidalforsøkere. Sammenheng mellom bakgrunnsdata og suicidal adferd. Stensil, Bergen.

Sundby, P. 1967. *Alcoholism and Mortality*. Universitetsforlaget, Oslo.

Ødegård, Ø. 1952. Mortality in Norwegian psychiatric hospitals, *Scandinavica*, 57:353–367.

Ødegård, Ø. 1967. Mortality in Norwegian psychiatric hospitals, 1950–1962. *Acta Genetica*. 17:137–153.

six

SUICIDE IN FINNISH CULTURE

K. A. ACHTÉ, M.D. and J. LÖNNQVIST

Finland belongs mainly to the same cultural sphere as her western neighbor countries, Denmark, Norway, and Sweden. Racially and linguistically, however, the Finns differ from the other Scandinavian peoples. The Finns migrated from eastern Europe, over land from the east and by sea from the south, to what is now Finland. Before arriving in Finland the Finns had intermixed racially with other eastern European peoples, and after entering Finland they were able to absorb the Lapps and the mixed Germanic-Ugric population that had previously inhabited the country. Later Finland also received inhabitants of Germanic origin from the west, and the Finnish population in the eastern parts of the country received cultural influences from east European peoples. According to current theories, Finns in the eastern parts of the country belong mainly to the east European race while those in the western parts of the country belong to the Nordic race. However, the racial boundaries are fluid between the population of Finland and that of the rest of Europe.

Linguistically the Finns belong to the Finno-Ugric peoples. Supposedly, a primordial Finno-Ugric people was living within extensive territories in eastern Europe some 4,000 or 5,000 years ago. The Finnish language differs completely from the other Scandinavian languages as well as from the Russian language, thus isolating the Finns linguistically from all their neighbors. A Swedish-speaking minority, which now accounts for about 6 percent of the total population of Finland, has played an important part in the economic and cultural life of the country.

Finland was a part of the Swedish Kingdom for over 6 centuries, until 1809, when it became a part of the Russian Empire as an autonomous Grand Duchy. In 1917 Finland declared itself independent and experienced a bloody civil war shortly afterwards.

A relatively large area of Finland is sparsely populated. There are approximately 4.5 million inhabitants in the country, one-half of whom live in urban areas. Agriculture and forestry have played a major part in the Finnish economy, especially during the interwar period. However, during the past decades Finland has industrialized rapidly. The climate is cool and the outward conditions of life are rather austere. Protestant Christianity formerly exerted a crucial influence on Finnish culture, and its impact is still visible as a strain of asceticism and as a kind of austerity in manner.

The psychiatric service in Finland has been strongly institution-centered. There have been no psychiatric wards in the general hospitals and psychiatric outpatient services have been poorly developed in many parts of the country. This institution-centered approach has led to the creation of an extensive network of psychiatric hospitals. At present there are 4.1 psychiatric hospital beds per 1,000 population in Finland, with the corresponding figure for Helsinki, the capital city, being 4.5. Psychiatric outpatient services outside the regular office hours are available only in Helsinki. The institution-centered orientation typical of psychiatric care in Finland has also molded the attitudes of the public, *e.g.*, seeking psychiatric help has, until recently, meant facing the threat of being confined in a psychiatric hospital. At present, however, the psychiatric outpatient service is strongly developed and differentiated. In relative terms, the number of doctors working on the psychiatric services is among the highest in Europe.

SUICIDE RATES

The Finnish statistics on suicide, dating back to 1751, are among the oldest in the world. Suicides were quite infrequent in Finland during the Swedish era, up to 1809, the annual rates per 100,000 population varying between 1.0 and 1.8. In the 19th century the trend was upward and the annual suicide rate per 100,000 averaged 4.8 during the 1890's. The rise was very sharp in the early decades of the present century and in the 1930's the Finnish suicide rates for the first time exceeded those of the other Scandinavian countries. The rates were highest in 1930 and 1931, viz., 23.1 and 23.4 per 100,000, respectively. During World War II and the immediate postwar years the suicide figures were below those recorded in the 1930's. Since 1955 the rate has averaged about 20 per 100,000 per year, varying between 19.2 and 22.4.

The rate for men was highest in the years of the depression, in 1930 to 1932, and before the outbreak of the war in 1939, namely, about 40 per 100,000. Since 1955 the rate for men has varied between 30 and 37.

The rate for women has risen more obviously than that for men. In 1924 to 1954 it ranged from 5.1 to 7.6 and since then has varied between 8.0 and 9.9 per 100,000.

The rates for the younger age groups have remained comparatively constant, or have even declined slightly since the 1920's, whereas those for the older groups have risen slowly but steadily with time.

The reliability of the earlier suicide statistics generally has been regarded as doubtful. The apparent rise in the frequency of suicide in Finland since the 18th and 19th centuries may have been partly spurious, reflecting an improvement in the gathering of suicide statistics during the period of independence, but this cannot possibly be the sole explanation. On the contrary, it is obvious that suicide rates have actually risen. The present day Finnish suicide statistics can be considered reliable. The law demands that the authorities be notified of every case of death which is equivocal in nature, or in which violence is suspected to have been the mode. In Helsinki, for instance, a medicolegal autopsy is performed without exception in every case of suicide or suspected suicide.

SUICIDE IN PREVIOUS LEGISLATION AND ECCLESIASTICAL PRACTICES

The oldest written laws in Finland during the Swedish rule contained no stipulations relating to suicide. The first law to mention suicide was the General Law of 1442, which treated suicide as a crime against the State. Suicide fell within the sphere of criminal law and thus did not come within the jurisdiction of the Church. If the judge was satisfied, after a trial had been conducted by the lay members of the court, that the suicide had been "insane," he was to be buried outside the churchyard, without traditional funeral ceremonies. If the judge was satisfied that the suicide had been "of sound mind," the corpse was to be burned on a pyre in the forest. The burning of the corpse was later replaced by a burial conducted by the executioner.

From the late 17th century on, suicidal attempts were dealt with as crimes of violence which were punishable by fine or public ecclesiastical chastisement. The Code of 1734 prescribed heavier penalties for suicidal attempts: imprisonment with a bread and water diet or flogging.

The Church Act of 1686 required that it be determined before burials if the deceased had committed suicide. A royal decree from 1726 stipulated that an autopsy should be performed in cases of sudden death, and according to another decree in 1739, the body of any person found dead was to be examined for the possibility of suicide.

The new Church Act of 1868, established in 1870, did away with the shameful burial of suicides. Nevertheless, those who had committed suicide were to be buried "in silence." The provisions relating to suicide in the Church Act of 1868, were apparently influenced by an article by R. E. Lagus, Lecturer in Civil and Roman Law (1861). The author wrote strongly against the view that suicide is a criminal act. He argued that the punishment did not apply to the person concerned, nor did it serve as a deterrent. In his opinion, suicidal attempts also should not be penalized; those making such attempts did not need punishment but treatment. Early in this century the Finnish sociologist Edward Westermarck (1908) hypothesized that the punishment of suicide was related to Christianity and that when religion lost ground, the punishments also became milder. It has only been since 1910 that a government decree became effective which stated that those who had committed suicide were to be buried as other deceased persons.

SUICIDE IN FINNISH FOLKLORE

There have been various popular beliefs concerning the act of suicide and about those who commit suicide. Guilt feelings and general fear have been associated with suicide. It was formerly believed that certain supernatural events could be harbingers of suicide or were connected with the act itself. It was believed that the soul of the suicide might haunt both men and animals near the place where he had killed himself. Ghosts, supernatural animals, and rare birds were, it was believed, omens portending suicide. Tales have related that before a suicide, a big black or red dog, a peculiar squirrel, or a hare had been seen. Sometimes only strange sounds have been heard, such as the howling of a dog or wild laughter. Sometimes the Devil was seen in the shape of some animal before a suicide. If the suicide had led an evil life, the Devil might come to fetch him with a horse. It was further believed that the Devil might give advice on how suicide should be committed. At the time when somebody killed himself, loud bangs were sometimes heard, the earth shook and objects were displaced.

According to ancient Finnish beliefs it was important that other people have time to be reconciled with a dying person. Because the one who committed suicide died unexpectedly, his soul was restless and kept haunting his survivors. One popular belief was that the corpse of the suicide was unusually heavy. There are numerous tales relating how horses were unable to draw the coffin of a person who had committed suicide or how men had been unable to lift it, no matter how much they tried. Nevertheless, the corpse could be made lighter by magic and could then be buried.

It was quite generally believed that the spirit of the suicide did not find peace but instead wandered near the place where the suicide was committed, frightening and disturbing people. The suicide might appear to the survivors in his own shape and even talk to them. More often, however, only an indistinct ghost was seen. Sometimes he appeared in the shape of some strange animal.

Places of suicide generally aroused fear in people, sometimes for hundreds of years. Special names were given to such places and tales referring to them were passed from generation to generation. People were afraid of passing such places, particularly during dark hours. The horse was believed to have a special ability to sense the presence of the spirit of the suicide in these places. It might happen, for instance, that the horse would refuse to pass a tree on which someone had hanged himself. There were ghost stories according to which the spirit of a suicide often appeared to people, asking them to pray for him, and it often happened that if the people prayed for him, the haunting came to an end (Achté and Lönnqvist, 1972).

SUICIDE IN ANCIENT FINNISH POETRY

An important part has been played in Finnish culture by *Kalevala*, the Finnish national epic, and by ancient popular songs. They have formed a significant source of inspiration for later artistic production in Finland; a part of Jean Sibelius's work, for instance, was strongly influenced by them. Suicide is a theme often found in ancient Finnish poetry. It is meaningful to consider these songs and poems, because they provide us with information concerning the Finn's previous attitudes about suicide. Furthermore, as these poems and songs have been passed from one generation to the next, they have obviously molded people's views of suicide.

In the *Kalevala* (an English translation is available, 1966) three suicides are described. Canto IV, "The Fate of Aino," contains a description of the suicide committed by a young girl named Aino, and another two suicides are described in Canto XXXV, "Kullervo and His Sister" and Canto XXXVI, "The Death of Kullervo."

Aino is obliged, against her own will, to marry the old and famous seer Väinämöinen. She is depressed and says that she prefers to die rather than marry him. Because her mother takes no heed of her feelings, Aino leaves home. She reaches the banks of a lake, where she sees three water-nymphs bathing. Aino's vision is described as unreal and supernatural. She tries to swim out to the water-nymphs, reaches a rock in the waves, and climbs upon it. The rock sinks in the waves and Aino is drowned. The survivors' reactions are described in the rest of the canto. Aino's mother is depressed and ruefully warns others against ever urging their daughters into a marriage that repels them. Väinämöinen, also depressed, goes fishing where Aino was drowned. He gets a strange salmon-trout, but the fish escapes him and proves to be Aino, who scornfully refuses to return to the old man. Aino's brother decides to avenge his sister's tragic destiny upon Väinämöinen and tries to kill him but fails in his attempt. Aino's suicide is described with understanding and the tenor of the ballad can even be said to be didactic. The survivors' reactions are typical. The mother feels guilty, regretful, and depressed. The brother also has guilt feelings but is aggressive and revengeful, Väinämöinen, finally, does not admit the loss but tries to regain the lost object.

The poems dealing with Kullervo are among the most impressive and dramatic in the whole *Kalevala*. Kullervo is a youth who has lost his father in war and has had to live with his father's enemies ever since infancy. Kullervo is described as an embittered and hostile young hero who feels himself called upon to avenge the losses and injustices he has suffered. When he grows up, Kullervo comes to know that his parents, brothers, and sisters were not killed in war. He finally finds his parents and then learns that his elder sister was lost in the woods when gathering berries and is apparently dead. Kullervo stays to live with his parents. On a journey he meets a maiden and, using the precious things he has with him as a lure, he succeeds in having her follow him and in seducing her. They shortly learn, however, that the maiden is his lost sister. Kullervo's sister says it would have been better for her to die in the woods, so that she would never have met her brother. She flies from Kullervo and throws herself into a torrent, where, in the words of the poet, she finds "refuge" and "compassion" in death. Kullervo now deliberately exposes himself to the danger of death by setting out to war in order to complete his revenge. After avenging himself upon his enemies Kullervo returns to the place where he met his sister, sets the handle of his sword firmly in the ground, and throws himself upon the point of the sword. The Kullervo poems provide a lively description of brutal masculine hatred, bitterness, revenge, and destructiveness, which, after devastating everying else, turn the man against himself.

Elina's Death is another ballad in the so-called Kalevala meter but it does not belong to the *Kalevala*. It is the most dramatic of all Finnish folk songs and is based on historical events that took place near the end of the 14th century. A judge and lord of a manor, upon the deceitful instigation of another woman who is in love with him, and who convinces him of his wife's infidelity, burned his innocent young wife and little son (Juvelius, 1930). When he later learns the truth he commits suicide by riding his horse into the sea, the other woman following him. It is impressive that the ballad survived in the memory of the people of the districts surrounding the manor for almost 400 years. It was not until late in the 18th century that it was first written down. Although the ballad is based at least partly on historical events, it may also have been influenced by the old Nordic heroic poetry. What is important is that the theme—murder committed out of jealousy, and its atonement through suicide—has been handed down by tradition from generation to generation, from late in the 14th century up to our own time. The attitude about suicide in the ballad is one of complete approval: evil begets the punishment it deserves.

There are numerous examples of suicide in more recent folk songs also. The reason for suicide is almost invariably the infidelity of the beloved one. Most of these songs are romantic and tragic in nature. The attitude toward suicide in them is understanding and approving. To past generations these songs were comparable to the present day hits and comics. They depict suicide as a dramatic and romanticized event with which anybody may identify in one way or another.

POLITICAL SUICIDES

Eugen Schauman's assassination of the Russian Governor-General Bobrikov in 1904 and his consequent suicide was not only an historic event but also reflected the attitudes of the people (Anttila, 1969). Eugen Schauman was born the son of a general, and in his youth had lived both in Russia and in Finland. When the family returned to live in Finland, his father became a Senator. His mother was the daughter of a bishop. The upbringing that Eugen received at home was emphatically patriotic. After completing secondary school in 1895 he studied law, graduated in 1899 and entered the civil service. Schauman has been characterized as a quiet and lonely person inclined to feelings of inferiority. He was hard of hearing and eschewed gatherings of people. He took an interest in outing and sports, particularly in shooting, in which he was skilled.

Like a vast majority of his educated compatriots, Eugen Schauman experienced the Russians' wielding power in Finland as oppressors, feeling that "marksmanship will prove necessary, as the relationships with our oppressors cannot be settled without an armed conflict." An incident in 1902 foreshadowed, in a sense, the later event. During a street melee' Eugen Schauman, who was passing by, was whipped by Russian Cossacks and, in an outburst of anger, he struck one of the Cossacks with a knife. However, for some reason or other the Cossack was not seriously injured and Eugen Schauman managed to escape.

The idea of assassinating the Russian Governor-General gradually ripened in Schauman's mind. He severed relationships with other persons one after another and put his affairs, including his will, in order. In his diary he wrote that it was "terrible to put a human being to death. With my own life will I atone for my crime. After making this decision I have attained peace, and I will now go to death calm and gay."

On June 16, 1904, in accordance with his premeditated plan, Eugen Schauman walked to meet the Governor-General Bobrikov in the corridor of the Senate building and shot him at a close range three times in the chest. Immediately afterwards he aimed his pistol at his own heart and fired it twice. Death followed at once.

A letter addressed to the Czar was found in Schauman's pocket. In this letter he wrote as follows, "My own life will I sacrifice at the same time, with my own hand, in an attempt to make Your Majesty even more convinced that there are serious drawbacks in the conditions prevailing in the Grand Duchy of Finland, as well as in Poland and the Baltic provinces, and, as a matter of fact, in whole Russia." In his letter Schauman further assured that he had acted strictly on his own, without the support of any conspiracy. He concluded the letter by once more appealing to the emperor, "I entreat Your Majesty to find out what that state of affairs is actually like in your empire."

The following excerpt from a handbook of history characterizes the attitudes that prevailed at that time, as well as typifying the way history was written in the early years of Finland's political independence, "The large majority of the people of Finland felt relief now that the oppressor had been done away with." The murder committed by Schauman was very generally regarded as justified, and he himself became a hero worshipped particularly by university students. Some "official" opinions in the opposite direction were also expressed, though rarely, stating that the act was a murder and that "all who take the sword will with the sword perish."

Although the Russians tried to prevent it, Schauman's grave became a place of pilgrimage and later was transferred to another locality with festive ceremonies. A magnificent monument was erected by university students on his grave. The attitudes of the early decades of independence are characterized by the fact that later, in 1934, a plate was attached to the wall of the government palace near the place of assassination and suicide, with an inscription *Se pro patria dedit* (He gave his life for his fatherland).

Obviously, the strongly patriotic and apparently anti-Russian environment in which Schauman grew up, in combination with intrapersonal factors, led him to murder and suicide. The personal nature of Schauman's motives for his deed is evidenced by the fact that, although he learned shortly before undertaking it of a conspiracy for Bobrikov's assassination, he expressly asked permission to try first to commit the act unaided. In his own eyes, the lonesome civil servant became a remarkable personage even before he had completed the act, as soon as he had made up his mind. Judging by what Schauman wrote in his diary, the planning for the act, as well as the act itself, clearly brought him satisfaction and pleasure. Unfortunately, we do not have enough information about his childhood experiences, especially his relationship to his father, to be able to identify the individual dynamic factors underlying his act. Because of the attitudes of the people, and particularly those of young, educated people, the murder became a legitimate act of liberation and the suicide a heroic death—just as Schauman himself also apparently felt (Juva, 1937).

Finland's declaration of independence was followed by a bloody civil war early in 1918. Typical of the first decades of independence up to World War II, there were strong emphases placed by certain student and rightist circles on patriotism, anti-Soviet attitudes, and the "Greater Finland" ideology. The Akateeminen Karjala-Seura (Academic Karelia Society or AKS), founded by university students, was the most prominent proponent of these aims and ideals.

During the Civil War of 1918, two parishes of Russian East Karelia, Repola and Porajärvi, the population of which was linguistically Finnish, were occupied by Finnish troops. The Finnish Government appointed as its representative in these parishes Bobi Siven, born in 1899. On October 14, 1920, a Peace Treaty was concluded between Finland and Soviet Russia, whereby the parishes of Repola and Porajärvi were to be returned to Soviet Russia. Bobi Siven, serving as the sheriff in these two parishes, wrote a letter to Finland's foreign minister, stating that he could not possibly leave the tribe entrusted to him to the hands of a foreign power. He further announced in this letter that he was going to kill himself to protest the ceding of Repola and Porajärvi to Soviet Russia. In the letter he also expressed the hope that his suicide would serve the task of atonement. It would, he hoped, encourage the future annexation of Karelia to Finland. Bobi Siven shot himself at Repola on January 12,

1921, at the age of 21, and he was buried a few days later in Helsinki where he had been born. The burial became a festive occasion attended by university students representing the extreme right, and Bobi Siven became a kind of martyr and saint, worshipped by the rightist students of the 1920's and 1930's. The bullet that he had shot into his heart was later buried in the white and blue ribbons of the flag of the AKS (Virkkunen, 1941).

NATIONAL IDENTITY

It is quite questionable whether it is legitimate at all to speak of the national character of a people in any scientific sense. The view that it is legitimate to speak of a national character of the Finns rests largely on the Finns' own prejudices. The Finns themselves consider that their national characteristics include features such as sullenness, feelings of inferiority, stamina or toughness, an inclination to an unreasonable use of alcohol and to conflicts. Obviously, it would be more fruitful to speak of national identity than of national character, as Erik H. Erikson has done in describing American and German identity (1950). The achievement of independence in 1917, the consequent Civil War of 1918, and the war of 1939 to 1944 engendered notable identity crises for the Finnish nation. The period following World War II has been a kind of clarification of the national features during which the Finns have become conscious of the existence of a national identity.

Although we cannot speak of a national character proper, it may still be legitimate to list a number of character traits quite generally met in the Finns. One might list, for example, industriousness, an emphatic demand for equality, difficulty in expressing one's own emotions, a degree of sulkiness and introversion, an inclination to regard positive and warm feelings in the male as a sign of weakness, and rather violent drinking habits. Finns are considered to be good soldiers. (A high aggression potential and, in particular, difficulty in finding natural outlets for their aggressions can also be regarded as typical of Finns.)

The Finns are obviously prone to depression, the relatively violent drinking habits and high suicide rates in Finland being manifestations of this proneness. One factor underlying this inclination to depression is, it would seem, the strict child-rearing tradition. Until very recently the view was generally held that a boy must never cry: the masculine ideal is a "superman" who does not reveal his feelings. When a Finnish man is unable to live up to such ideals, there is danger of depression and self-destruction.

AGGRESSION PROBLEMS

The Finnish suicide rates are among the highest in Europe, and, as far as murder and manslaughter are concerned, Finland is also one of the European countries with the highest figures for crimes of violence. The extreme forms of violence, *i.e.*, murder and manslaughter, have increased during the last few decades in several western cultures, *e.g.*, in Canada, the United States, West Germany, Norway, the United Kingdom and Sweden. There are, however, Western countries, including Finland and Denmark, where the frequency of murder and manslaughter has declined sharply. Comparisons concerning crimes of violence other than those leading to death are difficult, but it would seem that violence has been on the increase in most industrial countries, including Finland. In Finland, the number of crimes of violence of the latter type recorded by the police has grown 2-fold over the past ten years, whereas the number of suicides has remained virtually the same. The suicide rate has in fact been comparatively constant since the 1920's, whereas the homicide rate has steadily declined. In the 1960's the suicide rate was 10 times the homicide rate.

The prevailing norms of the Finns forbid the expression of aggressions and tensions, and the view has often been advanced that this accounts for their violent drinking habits. However, there is no conclusive evidence showing that the norms concerned are a distinctive characteristic of the Finnish culture alone. It has been assumed that Finns are inclined to interpret positive feelings as a sign of weakness and aggressiveness as a sign of strength and masculinity.

Several Finnish studies have revealed that those who attempt or commit suicide also tend to be characterized by a high degree of outwardly directed aggression. Finnish homicides resemble suicides in several respects. Only one-tenth of the homicides are women. Half of those found guilty of homicide are over 35 years of age, and about 80 per cent of them are laborers (belonging to the two lowest social groups, according to the Finnish classification). The victims of homicide resemble in many respects the homicidal offenders, often being persons close to the latter (Aromaa, 1972).

Obviously, many serious aggression problems have been and still are inherent in Finnish culture. The presence of such problems in a given community is generally related to interpersonal and social structural factors (Littunen, 1972). On the other hand, there are individual variations in the arousal and intensity of aggression; some people tolerate frustration better than others. How, then, is aggressiveness discharged? It would seem that the way that Finns vent their aggression is strongly influenced by the norms and values of the community, both at the level of the entire society and within small groups. In our opinion, an individual's childhood experiences, in particular, are among the factors with most impact upon the way in which he learns to discharge his aggressiveness. In Finnish families it has traditionally been forbidden for children to behave aggressively, although they often have much opportunity to witness violent features in their parents' behavior. In consequence, their attitudes about the discharge of aggression become ambivalent. On the one hand, they learn aggressiveness and to identify with it; on the other hand, they do not receive any training in its normal discharge.

THE IMPACT OF GEOGRAPHICAL, CLIMATIC, AND ENVIRONMENTAL FACTORS ON SUICIDES

The Finns have become accustomed to life in comparatively unfavorable geographical and climatic conditions. The ground is covered by snow almost half the year. The summer is rather short and the weather during these months is often quite variable, although it may sometimes be very warm and sunny. The autumn and winter months are dark, whereas the short summer is very bright, the summer nights being short. The various seasons of the year differ rather sharply from one another, and this also affects people in a variety of ways. For numerous people the early spring is a period of occurrence of depressions. Suicides also increase in frequency during spring and early summer, although not very markedly. Another slight rise in their frequency takes place late in the autumn. During the long and dark winter, by contrast, suicides are least frequent. These seasonal variations are not great but they have persisted consistently since the beginning of this century.

As stated previously, geopolitically, Finland has been a borderland between East and West throughout its history. It has been influenced by both East and West, which has enriched the Finnish culture and given it cosmopolitan color, despite its otherwise original and isolated character. Unfortunately, Finland's situation as a buffer zone between East and West has also meant that conflicts and aggressiveness have for centuries formed a part of the people's life.

Finland was for a long time under foreign rule, at first Swedish and then Russian, and has been independent only for slightly over 50 years, but the people of Finland have nevertheless had an opportunity to lead a relatively free and independent life compared with most of the other small nations of Europe. There have been and there still are considerable socioeconomic differences between groups of people in the country; yet, by international standards, social security is notably good in Finland. Finland is still in the process of transition from a traditional agrarian society, security-producing in several ways, to a modern industrial society typified by high mass consumption. The process of social change has been powerful and social mobility considerable. However, one consequence of this has been that in the remote parts of the country the living conditions have grown relatively more difficult. Much unemployment has occurred, and migration to urban centers and emigration from the country have taken place on a larger scale than ever before. Low standards of living and rapid social change have had an unfavorable influence on the mental health of people. It would seem, however, that of these two, a low standard of living is more noxious to mental health than is the process of social modernization (Hirvas, 1966).

In this century there have been more suicides in cities and towns than in the countryside in Finland. However, the difference has diminished, though not totally disappeared, during the past few decades. On the other hand, the changes that have occurred in the conditions prevailing in urban centers are not clearly reflected in the suicide statistics. For instance, in Helsinki, the capital city, suicide rates have been approximately the same for decades, despite the fact that Helsinki has grown greatly and changed in character.

In Helsinki the suicide rates are highest in the central parts of the city, and in sections with high percentages of members of the lowest social class, of people living alone, and of people who have received psychiatric hospital treatment. The suicide rate for the lowest social class is about twice the rate for the other social classes. The reasons for this difference are still obscure. One hypothesis has been that the restrictions on a life characterized by a low socioeconomic position–including the relatively high occurrence of psychic disorders such as schizophrenia, the difficulty in receiving psychiatric services, and various attitudes toward mental health–are among the factors making for a high suicide rate.

THE IMPACT OF CULTURE ON THE METHODS OF SUICIDE

In Finland the four most usual methods of suicide have for a long time been hanging, shooting, poisoning, and drowning. Hanging has ranked and still ranks first in frequency among the methods of suicide and is used by about 40 percent of those who commit suicide. The method is used particularly by men whereas poisons are used more frequently by women. In Helsinki, self-poisoning has also become increasingly more common with men and now ranks before hanging as a method for suicide. Hanging as a means for suicide is used more frequently by old than by young people and significantly more often in the lower than in the upper social groups.

In the 1930's suicides by poisoning accounted for less than 10 percent of all suicides. Since the 1950's their proportion has been in excess of 20 percent and they have ranked second, after suicides by hanging. Almost half, and in Helsinki already over half, of the women who kill themselves use poison. The use of poisons is definitely less frequent among men, with less than one-fifth resorting to them. Judging by the trend observed in Helsinki, the use of poisons can also be expected to become the most frequent method of suicide among men in the whole country. Apart from being a method used more often in urban than in rural areas, poisoning is slightly more frequent in the upper social classes and among young people as compared with the lower social classes and old people.

Up to the 1940's one-third of all suicides in Finland were committed by firearms, and the use of firearms or explosives still accounts for a fifth of the total number of suicides today. Women do not use firearms often, whereas among men the use of firearms continues to rank second among the methods of suicide. Suicides by shooting are also most frequent in groups of people who have firearms at their disposal; *e.g.*, they are relatively frequent in the countryside, among members of the highest social group in Helsinki, and in such small groups as conscripts and the permanent personnel of the armed forces. They are also slightly more frequent in the younger than in the older age groups.

In Finland, a country of tens of thousands of lakes, drowning has only accounted for slightly less than one-tenth of all suicides during this century. Among men, suicides by drowning have been comparatively rare, whereas among women they continue to account for over one-fifth of all suicides. As a method of suicide, drowning is approximately as frequent in Helsinki as in the rest of the country.

Jumping from high places as a method of suicide was very rare until the 1950's and is also rather infrequent today. It provides, however, an example of the influence of the cultural setting on the means of suicide. It has become a problem only after the erection of high buildings and is found much more often in Helsinki than elsewhere in the country. For some reason or other, it is also a method used much more often by women than by men.

Suicide by cutting and stabbing has never been frequent in Finland during this century. While it was somewhat more frequent during the first decades of the century, in the past few decades they have only accounted for a few percent of all suicides. This may have been because violent methods of suicide in general have become less frequent, but it may also partly reflect the improved efficiency of surgical treatment.

The role played by medical treatment is seen most clearly in the fact that the frequency of suicides by poisons has not risen, despite an apparent increase in suicidal attempts by means of poisons. According to one study (Ekblom and Frisk, 1959), 13 percent of those admitted to the hospital in Helsinki for suicidal attempts by persons in 1950 to 1952 died; 10 years later the corresponding proportion was, owing to efficient modern methods of treatment, no more than 1 percent (Achté and Ginman, 1966).

PRESENT ATTITUDES ABOUT SUICIDE

As already stated, suicide was formerly considered to be a criminal mode of behavior. The Church also did not approve of suicide. In the past, religion and the Church were important sources of norms. Moreover, the Church was in a position which permitted it to use various sanctions to prevent behaviors departing from its norms and to promote behaviors consistent with these. The official norms of the Church were conducive to a uniformity in the behavior of the people everywhere in the country, where all inhabitants traditionally were members of the Evangelic Lutheran Church. Freedom of religion has been in force in Finland since 1922, but over 90 percent of the population still belongs to the Church. Nevertheless, in Finland as in most other industrialized communities, a powerful secularization has been in process and the importance and influence of the Church have diminished considerably. The Church no longer serves as a source of norms, and the people's attitudes toward religion are generally indifferent. It is difficult to estimate the extent to which the simultaneous increase in the frequency of suicide can be ascribed to this decline in the importance of religion and the Church, yet it seems obvious that this has played an important part.

The attitudes of the Finns toward deviant people in general, and toward psychiatrically disordered people in particular, have traditionally been rejecting. What people have expected of psychiatric treatment has been that it should protect the healthy majority from the deviant few. Thus, from the patient's point of view, psychiatric treatment came to mean isolation as a form of punishment rather than therapy. There has also been a tendency for people to view psychiatric disorders as a consequence of sin. The psychiatric patient's relatives were ashamed of him and tried to conceal the case from other people. Warding-off attitudes, shame, and attempts to keep the cases secret are even today often associated with psychiatric disorders.

Today, suicides and suicidal attempts are likely to evoke "mixed feelings" in people. Suicide is still largely taboo; it exists but it is not spoken of often. There are no definite norms comparable to those which prevailed formerly. Suicide is even generally approved of, as it is felt that it is every individual's democratic right to be free to decide about his own affairs, and people often try to understand the motives of those who commit suicide. At the same time, however, the individual suicide may arouse feelings of shame, guilt, and aggression and give rise to moralizing and to thoughts about insanity. Efforts are often made to keep a suicide secret even to the deceased person's near relatives, to say nothing of other people. Such powerful efforts at repression cause additional problems in the survivors as, normally, suicide is a matter that will not be worked through.

The problem of suicide in Finland is chiefly a problem of the Finnish male. Three-quarters of all suicides in Finland are committed by men. In Helsinki, however, the corresponding proportion is only two-thirds, and thus, in the rest of the country men outnumber women even more definitely among those who commit suicide. It should also be mentioned that in the older age groups the suicide rates of men exceed those for women still more clearly than in the younger age groups.

Suicidal men have sought psychiatric help before committing the act less often than suicidal women. About 29.2 percent of the males compared with 44.5 percent of the females who committed suicide in Helsinki in the years 1956 to 1965 had been under psychiatric treatment (Achté and Lönnqvist, 1972). A fact that may partly explain this difference between the two sexes is that many of the male suicides had had alcohol problems; *i.e.*, they had been affected by psychic disorders of a sort for which people formerly did not often come for treatment. Furthermore, because of the prevailing role expectations it was more difficult for a man than for a woman to come to a psychiatric hospital for treatment. The Finnish male often finds a kind of substitute for treatment in alcohol.

The Finnish male also apparently experiences it as more difficult than the Finnish female to mark himself off as psychically ill, as "a weak individual who is in need of care." Such role allocations and role assumptions, in combination with a consequent tendency to ward off psychic problems, may partly explain why the suicide rates of men exceed those for women.

The altered position of women in society appears to have increased their proneness to commit suicide. Women have increasingly left the sphere of home and have begun to participate more in the activities of the rest of the community, and this has faced them with more conflicts and more frequent tensions than before. In Finland the proportion of women employed outside the home is higher than in many other European countries. Of the female working age population of Helsinki, 58 percent were gainfully employed in 1960; in Boston, for example, the corresponding proportion was 33 percent (Sweetser, 1962; Alanen, 1966). The rising divorce rates may be another consequence of the altered system of norms, which may also make for an increased frequency of suicide among women. In 1969 the divorce rate in Finland was 1.3 per 1,000 population; the corresponding rate for the United States was 2.9 in 1968 and in 1966 the divorce rate in Sweden was 1.3.

In Finland, too, the number of suicidal attempts is estimated to be about 10 times as high as that of suicides. It would seem, although there is no conclusive evidence in support of this conjecture, that the frequency of suicidal attempts has risen in recent years. In Finland, as elsewhere, a majority of those who attempt suicide are women, and people who attempt suicide unsuccessfully are definitely younger on an average than are those whose attempts lead to death. Our study dealing with persons who had attempted suicide by poisons in Helsinki in 1963 (Achté *et al.*, 1972) yielded certain interesting findings concerning treatment and suicidal attempts. Half of our subjects had sought psychiatric help before their suicidal attempts and one-third had been under psychiatric hospital treatment. One-fourth of the patients reported anxiety and dejection for no apparent outward cause as the reason why they attempted suicide. Over half of the female subjects stated that they had attempted suicide because of family conflicts, marital problems, or disappointment in love, whereas a majority of the males gave various social reasons. Two-thirds said that they had made the attempt on the spur of the moment, and half of the subjects were inclined to belittle the significance of their attempts. Only one-tenth expressed dissatisfaction at the failure of their attempts.

Eight years later, in conducting a follow-up, we were surprised to find how large a proportion of the patients either denied ever having attempted suicide or else wanted to forget the matter altogether and therefore refused to be interviewed. Although such patients were in the minority, they were enough that we were obliged to give up the study in the planned form.

In Finland those who have attempted suicide receive treatment at the outpatient clinics and departments of intensive treatment of general hospitals. There are no psychiatric departments in Finnish general hospitals, nor is the use of psychiatric consultants at general hospitals sufficiently well organized as yet. As a result, the care of patients who have attempted suicide generally consists in primary somatic treatment alone, with no psychiatric continuation treatment. Only in Helsinki is there a poisoning department operated in connection with a psychiatric hospital and is there satisfactory psychiatric consultation service for the other hospitals.

Physicians' therapeutic attitudes toward those who had made suicidal attempts were previously often typified by reliance on institutionalization and by an "isolation and preventive custody" approach, and the appeal inherent in such attempts was not always understood. Today, efforts are being made to provide everybody who has attempted suicide with an opportunity for adequate psychiatric treatment and, in particular, for some psychotherapeutic response to his suicide problems.

When the writers examined the attitudes of the survivors, certain typical attitude patterns were found. The first point to attract attention was the surprisingly large number of cases where the suicide had not had a single person close to him, so that there was nobody to be interviewed. Moreover, there were relatives who refused to discuss the matter, and there were others who, although they did not refuse an interview, made it clear that they would have preferred to forget the matter altogether. A few of the interviewed relatives insisted that instead of committing suicide the deceased had met a natural death, thus making the situation embarrassing both to the interviewer and to themselves. Many of the persons interviewed exhibited an understanding and empathic attitude toward suicide, and their attitude toward the study was marked by a willingness to cooperate. The instances were very numerous in which the interviewed person had been estranged from the suicide to such an extent that the act obviously did not move him strongly. Repeated suicidal threats and attempts had in some cases apparently estranged the relatives, as it were, and made them indifferent over the course of the years. Nevertheless, the suicide had often come as a surprise to the relatives, even when its threat had been apparent in the form of previous attempts. The relatives had experienced the previous attempts as irritating demonstrations, and the appeal for help inherent in such attempts had obviously aroused no response. Finally, there were those whose attitudes to the deceased were overtly hostile and who felt that the suicide had meant "a bad end to a bad life." A further surprising observation was that many relatives were bitter toward the doctors and the institutions who had been responsible for the care of the deceased person, often accusing these of giving the wrong kind of treatment.

The above examples show that the attitudes toward suicide vary widely and that it is difficult and even inappropriate to present any final generalizations concerning them.

REFERENCES

Achté, K. A., and Ginman, L. 1966. Suicidal attempts with narcotics and poisons. *Acta Psychiatrica Scandinavica*, 42:214–232.

Achté, K. A. and Lönnqvist, J. 1972. Cultural aspects of suicide in Finland. *Psychiatria Fennica*, 291–294.

Achté, K. A., Lönnqvist, J., Niskanen, P., Ginman, L., and Karlsson, M. 1972. Attempted suicides by poisoning with an eight-year follow-up investigation. *Psychiatria Fennica*, 321–340.

Alanen, Y. 1966. The family in the pathogenesis of schizophrenic and neurotic disorders. *Acta Psychiatrica Scandinavica*, 42: Suppl. 189.

Anttila, I. 1969. Assassination in Finland. In J. F. Kirkham, S. G. Levy, and W. J. Crotty (Eds.), *Assassination and Political Violence*. A report to the National Commission on the Causes and Prevention of Violence, Vol. 8, U.S. Government Printing Office, Washington, D.C.

Aromaa, K. 1972. Väkivaltamme (violence in Finland). *Mielenterveys*, 1–2:13–26.

Ekblom, B., and Frisk, M. 1959. Den vid suicidförsök angivna subjektiva orsakens relation till recidivfrekvensen (Relation of the immediately stated subjective cause of suicide attempts to the frequency of recidivation). *Nordisk Medicin*, 62:1176–1182.

Erikson, E. H. 1950. *Childhood and Society*. Norton, New York.

Hirvas, J. 1966. Identity and mental illness. In *Transactions of the Westermarck Society*, Vol. XII, Turku.

Juva, E. W. 1937. Suomen kansan aikakirjat, IX osa (Chronicles of the Finnish people, Vol. IX). Otava, Helsinki.

Juvelius, E. W. 1930. Suomen kansan aikakirjat, I osa (Chronicles of the Finnish people, Vol. I). Otava, Helsinki.

Kalevala. 1966. English translation by W. F. Kirby. Everyman's Library, London.

Littunen, Y. 1972. Väkivalta, yhteistyö, yhteiskuntarakenne (Violence, cooperation, social structure). *Mielenterveys*, 1–2:6–11.

Sweetser, F. L. 1972. Press interview in Helsinki.

Virkkunen, P. 1941. Suomen taistelevan armeijan henki (The spirit of the fighting Finnish army). Otava, Helsinki.

Westermarck, E. 1908. Suicide. A character in social ethics. *Sociological Review*, 1:12–33.

seven

SUICIDE IN SWEDEN AND THE UNITED STATES

KJELL ERIK RUDESTAM, PH.D.

Editor's note–,

The following is a condensation from three separate articles written by Dr. Rudestam on a study comparing completed suicides in Sweden with completed suicides in Los Angeles.[1] It is similar to the chapter by Farberow and Simon that reports their study of completed suicides in Vienna and Los Angeles, in that both studies used the same procedures and instruments for investigation. The latter was a standardized interview protocol covering the following areas: identifying information about the decedent and the respondent, details of the suicide act, communication of suicide intent, motivations and intentions, and demographic information, including medical, psychiatric, behavioral, marital, sexual, social, occupational, residential, family, and religious data.

In each country cases were drawn until a total of 50 interviews were completed. Contact was sought with a close living relative of the deceased approximately 2 months after death. The interviewers were professional workers from the mental health field, experienced in the interviewing of suicidal patients. Because of unavailability of knowl-

---

[1] Grateful acknowledgment is made to each publisher listed below for permission to reprint in part from each:

Stockholm and Los Angeles: A cross cultural study of the communication of suicidal intent. *Journal of Counseling and Clinical Psychology*, 1971. 36(1):82–90; copyright (1971) by the American Psychological Association. Reprinted by permission.

Demographic factors in Sweden and the United States, *International Journal of Social Psychiatry,* 1972, 18-2, 79–90.

Some cultural determinants of suicide in Sweden, *Journal of Social Psychology,* 1970, 80:225–227.

edgable informants, inability to contact significant others who did exist, and the refusal of some friends and relatives of the deceased to cooperate, 31 cases in Stockholm and 36 cases in Los Angeles were excluded from the study.

The intensive investigation of a sample of cases of suicidal death taken from separate countries could provide the basis for evaluating how many suicidal phenomena are universal and how many reflect distinct, sociocultural processes. As a step in this direction, the present study was designed to compare data from established cases of suicide in Stockholm, Sweden, and Los Angeles, California, using identical methodology.

Sweden traditionally has had a rather high suicide rate (20.1 per 100,000 in 1966). Urban suicide rates are almost always higher than corresponding rural figures so that Stockholm's rate was 23.6 per 100,000 in 1967, somewhat higher than Los Angeles County's frequency of 17.9 per 100,000 in 1967, which in turn is considerably above the United States national rate of about 11.0 per 100,000. It is well known that the certification of suicide differs widely in both methodology and reliability across countries and even cities (Stengel and Farberow, 1968). Although Stockholm and Los Angeles have superior and similar certification procedures, limitations of time and money, coupled with the particularly vexing increase in difficult-to-interpret drug overdose, help to distort and, most likely, to lead to underestimates of suicide statistics in both cities.

The bulk of research on self-destructive phenomena conducted in Sweden has taken place within the hospital setting. Social and medical history data have been amassed on several samples of patients incarcerated in the hospital for attempted suicide (Dahlgren, 1945; Ettlinger, 1964; Ettlinger and Flordh, 1955; Jasson, 1962). The only comparative study of the Swedish suicide problem known to this author is a provocative exploration by Hendin (1965). He wove a highly publicized net of interesting speculations about the Scandinavian suicide paradox, *i.e.*, the fact that Sweden and Denmark regularly have high suicide rates, whereas Norway boasts one of the world's lowest frequencies. To explain this paradox, Hendin gathered data from a series of depth interviews of suicide attempters who were temporarily in residence on medical and psychiatric wards in Scandinavian hospitals. In Sweden Hendin placed the blame for suicidal behavior squarely on the shoulders of the deleterious effects of child-rearing practices, reinforced by the psychosocial attitudes of the culture.

A formidable limitation to Hendin's study and the work of others is that suicide attempters cannot be considered to be carbon copies of the general population of suicide cases. Data from the studies of Shneidman and Farberow (1961*b*), Ettlinger (1964), and Stengel (1952) confirm significant differences between these two groups, *i.e.*, attempted and completed suicides, and it is well known that an attempted suicide is frequently planned precisely as an attempt. With this limitation in mind, we systematically interviewed friends and relatives of completed suicide cases and, in so doing, sampled those citizens who actually become suicide statistics.

The method chosen to collect data on completed suicide cases in both Stockholm and Los Angeles was the "psychological autopsy." Initially conceived as a device by which to investigate equivocal cases of suicide on behalf of the coroner's office of Los Angeles County, an "autopsy" consisted of interviewing significant friends and relatives of the deceased to learn about suicidal communication, current and previous stresses, psychiatric and medical history, and general "life style" of the victim (Litman *et al.*, 1963). It was found that these data, unavailable to the medical examiner and police investigation team, were useful for more valid certification of death. A preeminent feature of the psychological autopsy is that it lends itself to cross-cultural comparisons. Data from the psychological autopsies permitted intercultural comparisons to be made on a great number of variables relating to the suicide act and the developmental history of the decedent.

RESULTS

The mean age of the decedents in Los Angeles was 46.0 and in Stockholm, 47.6. Twenty-seven victims in each city were men and 23 were women. In actuality, the male-female suicide ratios for Los Angeles County in 1967 and greater Stockholm in 1966 (latest figures available) were 59.0 and 59.0, respectively. There is no significant difference between this ratio and the 54.0 proportion derived from the samples used in the intercultural study. The respondents tended to be somewhat younger than the decedents, *viz.*, mean of 41.0 years in Los Angeles and 44.5 years in Stockholm. In each sample, quite coincidentally, 18 informants were men and 32 women. Virtually all of the respondents had known the deceased for a considerable period of time, including about 75 percent who had maintained contact for over 10 years. The majority of the respondents had experienced relatively recent contact with the victims. Eight persons in Los Angeles and seven in Stockholm had actually seen the decedents less than 1 hour before their deaths, while 80 percent had talked to the victims within 48 hours preceding the deaths.

CIRCUMSTANCES OF DEATH

On the whole, suicide in Los Angeles and Stockholm takes place in the victim's home. Approximately one-half of the time it was the respondent who discovered the victim and almost one-half of the time the discoverer was a relative of the deceased. Slightly over 50 percent of the suicides in Stockholm were due to drug overdose, most frequently of a barbiturate variety. This compares with 34 percent drug overdoses in Los Angeles. On the other hand, a full 42 percent of deaths in Los Angeles were attributed to firearms, while only two gunshot deaths were reported in Stockholm, ($p < 0.01$). It is significant that in each culture drugs were the method chosen primarily by women ($p < 0.01$), while firearms were selected almost entirely by men ($p < 0.01$). Less prominent methods of suicide were hanging (16 to 18 percent) and domestic gas (eight cases in Stockholm). The difficult accessibility of guns due to rigorous licensing procedures in Sweden is reflected in the infrequent use of firearms in the suicide statistics (4 percent in this study). One might predict that thoughtful gun control legislation would reduce suicide rates in the United States. Since ambivalence has been shown to be a common characteristic of the suicide threateners (see, for example, Farberow and Shneidman, 1961), readily available and highly lethal means probably increase suicide rates. Note that this study cannot be used to confirm these suspicions, since the suicide rate of Stockholm is not lower than the rate in Los Angeles. Likewise, domestic gas is lethal in Stockholm and accounted for 16 percent of the suicides there. Depoisoning the gas in Sweden would not attack the "cause" of suicidal ideation but might avert some of the effect, *i.e.*, reduce the rates.

Precisely 16 decedents from each country had been drinking just prior to their deaths. This information was confirmed by toxicological reports from the coroner's offices in each city.

SUICIDE NOTES

Twenty-three of the decedents in Los Angeles and 20 of the decedents in Stockholm left suicide notes in the vicinity of their deaths. These notes were written for a variety of purposes and sometimes served multiple functions. In Los Angeles the notes predominantly provided instructions for others to follow (18) or helped to explain the decedent's motivation for taking his life (14). The notes in Stockholm incorporated these messages too but more often expressed feelings of sadness or depression (13).

MEDICAL INFORMATION

Medical status is considered to be particularly pertinent when evaluating suicide potentiality. The data suggested that the Swedish victims were in poorer health than the Los Angeles victims were: 34 percent of the Stockholm sample was rated as being in "poor" health compared with 18 percent of the Los Angeles group ($p < 0.05$). Furthermore, 18 of the Swedes had evidenced a recent change for the worse in physical health, compared with only 8 such deleterious changes among the Americans ($p < 0.05$). As a perhaps more important index of medical status, 57 percent of the Swedish decedents were reported as having regarded their own health as poor, independent of the actual medical situation. This finding compares with only 33 percent of the Los Angeles decedents viewing their health as poor ($p < 0.05$).

There was no significant difference between the two groups regarding the victim's last visit to a medical doctor. Twenty-eight percent of each group of respondents reported that the decedent had had contact with a doctor during the week preceding his death. Forty-four percent in Los Angeles and 60 percent in Stockholm had established contact within a month preceding death. Somewhat more of the Swedish sample (about 32 percent) were taking medication in the form of tranquilizers and sleeping pills, while approximately 30 percent of each sample had had surgery within the preceding 5 years.

PSYCHIATRIC INFORMATION

It was expected that individuals who ultimately commit suicide would often come to the attention of the mental health community. Thus, 40 percent of the Los Angeles decedents had had at least one psychiatric contact (including psychologists and psychiatric social workers) for consultation regarding emotional problems, while 59 percent of the Stockholm victims had sought this kind of help. Moreover, 22 percent of the Americans were advised to seek help but did not go; only 14 percent of the Swedes refused to go when it was recommended. Of these psychiatric contacts, 75 and 69 percent were made during the last year, in Los Angeles and Stockholm, respectively. A very high percentage of the Swedish sample had actually been hospitalized in a psychiatric facility (42 percent). The comparable figure for Los Angeles was 28 percent. Finally, between 24 and 30 percent of the suicide victims had undergone outpatient psychiatric treatment, either in addition to hospitalization or irrespective of it.

BEHAVIORAL SYMPTOMS

Several interview items dealt with behavior symptoms subsumed under the heading of depression, schizophrenia, cerebral brain syndrome, alcoholism, personality disorder, neurasthenia, and manic-depressive syndrome, although they did not purport to be diagnostic. Both groups of victims rated high on the depression scale, which included references to sleeping difficulties, loss of appetite, feelings of hopelessness and worthlessness, and withdrawal from people. Few individuals displayed characteristic schizophrenic symptoms and fewer still evidenced the characteristics of brain injury, personality disorder, or manic-depressive syndrome.

Thirty-six percent of each sample were described as having had drinking problems, while about 30 percent of each group had been drinking greater quantities of alcohol sometime in the past. A scale of alcoholism (Jackson scale), applied to the problem drinkers, suggested that the severity of alcoholism among the drinkers was not significantly different between the two cultures.

MARITAL INFORMATION

Thirty-one of the victims in Los Angeles were legally married at the time of their deaths, including nine who were separated. This figure compares with 19 decedents in Stockholm who were married at the time, including six who were separated. A larger number in each city had previously been married. More of the decedents in Los Angeles than in Stockholm had had previous marriages ($p < 0.05$). Marital conflicts were reported as frequent, and between 63 and 60 percent of the respondents (Stockholm and Los Angeles, respectively) stated that their spouses were often in need of attention or reassurance.

An assessment was made of recent changes in marital adjustment. A majority of spouses reported that their marriages had been deteriorating during the year prior to the suicides. This change was equally evident in both countries. In 15 cases in Los Angeles and 10 cases in Stockholm divorce had been considered during the preceding year. As expected, this measure was most frequently considered by the respondents. In 14 instances, eight in Los Angeles and six in Stockholm, divorce proceedings had actually been initiated. These figures are rather high when one considers that the base rates for a divorced marital status are 3.1 percent of the population in Sweden (1967) and 3.8 percent in Los Angeles County (1960 census). In five cases in each country the decedent had threatened to commit suicide to avoid divorce.

A small number of cases were widows or widowers (10 in Los Angeles; four in Stockholm). In comparison, the base rates for widowhood in Los Angeles and Sweden are 6.0 percent (1960) and 7.3 percent (1967), respectively. About one-half of the spouses had died less than 1 year preceding the decedent's suicide, setting the stage for a recent period of potentially severe grief. In fact, between 30 percent (Los Angeles) and 50 percent (Stockholm) of the survivors did react poorly to the loss of their mates. A majority often talked about their late spouses just prior to their own deaths.

Eighteen decedents in Stockholm and eight in Los Angeles were single at the time of their deaths. This difference accurately reflects the base rates for single marital status in Los Angeles (14.4 percent, 1960) and Sweden (27.0 percent, 1967). It was more likely for single decedents in Sweden than in the United States to have been dating often, *i.e.*, 10 or more times per month, or going out steadily with someone. In Stockholm only 35 percent of the decedents voiced negative, indifferent, or hesitant views toward marriage, while in Los Angeles, 67 percent held such attitudes, although the sample size for Los Angeles was rather small.

SEXUAL INFORMATION

Sexual information was not always elicited from the respondents, owing to their lack of knowledge and/or deliberate suppression of facts. Nevertheless, evidence indicated that about 42 percent of the Stockholm residents and 48 percent of the Los Angeles inhabitants were experiencing some difficulties in sexual adjustment at the time of their deaths. The chief causes of maladjustment in each country appeared to be frigidity, impotence, or premature ejaculation. In 11 instances in each city the respondent, generally the spouse, admitted that his/her partner's sexual interest had recently waned. This compared with only two cases in Los Angeles and one case in Stockholm in which the decedent's sexual interest had changed for the better. Eight Swedes and nine Americans had verbalized their sexual problems to their spouses or lovers.

SOCIAL INFORMATION

Results suggested that somewhat more of the suicide victims in Los Angeles more frequently participated in organized social group activities than decedents in Stockholm did (29 versus 20). Perhaps more important are the ways in which the decedents perceived themselves as relating to other people. Only five individuals actually spoke of an inability to get along with other people, but many complained of being misunderstood and unappreciated. Eighteen informants in Stockholm and 15 in Los Angeles responded affirmatively to the question, "Did P (the decedent) use to say that 'nobody understands me'?" Likewise, a substantial number, particularly in Sweden, were apt to remark that "nobody cares." Finally, 40 percent of the victims in Los Angeles and 56 percent in Stockholm experienced a change for the worse in their attitudes toward and their contact with friends during the last year of their lives.

OCCUPATIONAL INFORMATION

Eight levels of occupational position, ranging from unskilled worker to corporation executive, were taken from Hollingshead and Redlich (1958). The majority of suicide cases in each sample were characterized as representing the middle income, skilled worker, and small business or clerical levels of employment. Seven Swedish decedents and five American decedents were unemployed during the preceding 5 years. Illness, dissatisfaction, and other reasons for temporary unemployment were much more prominent than the inability to find an available job, especially in Sweden.

Fifty-three percent of the Swedes and 44 percent of the Americans had maintained the same job during the past 5 years. This can be compared with the three or four decedents in each country who showed marked occupational instability, shuttling around to five or more jobs during this period of time. A rather high percentage of decedents had held their latest jobs less than 1 year (Los Angeles: 35 percent; Stockholm: 47 percent). A somewhat higher number of Los Angeles victims reported being dissatisfied with their latest jobs (41 percent) compared with the disenchantment of Stockholm's victims (29 percent). Yet, a greater number of Swedish decedents had work habits which deteriorated during the last 6 months of their lives (47 percent) than the number of Los Angeles victims who experienced changes for the worse (19 percent) ($p < 0.05$).

FINANCIAL INFORMATION

Related to occupational performance is financial status. The primary source of income for most victims was their own employment. On the other hand, twice as many Los Angeles decedents as Stockholm decedents were receiving monetary assistance from their spouses or lovers ($p < 0.05$).

Exactly 15 persons in each country were dependent upon public or private pension funds for financial support.

The majority of victims in each sample could be classified as lower middle class with regard to personal yearly income. On the average, the Los Angeles group earned more money: 46 percent of them made over $5,000 as personal yearly income, compared with 26 percent of the Swedish group over $5,000 ($p < 0.05$). Note that income is expressed in terms of American dollars based on the current rate of exchange, not in terms of buying power. Figures used do not, of course, reflect government benefits, *e.g.*, free medical assistance, granted in the respective countries. A more promising measure of financial status was money problems experienced by the decedents during the past year. In only 10 percent of the cases in Los Angeles and 5 percent of the cases in Stockholm were victims beset with increased financial woes during that period of time. Problems that did occur were likely to be loss of income, debts, and unmanageable expenses. In all cases these numbers were somewhat higher for the Los Angeles sample.

RESIDENTIAL INFORMATION

Residential data indicated that 44 percent of the Los Angeles group and 28 percent of the Stockholm group had moved within 1 year prior to their deaths. This compares with base rate data for Stockholm of 10.8 percent who moved during the year 1966, including those who moved out of the city or to another residence within the city. It was also more common for the decedents in Los Angeles to move around more frequently than the decedents in Stockholm did, suggested by the fact that 32 percent of the former group had moved two or more times during the previous 2 years, compared with a figure of 6 percent for the sample from Stockholm ($p < 0.01$). However, about one-third of the decedents in each city were planning to move at the time of their deaths.

FAMILY INFORMATION

Most informants were able to provide some information about the decedent's family. In four instances in each city the decedent was an only child, whereas he had at least three brothers and/or sisters 49 percent of the time in Los Angeles and 59 percent of the time in Stockholm. A majority of decedents in each city lived with both parents until the age of

16. But in 18 instances in Los Angeles and 20 cases in Stockholm the parents were separated through death, divorce, or desertion, making it impossible for the children to live with both parents during their childhood. Most of the decedents from each sample left home between the ages of 15 and 19. Heavy drinking was a problem for a number of parents, including nine fathers of Los Angeles decedents and 12 fathers of Swedish decedents. A small number of parents were known to have been hospitalized for mental illness at some point in their lives, but there were only three instances of known suicide among parents of future victims.

RELIGIOUS INFORMATION

Virtually all of the Swedish suicide victims were classified as belonging to a Protestant denomination, the Lutheran state church of Sweden, while slightly fewer than half of the Los Angeles decedents were affiliated with Protestant churches ($p < 0.01$). A very sizable cultural difference appeared in the intensity of religious participation. Specifically, 80 percent of the Swedish decedents were judged to have had no interest in religion and only one Swede had actually been an active church member. These figures were in dramatic contrast to the six Los Angeles decedents who professed to have had no interest in religious ideology ($p < 0.01$) and the eight active church members from this group ($p < 0.05$). Finally, 10 individuals from the Los Angeles sample gave evidence of having had an increasing concern for religious matters during the last 6 months of their lives; only one Stockholm resident acknowledged a similar increase in concern ($p < 0.01$).

In summary of the demographic aspects, it was found, first of all, that close survivors of suicide victims in Stockholm and Los Angeles were prepared to discuss the events and issues surrounding the death with a concerned and open-minded research worker. The interview was, in fact, seen as a beneficial therapeutic experience by several respondents. A great number of cultural similarities appeared in the data. This finding was not entirely unexpected, since Sweden and the United States have in common a democratic government, a high standard of living, a progressive morality, and an inheritance of the Protestant ethnic.

It should be stressed that these data cannot be taken to represent suicide cases among the general populations of Sweden and the United States. They did compose a complete time sample of the suicides in Stockholm and Los Angeles during a given year and probably generalize well to the populations of these cities. Generalizing to other geographical areas and away from large urban centers of the respective countries must be done with caution.

COMMUNICATION OF SUICIDAL INTENT

Part of the study focused on the question of suicidal intent and its communication in the two countries. It has been the experience of crisis clinics and mental health agencies in recent years that suicidal individuals communicate their despair and their intentions in both direct and disparately subtle ways. Since most people doubt that a serious wish to die would be verbalized, the intentions of a suicidal individual are commonly questioned. Yet the presence of communication elements in suicidal behavior is well documented. Tuckman and Lavell (1958), in a study encompassing completed suicides in the city of Philadelphia, found that 13 percent of the victims had threatened suicide prior to the act and that 25 percent had shown suicide potential by having threatened or by having previously attempted suicide. Somewhat higher estimates have been given in studies by Yessler *et al.* (1961), Robins *et al.* (1959), Vail (1959), and Friel and Frank (1958). The highest published figures have been reported by Dorpat and Ripley (1960), who found, in a study of suicide in the Seattle area, that 43 percent of the decedents had voiced a specific intent to terminate their lives, while 83 percent had communicated some suicidal ideation.

Inseparably coupled with the verbal or nonverbal messages of the potentially suicidal sender is the response of the receiver. There is reason to believe that suicidal communications that are accepted with realistic appraisal and sympathetic understanding by significant others have gone a long way to subvert self-destructive acts (Farberow and Shneidman, 1961). This belief has served as the *raison d'être* for the daily activities of suicide prevention services over the world.

Suicide attempts are thought to serve notice to significant others that the attempter sees himself as suffering from personal problems which have only extreme and desperate solutions, In this way, unsuccessful suicide attempts have communication value. According to the respondents, approximately one-half of the victims had been involved in prior suicide activity (Los Angeles, 24; Stockholm, 25), including nine individuals in each city who had made multiple previous attempts. The majority of the attempts occurred more than a year before the respondents' deaths, which may have had an effect on the way in which recent communications were evaluated. About two-thirds of the attempts in each city were drug overdoses. Medical or surgical treatment was received by a majority of the attempters as a result of their action (Los Angeles, 20 per 24; Stockholm, 16 per 25), and 10 persons in each city were accorded psychiatric aid.

Direct communication of suicidal intent refers to a statement made by the decedent noting in explicit terms that he had planned or considered killing himself. Twenty-one of the Los Angeles group verbalized a suicide threat to precisely one person, while seven more threatened to more than one person. These data compare with 22 Swedish decedents who threatened directly to one person and 11 additional victims who spoke to more than one person. All in all, 62 percent of the victims were known to have made direct suicide threats at some time, the majority of which were made to relatives and close friends. Ten decedents in Los Angeles and eight in Stockholm had apparently threatened on only one occasion. A high proportion of the Stockholm group were known to have communicated this message four or more times (18 compared to 6 in Los Angeles, $p < 0.01$). More of the Los Angeles group threatened on the actual days of their suicides (7, compared to 2 in Stockholm), but more Stockholm residents threatened between 2 days and 1 month of the time of their deaths (Los Angeles, 7; Stockholm, 21; $p < 0.01$).

A less direct form of verbal threat was to talk in general about the subject of suicide and give evidence of a preoccupation with the death of oneself and/or significant others. Twenty-one of the victims in Stockholm and 17 of the victims in Los Angeles communicated their suicidal intentions on this level. There were no significant differences between the two countries in the number of times the decedent participated in such talk; however, most decedents did repeat these verbalizations.

A more infrequently acknowledged kind of suicidal communication is the suggestions that one does not plan to "be around" anymore. This can take the form of a direct verbal statement in which the potential suicide victim says that he will not live much longer or that he expects to be dead at a particular time in the future. Verbal threats that were coded as indirect statements of suicidal ideation might include a proposal. "There is no point in planning for my birthday next week." "Action hints" referred to actions which led directly to the individual's death, such as purchasing a gun prior to the event, as well as to actions that could be suggestive of suicide planning but would not directly lead to such fate. An example of the latter would be a victim who recently withdrew his life savings from the bank shortly before his death.

A total of 22 decedents in Los Angeles and 38 decedents in Stockholm ($p < 0.05$) had verbally suggested–directly or indirectly–that they would not be around much longer. A majority of these individuals were credited with only indirect statements to this effect (Los Angeles, 15; Stockholm, 24). A smaller number of decedents had provided action clues that were interpreted as meaningful by the respondents. Seven of these acts occurred among the Stockholm sample and 13 took place among the Los Angeles group. Fourteen victims in Los Angeles and 14 victims in Stockholm made noteworthy presuicidal preparations by making out a will, putting affairs in order, or taking out life insurance recently. Although these were actions contributing to suicide planning, they differed from communicative action hints in that they were not discovered until after the suicide occurred.

RESPONSES TO SUICIDAL COMMUNICATIONS

It is apparent that a high percentage of the victims were heard to verbalize suicidal ideations. Equally important were the reactions of the receivers of these communications. Respondents were first asked how they felt when the victim spoke in this way to them, that is, when the victim revealed his suicidal intentions. Since 40 decedents in Los Angeles and 42 decedents in Stockholm, two nearly equal groups, did communicate some measure of suicidal intent (direct verbal communication, talk of suicide in general, or hints of suicidal ideation) to the respondents in the study, intercultural comparisons on the response data were applicable.

The dominant feeling states of the respondents were denial and concern, and these two emotions were not always mutually exclusive. Specifically, 19 of the respondents in Los Angeles and 19 in Stockholm did not at any time believe the suicide content of the messages they were receiving. Quite often this disbelief took the form of blatant denial of a very direct suicide threat. Seventeen respondents in Los Angeles and 30 respondents in Stockholm ($p < 0.05$) felt concern for the decedent on receiving a communication of suicidal intent from him. There was a sizable overlap here, so that respondents could concomitantly evidence extreme skepticism about suicide possibilities and concern and sympathy for the individual's problems. The third most popular response to suicidal communication was fright, acknowledged in nine cases in Los Angeles and 16 cases in Stockholm. Fright was the dominant response in those instances in which the respondent tended to believe the communications and dreaded the eventual outcome. Other strong feelings reported by the respondents included surprise or shock, depression, anger, expectation, and unconcern, but these feelings were recorded in a minority of cases and did not yield significant intercultural differences.

Informants were further asked to describe what they did upon hearing the suicidal communications of the decedents. One possible response, favored in 17 instances in Los Angeles and 16 instances in Stockholm, was to ignore or deny the threat completely and go on as things had been before. On the other hand, 22 respondents in Stockholm and 15 in Los Angeles tried to argue or reason the decedent out of carrying through with his intentions. In 14 cases in Stockholm and 12 in Los Angeles, the respondent either suggested that the decedent seek help for his problems or, in some instances, actually sent or took him for help. Other possible action responses, used in a minority of cases, were rejection, avoidance or withdrawal from the threatener, ridicule, consultation with professional help, or consultation with nonprofessional help about how to handle the situation. Note that it was perfectly possible to acknowledge the suicide threat on the feeling level and deny or ignore the possibility in one's resultant behavior, that is, by not doing anything about it.

Respondents were also asked how other friends and relatives reacted to the decedent's threats. The informants were aware of the reactions of others in 24 cases in Los Angeles and 34 cases in Stockholm. In these instances, the listeners ignored or denied the content of the communications in 67 percent of the cases in Los Angeles and 7 percent in Stockholm; that is, the respondents saw themselves as being more attuned than others to the decedents' needs.

COMMUNICATION

With 56 percent of the victims in Los Angeles and 60 percent of the victims in Stockholm known to have communicated their suicidal intent directly to significant others, the data demonstrate that verbal threats of suicide among those who go on to take their lives are at least as common in Stockholm as in Los Angeles. A majority of these threateners repeated their warnings, and a majority of the threats in each city occurred within a month preceding death. These figures are rather similar to those of Robins *et al.* (1959), who found that 41 percent of their decedents had voiced a specific intent to terminate their lives; two-thirds had done so repeatedly, and three-fourths had done so within a year preceding their deaths. On the other hand, the estimates of the direct communication of suicidal intent made by Friel and Frank (1958), Tuckman and Lavell (1958), and Yessler *et al.* (1961) are considerably lower. It is suspected that the figures of 56 and 60 percent are actually lower limits for at least two reasons; a) the friend or relative who was interviewed may not have been aware of all instances of communication of intent with other significant members of the decedent's environment; b) some respondents may have held back information about threats made to them to avoid being accused of failing to respond to and aid the decedent. These lower limits are consistent with Shneidman and Farberow's (1961*b*) estimate of a 75 percent rate of threats or attempts within the United States, and thus their estimate can be seen to generalize to the city of Stockholm, Sweden.

More subtle forms of suicidal communication were found in a great number of cases. About 45 percent of the victims had talked about suicide or death in general some time before their deaths. Forty-four percent of the decedents in Los Angeles and 76 percent of the decedents in Stockholm had given verbal hints of suicidal ideation to the respondents. This difference was statistically significant beyond the 0.05 level of confidence and showed that such communications are even more common in Stockholm than in Los Angeles, Robins *et al.* (1959), in a study conducted in St. Louis, reported a comparative figure of 69 percent. Action hints were much less common than verbal hints and somewhat more frequent in Los Angeles (24 to 12 percent) than in Stockholm. It is very possible that respondents are not as sensitive to nonverbal forms of communication as a way of expressing feelings as they are to clearly phrased verbal messages.

In summary, respondents in 82 out of 100 cases admitted that the decedent had communicated his suicidal intent either directly or indirectly. In addition, 48 percent of the victims in Los Angeles and 50 percent of the victims in Stockholm had made previous suicide attempts. Most investigators do not consider previous attempts with their figures for suicide threats. One exception is Dorpat and Ripley's (1967) review article in which they estimated that between 20 and 65 percent of suicide victims have previously attempted to take their lives. Results of this study were consistent with those estimates.

SEX FACTOR IN COMMUNICATION

There was an interesting sex factor in the degree to which decedents communicated their suicidal intent and the manner in which significant others responded to these communications. The caseloads of most suicide prevention agencies in the United States are heavily weighted with female patients, and it has been generally concluded that women have a stronger tendency to call for professional advice in times of suicidal crisis than men do. Results of this study indicate that, contrary to these expectations, men communicate their suicide intentions to friends and relatives just as directly and just as frequently as women do. The sex ratios of direct verbal communications of suicidal intent in Los Angeles and Stockholm reflect the sex ratios of the samples of 50 cases in each city very closely. The implication is that men do leave very direct suicide messages and that some other explanation must account for the types of patients who are likely to come in contact with prevention agencies. Two possible explanations are the following: a) men are willing to share their desperation with close friends and relatives during periods of crisis but are reluctant to discuss their problems with professional persons away from home; and b) the population of persons who come into contact with crisis clinics is largely composed of low lethality threateners. This last point is apparently true. Most individuals who contact suicide prevention agencies do not go on to complete suicide and, moreover, are rated as low risks (Litman *et al.*, 1965). Further support comes from the fact that women are credited with attempting suicide more often than men. (This may be a cultural difference, since more women had attempted suicide previously in Los Angeles while more men had attempted suicide previously in Stockholm.) The first argument is reinforced by the fact that more women than men in both Los Angeles and Stockholm had previously had contact with a psychiatrist for treatment of emotional problems.

RESPONSES

Support for the need for increased sensitivity to suicidal communication among laymen comes from the fact that responses to such communication were maladaptive, that is, denial, rejection, avoidance, or ridicule in both Los Angeles and Stockholm a majority of the time. There was no cultural difference in the number of respondents who failed to believe the threats and acknowledge the suicide possibilities. This figure was about 50 percent for cases involving both men and women. Even blatant suicidal behavior was viewed as a skeleton to be placed in the family closet rather than as a plea to be given professional or nonprofessional help. In the case of men, the same individuals who denied the suicide message also ignored the communication altogether and made no beneficial action response. On the other hand, about half of those who did not really believe that the female decedents intended suicide still took an interest in the communication to the extent that they argued or reasoned with the threatener and, in some instances, consulted with professional help. There seemed to be the unvoiced belief that it is more acceptable for women than for men to complain, even if such complaints take the form of suicide threats, and that such threats will be responded to, rather than withdrawn from, but more likely not on the level on which they were given. Direct suicide verbalizations may have been seen as inconsistent with the male role. The responses to men's threats were most often adamant denial, fright, and withdrawal, rather than arguing or reasoning.

Greater concern was verbalized by the respondents in Stockholm than in Los Angeles toward the victims. Yet even though suicidal communications were met with concern, which was appropriate, this concern seemed to make no impact on responsible behavior. In only about one-third of the cases in each city in which the victim directly communicated his suicidal intent was a professional mental health worker consulted. This means that respondents either do not know what an adaptive response is in such periods of crisis, do not feel that there is anyone who can help, or, as a third possibility, do not care enough about the victim's welfare to seek outside help. The results of this study are consistent with the finding of Robins *et al.* (1959) that lack of knowledge of what to do was very characteristic of those respondents who believed the message of suicide. The third response—apathy—was observed only in isolated instances, mostly in cases of those older women who were noted for their querulous and alienating behavior and constant meddling in the affairs of other family members, and in some cases of unreliable, dependent, middle aged alcoholic men who made life miserable for those around them. There is no doubt that a majority of respondents met the death of a close friend or relative with sadness, puzzlement, and difficult acceptance.

In summary, the study of suicide is complicated by its extremely low rate of incidence. Just as there is no way of preventing all traffic accidents without keeping all cars off the road, there is no method of screening out all potential suicides without disadvantaging the majority of the population. However, this study supplies empirical evidence that most suicidal individuals in Stockholm as well as in Los Angeles identify themselves to available listeners. This fact, acknowledged in the United States though rarely demonstrated in any systematic study of completed suicide cases, has determined the course of primary prevention in this country. Now it can safely be concluded that potential suicides in Stockholm are presaged by similar communications of intent.

CULTURAL DETERMINANTS OF SWEDISH SUICIDE

Certain qualities of Swedish culture—*viz.*, secularism, pacifism, and egalitarianism—appear to have been reflected in the Stockholm suicide data. With regard to secularism, Sweden is heavily steeped in the tradition of the Protestant ethic with its emphasis on hard work, thrift, individual responsibility, and a middle class, this-world value orientation. In recent times growing materialism had coincided with the secularization of the church. The relative unconcern with traditional religion among Swedes today is illustrated by the very small number of decedents in the study who actively participated in church activities compared to those in Los Angeles ($p < 0.01$). Swedish secularism has also led to rather accurate suicide statistics, in contrast to scores of deaths that are miscertified as accidental or natural in many countries owing to strong religious denigrations of suicidal behavior. Furthermore, the emphasis on materialism as opposed to asceticism adds greater portent to performance failures among

Swedish men. Occupational and financial problems were mentioned in almost 50 percent of the male cases in Stockholm. Financial and occupational difficulties in the United States and Sweden are not considered salient according to established social norms and thus are more likely to result in psychological anguish and suicide than is the case in poorer countries, where physical discomfort is more likely.

The attitude of pacifism, exemplified by Sweden's long-established international neutrality, was reflected in the research data by the high proportion of passive compared to violent suicide (3.5:1), although the direct cause of this finding is probably the relative unavailability of firearms. This was clearly not the situation in Los Angeles, where gunshot wounds accounted for 42 percent of the deaths ($p < 0.01$).

Third, Swedish social and sexual egalitarianism has resulted in a very large middle class which has access to a wide range of governmental services. This study supports the fact that many suicide decedents had utilized available mental health facilities (58 percent). Finally, educational and occupational opportunities for a Swedish woman make it possible for a man to find himself materially, as well as emotionally, dependent upon her, and experiencing difficulty in maintaining his traditionally dominant role in the family. Some men, no doubt, are particularly sensitive to such dependency. Corroboration of this observation is suggested by a large number of men in Stockholm who prior to suicide complained about feelings of uselessness and being a burden to their wives or lovers (57 percent).

In summary, the findings suggest that, while several aspects of suicide are analogous in Stockholm and Los Angeles–*e.g.*, communication of suicidal intent–and while there are considerable cultural similarities between the two countries, one cannot fully understand the dynamics of suicide in Sweden without considering some of the unique cultural determinants.

REFERENCES

Dahlgren, K. G. 1945. *On Suicide and Attempted Suicide.* Lund, Lund, Sweden.

Dahlstrom, W. G., and Welsh, G. S. 1960. *THE MPPI Handbook*. University of Minnesota Press, Minneapolis.

Dorpat, T. L., and Ripley, H. S. 1960. A study of suicide in the Seattle area. *Comprehensive Psychiatry*, 1:349–359.

Dorpat, T. L., and Ripley, H. S. 1967. The relationship between attempted suicide and committed suicide. *Comprehensive Psychiatry*, 8:74–79.

Ettlinger, R. 1964. Suicides in a group of patients who had previously attempted suicide. *Acta Psychiatrica Scandinavica*, 40:363–378.

Ettlinger, R., and Flordh, P. 1955. Attempted suicide. *Acta Psychiatrica et Neurologica Scandinavica*, Supplement 103.

Farberow, N. L., and Shneidman, E. S. (Eds.) 1961. *The Cry for Help.* McGraw-Hill, New York.

Friel, P. B., and Frank, L. M. 1958. The management of the suicidal patient. *Annals of Internal Medicine*, 49:632–641.

Hendin, H. 1965. *Suicide and Scandinavia*. Doubleday, New York.

Hollingshead, A. B., and Redlich, F. C. 1958. *Social Class and Mental Illness*, pp. 390–391. Wiley, New York.

Jansson, B. A. 1962. A catamnestic study of 476 attempted suicides with special regard to the prognosis of equivocal suicides. *Journal of the American Medical Association*, 184:924–929.

Litman, R. E., Farberow, N. L., Shneidman, E. S., Heilig, S. M., and Kramer, J. A. 1965. Suicide prevention telephone service. *Journal of the American Medical Association*, 192:21–25.

Robins, E., Gassner, S., Kayes, J., Wilkinson, R. H., Jr., and Murphy, G. E. 1959. The communication of suicidal intent: A study of 134 consecutive cases of successful (completed) suicides. *American Journal of Psychiatry*, 115:724–733.

Shneidman, E. S., and Farberow, N. L. 1961*a*. Sample investigations of equivocal deaths. In: N. L. Farberow and E. S. Shneidman (Eds.), *The Cry for Help.* McGraw-Hill, New York.

Shneidman, E. S., and Farberow, N. 1961*b*. Statistical comparison between attempted and committed suicides. In: N. L. Farberow and E. S. Shneidman (Eds.), *The Cry for Help*. McGraw-Hill, New York.

Stengel, E. 1952. Enquiries into attempted suicide. *Proceedings of the Royal Society of Medicine*, 45:613–620.

Stengel, E., and Farberow, N. L. 1968. Certification of suicide around the world. In: N. L. Farberow (Ed.), *Proceedings of the Fourth International Conference for Suicide Prevention*. Delmar, Los Angeles.

Tuckman, J., and Lavell, M. 1958. Study of suicide in Philadelphia. *Public Health Reports*, 73:547–553.

Vail, D. J. 1959. Suicide and medical responsibility. *American Journal of Psychiatry*, 115:1006–1010.

Yessler, P. G., Gibbs, J. J., and Becker, H. A. 1961. On the communication of suicidal ideas: Some medical considerations. *Archives of General Psychiatry*, 5:12–29.

eight

SOME CULTURAL ASPECTS OF SUICIDE IN BRITAIN

MAXWELL ATKINSON, PH.D.

One way of considering the place of suicide in a particular culture is to examine how it is regarded in literature and the arts, religion, law, philosophy, media, public opinion, and so on. Viewed in these terms, the situation in Britain appears to pose something of a contrast. On the one hand, it can be noted that British culture has much in common with other Judeo-Christian Western European cultures, as well as with other English-speaking cultures in other parts of the world, and hence there will be a high degree of similarity between the way suicide is regarded in British culture and in the other related cultures. On the other hand, the presence of suicide as an important theme in English literature and philosophy, together with its illegality until 1961, seem to suggest that there may be something very special about the place of suicide in British culture.

This contrast poses some problems for the analysis developed in this chapter. Excessive or exclusive concentration on general features of the place of suicide in British culture is likely to involve repetition of many of the themes discussed in other chapters in this book. The very interrelatedness of different cultures also means that even features that appear special to Britain may also apply in some or all of the other similar cultures; an obvious example of this is the widespread availability of translated versions and performances of Shakespearian plays in other cultures. In addition to these difficulties is the more fundamental methodological problem involved in arriving at definite conclusions about how suicide is regarded in a culture; this problem emerges because different and sometimes contradictory interpretations of some particular cultural manifestation may seem equally plausible. In other words, there is the problem of choice between competing versions of the cultural significance of suicide. The following section attempts to illustrate this point with reference to some of the things that seem peculiar to British culture. The focus in the next section then shifts to a major change that has been taking place in the way suicide is viewed in Britain, but which seems to be shared in variable degrees with other related cultures, namely, the increased scientific interest in suicide and the emergence of a suicide prevention movement. Finally, the availability of alternative interpretations of the cultural place of suicide is considered again in the last section of the chapter as being itself of crucial cultural significance. In other words, the ways in which cultural knowledge and conventions are used by members of the culture in order to identify and make sense of suicidal phenomena are presented as being potentially the most important data to be analyzed if we are to arrive at an understanding of cultural aspects of suicide in Britain and other cultures.

ALTERNATIVE VERSIONS OF SUICIDE IN BRITISH CULTURE

As was noted above, it is tempting to regard the recurrence of suicide as a theme in English literature and philosophy, and its status as a felony until as late as 1961, as support for the view that there is something very special indeed about the place of suicide in British culture. The next step might then be to examine the details of the way suicide gets presented in literature, philosophy, religion, and law, and to claim such details as being in some way "typical" of the more generalized cultural status of suicide in Britain. By looking at some of the inferences and interpretations that can be made in this way, however, it can be shown not only that there may be several interpretations that can be claimed to be "typical," but also that the different interpretations may actually contradict each other. And it can be shown too, that, although it is possible to arrive at generalizations about the cultural significance of suicide, there are no clear procedures available for warranting one particular procedure as "correct," "better," or "more correct" than another.

We can begin to illustrate these points with reference to a central problem facing the cultural analyst, namely, how to assess whether a particular cultural manifestion—be it a play, painting, film, law, religious practice, or whatever—reflects some more generalized theme in the culture or is itself an initiator of that theme or cultural attitude. Hume's philosophical concern with the problem of suicide[1], for example, could be seen as stemming from some wider preoccupation with suicide that was characteristic of British culture at the time. Alternatively, it might be argued just as plausibly that it was Hume's interest that either triggered or influenced the wider preoccupation. Or a third version, taking both possibilities into account, could be argued: that Hume's work both reflected and instigated a broader cultural concern. The central methodological problem, however, is simply that of which version to opt for and why one should opt for one rather than another version. And, given that all three versions are based on the assumption that there was indeed some broader cultural concern with suicide that extended beyond the cloistered confines occupied by the intelligentsia of the day, there is the problem of establishing that this was actually the case. Furthermore, even if such a preoccupation could be established with some degree of definiteness, there would arise another problem relating to the question of how to assess the extent to which the particular set of attitudes survived or were modified during the subsequent periods of history.

Similar difficulties are involved in connection with the important place suicide occupies in Shakespearian drama. As Farberow noted earlier in this volume, suicide frequently occurs in Shakespeare's plays, which, given their supreme importance in English literature, is rich with inferential potential for the cultural analyst. Thus, we have already noted that this could be regarded as evidence that there is something generally very special about the place of suicide in British culture. By examining the way in which Shakespearian plays depict particular kinds of persons with particular problems in particular settings and circumstances, it could be argued that a set of contexts that can be regarded as "typically suicidal" in British culture have been successfully located. This theme could be further elaborated into a causal statement to the effect that such situations provide the British with a series of models of the kinds of problems and settings likely to lead to suicide, so that they will on occasion be able to see themselves in such situations and may accordingly be particularly prone to entertain the possibility of a suicidal solution.[2] One interesting example of this is the way in which suicide is depicted in many of Shakespeare's best known plays as the only honorable or logical next step for the character concerned; that suicide involves matters of honor could be interpreted as characteristic of British culture. Put another way, the kind of suicide defined by Durkheim[3] as "altruistic" suicide could be considered a typically British cultural form.

Plausible though such interpretations may be, alternative and indeed opposite versions of the Shakespearian evidence can be formulated that may be just as acceptable. One can, for example, point to the fact that, in Shakespeare's plays, most of the key characters who either contemplate or commit suicide are not British (e.g., Hamlet, Prince of Denmark; Cleopatra, Queen of Egypt; Othello, Moor of Venice, etc.), and stress their membership of *foreign* cultures. This could then be developed to support the view that suicide was regarded by Shakespeare as an activity typical of foreigners and hence as something that is essentially strange to British culture generally. In proposing such a version, it could be noted further that some of the methods of self-assault used by Shakespearian characters—such as falling on swords and applying an asp to one's bosom—were peculiar to other cultures and are not, and have never been, commonly found modes of suicidal activity in Britain. Thus, while the earlier interpretation of the Shakespearian evidence implied a possible causal effect by providing a set of models of suicidal situations, this interpretation could be claimed to have a preventive effect in the sense that the plays may teach the British to regard suicide as a rather bizarre feature of alien cultures.

An examination of how suicide is treated in English law can also generate alternative versions of the cultural significance of suicide. The illegality of suicide until the Suicide Act of 1961 seems at first to be an obvious indication of an especially strong disapproval of suicide within British culture in general and, more particularly, as far as its moral and religious codes are concerned. Thus, it is often assumed that, although some activities may be regarded as immoral or sinful, it is only the "really serious" ones that are officially prohibited by law, and hence that an inspection of the legal code is a good guide to the relative seriousness with which different kinds of activities are viewed.

Implicit in this is usually a further assumption, that laws come into being or remain on the statute books as a result of a general consensus among the members of the society as to what is right and wrong. Such an analysis, however, is difficult to sustain in relation to the law on suicide in England and Wales, for the origins of its status as a felony seem to have had little or nothing to do with any widely shared consensus about its moral undesirability. In the Middle Ages, the property of convicted felons was automatically forfeited to the crown, a consequence of which was that persons awaiting trial could effectively ensure that their property passed to their own families rather than to the monarch by committing suicide at some stage before being convicted for a felony. By making suicide itself a felony, therefore, this practice ceased to provide a way of depriving the crown of one source of revenue. Of course, it may have been that religious and moral leaders gave their support to the law against suicide both at the time and during later periods after the property forfeit rule had ceased to apply, so that it might be claimed that the law reflected both pragmatic and moral concerns. And the fact that the law was not changed until 1961 could be cited as support for the view that the felonious status of suicide indicated a deeply entrenched and widely shared taboo against suicide. Against this, however, reference can be made to empirical studies of the processes leading to changes in the law, some of which present a strong case for believing that the existence of organized pressure groups of "moral entrepreneurs" who feel strongly about some form of conduct is far more important than the existence of some generally shared moral consensus. Indeed, this line of reasoning becomes more plausible when the passing of the 1961 Suicide Act is considered, for, as is elaborated in the next section, it is noticeable that, by 1961, a powerful "mental health" lobby had developed in Britain, and it felt strongly enough about the inappropriateness of the then existing law on suicide to be successful in exerting pressure for change.

Given that the members of Parliament who debated and passed the Suicide Bill were the elected representatives of the people of Britain, it might be expected that the content of their deliberations would provide some useful insight into the ways in which suicide is regarded in British culture. Inspection of the Hansard records,[4] however, indicates that a great deal of time was taken up with debating a problem that most experts would regard as insignificant in relation to the normal patterns of suicidal activity in Britain: the issue of how to cope with survivors of suicide pacts who, when the original law was in force, were automatically liable for prosecution for an attempted felony (i.e., attempted suicide). The politicians seemed obsessed with the possibility of the proposed change in the law removing the alleged deterrent value of the old law, and the one thing they were apparently particularly keen to deter was the suicide pact. As a result of these fears, assisting another to commit suicide was retained as an offence, even though it does not appear to have been applied during the 14 years since the passing of the Act. Data such as these again point to the difficulties and dangers in constructing interpretations of the cultural significance of suicide. For in one sense, the parliamentary debates could be invoked to support the proposition that suicide pacts are a common enough feature of British culture for special provisions to be retained even after suicide itself ceased to be a felony. But, using other criteria, there is little evidence to suggest that suicide pacts are particularly frequent occurrences in Britain, or are more typically associated with British culture than with others.

One approach to doing cultural analyses is to examine legal codes for data relating to something other than what is officially sanctioned as right and wrong. Laws call for careful definitions of the activities they regulate, so that they can be readily recognized by those whose job it is to judge them. In relation to suicide, then, the law might be expected to provide some guide to the dominant cultural definition of suicide in the society in question. But, as I have suggested in more detail elsewhere,[5] a curious feature of the law on suicide in England and Wales is that such a definition is not easy to find. Indeed, given that it is closely tied in with the homicide law so that suicide, or *felo-de-se,* was, at least until 1961, the same as homicide except that the victim was the self, there is even some doubt as to whether that definition (i.e., killing the self with intent) still holds now that suicide is no longer a felony.

Particularly curious, for example, is the fact that the main legal handbook for coroners[6] contains no definition of suicide that would be readily recognizable to most members of the culture, but refers only to some rather obscure technicalities that are supposed to describe suicides. If, for example, one person aims a gun at another with intent to kill but the gun explodes and kills the gunman, then the death of the gunman is a suicide. The logic of this appears to be somewhat eccentric, although it may relate to the kind of reasoning that originally led to the outlawing of suicide, so that attempted murderers who killed themselves by mistake would nevertheless be guilty of a felony and hence forfeit their property to the crown. But whatever the origins of this definition, there can be little doubt that it has fallen out of use and that there are hardly any members of British culture (other than suicide researchers) who are aware of it. Indeed, it is interesting to note that it presumably could be used to apply to the deaths of members of the Irish Republican Army who have died as a result of their bombs exploding by mistake, and yet no such verdicts have been recorded in the several cases where this has happened in the last few years.

One other little known legal stipulation is that for a death to be a suicide, it must occur within a year and a day of the act of self-assault that led to the death, and here again it seems doubtful that there are many citizens of Britain other than lawyers who are aware of the constraint. The implication of all this, then, is that even what might appear to be relatively hard evidence about cultural definitions of suicide in Britain fails to provide much basis for any definite, generalizable conclusions about them.

At a more general level, the patterns of suicide in Britain as reflected in the official rates reveal some curious anomalies and contradictions. The individual countries–England, Wales, Scotland, and Northern Ireland–that comprise the United Kingdom are predominantly Protestant. Given the widely reported findings of correlations between high suicide rates and Protestantism as compared with other Christian denominations and other religions, one might therefore expect that there would be a tradition of high suicide rates in the countries of the United Kingdom. Yet compared with other Protestant countries, the suicide rates have been relatively low for a long period of time.[7] An interpretation of this rather odd state of affairs can be constructed with reference to the character of English Protestantism, for, apart from the brief period of rule by the Puritans following the execution of Charles I in 1649, the Church of England has been the established Church. Henry VIII, who initated the English Reformation was very untypical of the early Protestants and had, before his urgent need for a speedy divorce, been given the title "Defender of the Faith" by the Pope in recognition of his support for Catholicism against the attacks of the Protestants in the rest of Europe. Compared with other Protestant denominations, Anglicanism still has much more in common with Catholicism in terms of its structure, doctrine, and ritual. The main structural change was the substitution of the monarch for the Pope as head of the Church, but the paternalistic hierarchy of archbishops, bishops, parish priests, etc., that was normally associated with Catholicism was retained intact, just as enough features of the dogma and ritual remained for "high church" Anglicanism to be referred to as "Anglo Catholicism." In light of this, the noteworthy point is that theories aimed at explaining why some religions appear to afford more protection against suicide than others have tended to give most emphasis to structural features of the religions and the kind of communities associated with them. Thus Durkheim, one of the best known exponents of this position, contrasted the closely integrated communities of Catholicism and Judaism with the much looser structures typical of Protestant denominations.[8] The similarities between the Church of England and the Church of Rome, then, provide a possible interpretation of how relatively low suicide rates are found in a predominantly Protestant culture.

There are, however, at least two themes that can be developed to render this apparently persuasive argument more than a little dubious. The first is the low and ever decreasing level of religious activity in Britain. Compared with other similar cultures, for example, the United States, rates of church attendance in Britain are phenomenally low, and a strong case can be made for the proposition that secularization has proceeded more quickly and extensively than in most other Western European countries. Each year more churches have to close through lack of support, and many are literally in danger of falling down for lack of resources. The point about secularization is that lack of religion has also been found to be correlated with high suicide rates. Notable among theorists who have elaborated this theme was Thomas Masaryk, whose central proposition was that suicide rates were increasing in direct proportion to the increase in "irreligiosity."[9] So, just as Protestantism in Britain might be expected to produce a higher suicide rate, the relatively high level of secularization might have been expected to produce similar results.

The second complication that casts doubt on the claim that the relatively low suicide rates are related to the Catholic character of the Church of England has to do with the important religious difference between England and Scotland. Although there may be many similarities between Anglicanism and Catholicism, the Church of Scotland was founded on the Calvinistic teachings of John Knox and has remained unequivocally Protestant. Using this major difference between the Churches of England and Scotland as the basis for a cultural comparison, then, one would predict that Scotland would have a considerably higher rate of suicide than England and Wales. The statistics, however, have traditionally shown and still show a dramatic difference in precisely the opposite direction, with Scotland's suicide rate at about one-half that for England and Wales.[10]

The implication, then, is that something must be seriously wrong with the attempt to attribute Britain's relatively low suicide rates to religious differences—unless there are other cultural differences that might be invoked to solve the puzzle. Thus, the original theory might be retained if it could be shown that the statistics for the two parts of Britain were worthless for comparative purposes owing to different procedures of registering sudden deaths. As it happens, there is a marked difference between the systems for officially recording deaths as suicides in Scotland and England and Wales, and it is sometimes suggested that this is important in accounting for the differences in suicide rates. A contrast that has been singled out as being potentially significant is that the Procurator Fiscals, who are responsible for registering sudden deaths in Scotland, have the power to conduct their investigations in private, while the Coroner system in England and Wales ensures that a suicide verdict cannot be recorded without a public inquest. This, so the argument goes, makes it potentially easier for suicides to be concealed in Scotland as compared with England and Wales, although there is to date little evidence to support such a claim. It is interesting, furthermore, that similar features of the Swedish system for recording sudden deaths have been cited in support of just the opposite of this particular thesis, inasmuch as some have suggested that restrictions on public reporting of suicide cases in Sweden remove some of the supposed motivation behind attempts at concealment, and hence may contribute toward a higher official rate than otherwise might be the case.

As far as England and Wales are concerned, however, it can perhaps be more plausibly argued that the absence of a high suicide rate in spite of the pressures implied by Protestantism and secularization may relate to another feature of its legal culture. Two fundamental principles of English law are, first, a person is innocent until proved guilty, and second, guilt can only be established if the case against the accused is proved "beyond reasonable doubt." The English coroner system, in contrast with the medical examiner systems used in some other countries, is essentially a legal process, and the coroner's court is one of the oldest in the English legal system. The Suicide Act of 1961 means that any question of guilt must be removed in cases of possible suicide, but the principle remains that the case must be proved beyond reasonable doubt. Indeed, although it fails to provide a definition of suicide, the coroners' legal handbook does stress the need for positive evidence of suicide and for there to be no doubt remaining. This implies that the deceased must be given the benefit of the doubt if there is any hint of equivocality about a death, and it could be argued further on the basis of this that, were the principle not applied, more deaths would be officially recorded as suicides.

To this point, then, I have attempted to show how particular cultural aspects of suicide in Britain can be used to construct different and often opposing interpretations, each of which can sound more or less plausible. It may have been noted that no effort has been made to resolve the methodological problem of choosing between competing versions, a solution to which would have to establish one version as an "objective" or "accurate" statement of how it really is with respect to this or that cultural manifestation. The reason for avoiding making any such commitment was suggested at the start of the paper. It is simply that we know of no methodological procedure that enable such generalizations to be warranted in any absolute or definitive way. This may seem to imply a rather negative orientation to the problem of analyzing suicide in different cultures in that it suggests that there is nothing to be done other than to sit on the fence inspecting alternative versions, reviewing possibilities, but being secure all along in the knowledge that ultimately there is no solution to the problem of choice. This analytic impotence, however, lasts only as long as one retains faith in the feasibility of arriving at an "objective" description of a culture, as well as the assumptions about what a culture is that are implicit in the belief that such an enterprise is possible. To be more precise, what I am suggesting is that the model of a culture as a rather rigid collection of fixed objective attitudes, beliefs, rules, etc., that can be neatly mapped by any observer who takes the trouble, is analytically of limited usefulness. One reason for this is the problem of establishing a "fit" between the "map" or description of the cultural place of suicide, and the "real world" in which the objects constituting the culture are to be found. This is the problem that I have tried to illustrate by pointing to the availability of multiple versions. Moreover, a feature of descriptions is that they can never be complete; this poses the additional problem of how a description of a culture could ever be brought to a close.[11]

A way out of these dilemmas has been proposed by Garfinkel and other ethnomethodologists, who have reformulated the more usual ways of analyzing cultural and social phenomena.[12] Thus, rather than to conceive of the problem as one of describing a culture, they suggest that one should seek to analyze the ways in which members of a culture use and rely on cultural knowledge and conventions to make sense of the world. An example of the form such an analysis can take with regard to suicide is presented in the last part of this chapter, but at this point it may be noted that, viewed in these terms, the availability of multiple versions illustrated above ceases to have the rather negative implications referred to. The fact that we are able to construct and recognize alternative interpretations can itself be seen as a crucially significant aspect of a culture, in that it points, among other things, to our ability to make sense of potentially puzzling phenomena.

SUICIDOLOGY AND SUICIDE PREVENTION

At first, it may seem somewhat eccentric to consider suicidology and suicide prevention movements under the rubric of a paper on suicide in British culture. But to regard these as interesting cultural manifestations would seem less odd were the author writing at some time in the future, for just as we tend to look to written data from the past, so presumably might some future researcher look at similar material from our own era. And were he to do so, it seems highly probable that the most striking cultural relics of the 20th century would be the hundreds of papers and books written as part of a sustained attempt to study suicide scientifically. Thus, there is an important sense in which this book is itself interesting data from the point of view of assessing the cultural place of suicide at the present time. This section, therefore, is devoted to a brief consideration of the possible cultural significance of the developments in suicidology and suicide prevention.

Given what has been said so far, it might seem somewhat inconsistent to embark on such an analysis, so it should be noted that what follows is just one version of how these trends have emerged. Furthermore, given that the relationship between common sense and expert knowledge is crucial to the discussion in the final section of the paper, many of the issues touched on here have a direct relevance for what follows.

One way of conceptualizing the ways in which intellectual concerns with suicide have developed is to view them as a series of conflicts between different bodies of knowledge, where what has been at issue has been the question of which one is best equipped to interpret, comment on, and deal with suicidal phenomena. Thus, the writings of people like Donne and Hume can be seen as contributions to a debate between religious and secular morality, with the one stressing the supremacy of the will of God and the other the supremacy of the will of the individual. Subsequently, the appropriateness of philosophical conceptions of suicide as the ultimate way of exercising free will was to lose ground to another body of knowledge which, perhaps ironically, was itself spawned by philosophy. For rationalist thought and the technological and cultural changes brought about by the industrial revolution gave rise to the dream that scientific methods of inquiry could be applied to the study of individuals, behavior, society, and culture. As the social and behavioral sciences emerged, the earlier intellectual concern with free will came to be contrasted unfavorably with the deterministic orientation of the new "scientists," so that suicide ceased to be a matter of free choice and became a fact to be explained like any other. The assumption was, and to an overwhelming extent, still is, that diligent research could lead to the discovery of the laws governing suicide which, once found, could lead to successful prediction, prevention, and treatment. Within the emergent social sciences, disputes between the new disciplines quickly arose regarding which had the best way of explaining suicide, and it may be noted that Durkheim's classic study involved a sustained attack by a sociologist on his contemporary psychologists, and the debate between them continued in France for many years.[13] More recently, there have been similar disputes within the disciplines themselves with different schools criticizing each other and each claiming better access to the truth than the other.[14] In spite of the divisions and differences, however, almost all shared in the belief that a science of suicide was possible, and it can be regarded as a sign of faith in this, as well as an indication of how far the study of suicide has been professionalized, that the new word "suicidology" came into the English language.

All this of course is a gross oversimplification of a whole series of complex social processes in which the "victories" and "defeats" have never been complete. Thus, elements of the different conceptualizations and theories of suicide can and do coexist, so that it is perfectly possible for a British psychiatrist to regard the suicide of one of his patients as caused or determined by some identifiable personality abnormality or illness and, at the same time, view the suicide of an East European student as a rational and freely chosen protest against his society. Religious leaders may similarly preach against suicide yet still be prepared to recognize its status as a "medical problem" by referring people to psychiatrists. The concurrent availability of free will and deterministic models of suicide, furthermore, provides a choice that can be a source of great comfort to the surviving relatives and friends of suicides. To accept that a particular suicide was the result of a rational choice may involve a person in accepting responsibility for what happened, but to invoke some explanation that locates the causes elsewhere is one way of mitigating feelings of guilt.[15] The deterministic model has even penetrated the legal system, which depends almost exclusively on a free-will model of man in the assessment of guilt and responsibility Thus the rider "while the balance of the mind was disturbed," is often added to suicide verdicts by coroners. Some coroners also specify what it was that caused the balance of the mind to be disturbed. The interesting point about such phrases is that they do not publicly or officially certify that the deceased was mentally ill, but they do imply that there was some cause "in the mind" that was probably responsible for the act of self-assault. By so doing, the degree of responsibility on the part of those who might have been blamed via the use of the free-will model is reduced. In short, then, what is being suggested here is that, although members of British culture can invoke either a rational or a deterministic model of suicide, or both, there are grounds for believing that the former has lost ground to the latter during the present century.

As far as the struggle between "experts" on suicide is concerned, the issue has centered for the most part on which of the various deterministic models is the most appropriate, and most of the indications are that the victor is what can be referred to as a "psychomedical" model. Most of the investment in suicide research in Britain comes from the Medical Research Council, and most of the research is done in departments of psychiatry and mental health or in special units situated in mental hospitals. This "medicalization" of suicide is an interesting cultural phenomenon in terms both of medicine in general and psychiatry in particular. Thus, one consequence of the advances in preventive medicine has been the virtual elimination of the big killer diseases like smallpox, and tuberculosis; this in turn has resulted in a revision in the way death is regarded in British culture. Although in the past it was a normal feature of peoples' lives to lose brothers, sisters, parents, and other relatives at fairly frequent intervals, death now tends to be viewed as something that is appropriate only if it occurs in old age. Before that, it is something surprising and shocking, so that it is common to regard a person who dies during youth or middle age as having been cheated out of the now taken-for-granted right to live a long time, a right which the provision of free health services in Britain endorses in a most emphatic way. This common-sense orientation to death before old age has its expert equivalent in the medical profession, for doctors know about the death rates for different ages and from different ailments. One thing these tell them is that, since the eradication of the epidemic diseases, a small number of illnesses now account for almost all the deaths in the age range 20 to 60, and that suicide ranks with heart diseases and cancer as one of the statistically important contemporary killers. Thus, it is included as one of a collection of "illnesses" for which an effective prevention or treatment policy needs to be found. In short, it readily gets categorized as a "medical" problem, and within medicine itself, it gets to be categorized as a problem for the specialists in psychological medicine. To them it is of particular concern, for not only does it appear to be related to the other kinds of "illnesses" over which they have special rights, but is also the worst kind of failure their treatment can bring about. To be able to solve the problem, therefore, would presumably have immense dividends and might be regarded as the psychiatric equivalent of medicine's defeat of the epidemic diseases.

Given that the right to good health is such a deeply entrenched aspect of British culture that free health services are provided by statute, it might seem wholly consistent that a suicide prevention movement would emerge. But the fact that every major town in Britain is now served by a telephone emergency service provided by the Samaritans probably has very little to do with the National Health Service and in some ways confirms the view that different orientations to suicide coexist and that the victory of the psychomedical model in the struggle for the rights to explain and treat suicide has by no means been complete. In the origins, structure, and mode of operation of the Samaritans,[16] furthermore, there are continuities with other features of British culture, some of which have already been alluded to. The organization was founded by Chad Varah, an Anglican clergyman, while responsible for an East London parish which had no parishioners in the normal sense of the word. He responded very imaginatively to this situation by setting up an emergency telephone service backed up by the "befriending" of clients who seemed in need of it. The center was manned by lay volunteers and provided a model for the many subsequent branches that opened in other places. In contrast to suicide prevention schemes in several other countries, there was very little involvement of the new experts on suicide, and, indeed, professional psychiatry initially regarded the whole enterprize with a disinterest verging on suspicion. Even now there are very few psychiatrists who are actively involved with the Samaritans.[17] Similarly, although many of the branch directors and the national general secretary are, like Varah, clergymen, the organization contrasts with other schemes that started with religious backing in that it is explicitly not concerned with evangelizing its clients.[18] The unprofessionalized character of the Samaritans, together with the related respect for and reliance on common sense as a means of dealing with peoples' problems, can be construed as being in keeping with the British tradition of the "good amateur," which is itself a reflection of the cultural value placed on pragmatism.

The development of the Samaritans can also be understood with reference to another major cultural change which has already been referred to, namely, secularization. Cynics, for example, sometimes note that the structure of the Samaritans is a kind of mirror image of the Church of

England, with Chad Varah as the Archbishop of Canterbury and the branch directors as the equivalent of the clergy. While this version may not be very constructive, it is relevant to point to one of the ways in which the churches have responded to declining religious activism. Thus, they have increasingly attempted to become more involved in the community and with social problems outside the churches, and the emergence of the Samaritans can be viewed as one particular way in which the clergy and laity have responded to calls to engage in such work. The elaborate system of social services provided by the welfare state means that there are relatively few areas in which the churches can become active without overlapping with the professional services provided by the state, but suicide prevention is something which had not and still has not been included among the statutory developments. By focusing on this, then, the Samaritans were able to fill one of the holes in the "safety net" of the British welfare state. The telephone service they provide, furthermore, has tended to fill another gap that had not been anticipated and about which some leading Samaritans appear to have mixed feelings, for there is a sense in which they have become an unofficial clearing house for the official social services. Thus, in an analysis of statistics gathered by the Samaritans during a single year, Richard Fox and I found that by far the most frequently listed "presenting problems" of callers had to do with problems relating to housing, finance, and health, and discussions with members of the Samaritans suggest that callers' problems can often be dealt with by referring them to the appropriate official agency.

The kinds of assumptions that seem to underlie the activities of the Samaritans can provide some interesting insight into the kinds of common-sense knowledge and theories of suicide that are available to members of British culture. The idea of a telephone service for persons in despair appears to involve, as Sacks has elaborated with reference to an American scheme,[19] the assumption that persons likely to commit suicide are those who have no one to turn to other than some anonymous person on the other end of a telephone line. Similarly, the policy of "befriending" assumes that the potential suicide is someone without friends or who is isolated and lonely. Evidence such as this supports the view already hinted at and to be developed below that there is a degree of convergence between theories of expert suicidologists and the kinds of common-sense theories used by ordinary members of the culture. The view of the suicidal person as one who is isolated is remarkably close to Durkheimian theories of suicide which relate it to a low level of social integration. Similarly, the Samaritans' training programs reflect a concern with other "causal" connections that occupy the research effort of experts, in that they focus on things like sexual problems, alcoholism, drug addiction, and so on. In other words, the "findings" of experts to the effect that suicide is closely interlinked with other social and psychological problems are things that are known and used by the lay suicide preventers in their practical work.

Lest it seem that too much attention has been given to the significance of the Samaritans in relation to the place of suicide in British culture, it should be noted that there are good grounds for believing that the kinds of assumptions they have about suicide are shared more widely among members of the culture. Not only are their volunteers recruited from the general public, but their work has been given massive publicity in the form of a television drama series called "The Befrienders." The way that the program became a series is of special interest. The British Broadcasting Corporation (BBC) first ran six different plays together with the announcement that one of them would become a series and that the decision would be based on the popular response to each individual program. There is no way of knowing, of course, how far popularity was the deciding factor in discarding the others and presenting "The Befrienders" as the new series, but the important point is that the claim that it had been the most popular was eminently believable.

In this section, I have attempted to show that the development of suicidology and of a national suicide prevention movement contrast markedly with the situation in other countries in that they can be seen as reflecting rather different cultural trends and have emerged more or less independently of each other. Thus, the increased investment in suicide research is probably best understood with reference to the proportionate increase in the importance of suicide as a cause of death, the emergence of the social and behavioral sciences in general, and the growth of psychiatry within medicine in particular. The Samaritans, on the other hand, can be viewed as a particularly successful response to the Church's call for greater community involvement as a way of adapting to secularization, and as giving lay volunteers the opportunity to provide a service that is not officially available under Britain's elaborate welfare state framework. It has been suggested further that there has been a struggle between different bodies of knowledge as to which discipline has the best approach to the study of suicide and, by implication, which can claim to have a special right to speak about and deal with it. At a general level, two competing models of suicide were referred to, one which conceives of suicide as an outcome of rational choice and the exercise of free will, and one which views it as determined by objectified causes of which the individual may be unaware but which are locatable by experts and other observers.

Although it was suggested that free will and deterministic models can coexist side by side, it would seem that the 20th century has seen the latter become predominant, and the Suicide Act of 1961 can be viewed as the culmination of this trend. In holding persons responsible for their own actions, the law relies heavily on a free-will model of man, and the effect of the abolition of the criminal status of suicide was to redefine it as something for which persons could not properly be held responsible. Similarly, although it has been argued that the British suicide prevention movement, as manifested by the Samaritans, has differed from professional suicidology with regard to its reliance on common-sense approaches to suicidal phenomena, it would nevertheless appear that both share in an acceptance of a deterministic model of suicide. For the most part, suicide researchers regard expressed motives as being of only secondary importance compared with other alleged causes, and hence in effect deny the rationality of the persons being studied. In the same way, the apparently deeply entrenched view that suicide is something that ought to be prevented involves the assumption that the reasoning of the suicidal person is at fault. To recognize suicide as the result of a rationally-arrived-at choice would render preventive activity irrational, or at least anti-rational. In other words, the suicide preventers, in their attempts to stop people from committing suicide, and suicide researchers, in their attempts to find the "real" causes of suicide, are both involved in denying the validity of the grounds on which a person opts for a suicidal solution.[20]

CULTURE AS A MEMBERS' RESOURCE FOR UNDERSTANDING SUICIDE

To this point, an attempt has been made to show that it is relatively easy to construct more or less plausible generalizations about British culture and about the cultural significance of suicide. At the same time, however, it has been stressed that it is much less easy to see how any particular observation, description, or explanation can be warranted as "objective," "the truth," or "how it really is with respect to suicide in British culture." This is not to suggest that members of the culture have no conception of objectivity, truth, or methods for recognizing these, but rather that the recognition of some version of the world as "objective," "truthful," or "factual" involves them in the analysis and recognition of the methods used to produce the version as appropriate methods for producing objective, truthful, or factual versions in the settings in which they are invoked and for the practical purposes for which they are used. The scientist's problem, however, is that he believes in the availability of versions that are objective, truthful, or factual in some way and are independent of the particular settings in which they are invoked. By taking this as his purpose, he has to claim that his descriptions and explanations are qualitatively different from those available to and used by ordinary members of the culture in conducting their everyday affairs.

Although the principled adherence to the distinctiveness of the methods of social scientific inquiry and the results they produce may be central to sustaining a distinction between lay and professional reasoning, it has a number of consequences that severely limit the analytic scope of conventional social science. In the first place, the similarities between common sense and expert reasoning, and the versions of the social world they produce, tend to be largely ignored. Second, the fact that the experts themselves are also members of the culture in which their studies typically take place, and hence have access to the common-sense knowledge and cultural conventions available to any other member of the culture, tends to be regarded as a rather minor problem that is interesting only insofar as it might give rise to "bias" (which, in any case can allegedly be guarded against by the use of "correct" scientific cautions). Generally overlooked is that their membership in the culture might be interesting in that they are able to rely on and use their common-sense knowledge and methods of practical reasoning as an unexplicated resource in their "scientific" work consequently. This leads to a third point, which is that by overlooking the potential importance of their tacit use of common-sense knowledge and methods of reasoning, the possibility of regarding these as a *topic* worthy of analysis is not seriously entertained. That the methods of practical reasoning used by ordinary members of society in their everyday lives should be taken as the central topic for analysis by sociologists is, however, a central recommendation of the ethnomethodologists. Viewed in these terms, man ceases to be the kind of cultural dope who is depicted in conventional social science as being programed by the culture to act and respond mechanically to situations which confront him. Instead he is regarded as a cultural analyst engaged in an ongoing process of finding order and sense in the world. Rather than attempt to elaborate the ethnomethodological program in detail, my aim in this final section is to illustrate some of the issues involved with reference to studies of suicidal phenomena that, quite by chance, have been conducted by two of the founders of ethnomethodology in the United States and have been followed up in research done in Britain.

Although all members of a culture may from time to time become engaged in the analysis of suicidal phenomena, it is useful for illustrative purposes to begin with a situation in which this is a particularly pressing and dominant concern. A good example of such a setting is provided by the procedures for officially certifying sudden deaths, for here members of the culture are involved in deciding which of several possible descriptors is to be regarded as the "correct" or "objective" one. Harold Garfinkel, who coined the word "ethnomethodology," and whose work has been overwhelmingly important in its development, has formulated the problem with reference to the work of the Los Angeles Suicide Prevention Center in the following way:

> SPC inquiries begin with a death that the coroner finds equivocal as to *mode* of death. That death they use as a precedent with which various ways of living in a society that could have terminated with that death are searched out and read 'in the remains': in the scraps of this and that like the body and its trappings, medicine bottles, notes, bits and pieces of clothing, and other memorabilia–stuff that can be photographed, collected and packaged. Other 'remains' are collected too: rumors, passing remarks, and stories–materials in the repertoires of whosoever might be consulted via the common work of conversations. These *whatsoever* bits and pieces that a story or a rule or a proverb might make intelligible are used to formulate a *recognizably* coherent, standard, typical, cogent, uniform, planful, i.e. a *recognizably* rational account of how the society worked to produce these remains.[21]

An important implication of this is that deaths in general and suicides in particular are viewed as being the end product of some set of circumstances that are recognizable as "fitting" with the particular manner of the end. For a death to be recognizable as a "suicide" or an "accident" or whatever, some story about the person in question and the events leading up to the death are required such that the descriptor of the mode of death and the story can be seen as consistent with each other. Not all the available "remains" and "bits and pieces" referred to by Garfinkel will get included in the final story, as not all will be useful in the production of a coherent rational account. In other words, persons responsible for processing deaths necessarily have to be selective about what is included in or excluded from the official evidence relating to a particular case, a point which is exemplified in the following extract from an interview conducted with a British coroner's officer while he was typing up a statement taken from witnesses:

> Normally I don't think I could really take a story, even from you now so that every word you said would be in story book form, it would be impossible . . . interviewing some people, they don't know what I want so I've got to ask them . . . the way these statements have been taken is question, answer–er–question then answer. Sometimes you get, particularly some elderly women, and they bloody go on and on, so I've got to interrupt them . . . in this very one here–um–she was rambling on a bit, backwards and forwards and he, I was taking a statement off him and she was chipping in. You get two sides of the tale then. And you think 'well now, how do you play this?' So rather than taking two statements–you're only going to end up with two negative statements, one against the other. So you bring it all into like a proper perspective, as you think it is. It's a nice, well to me it's a nice story book finish.

> Sometimes I get mixed up. I've read it through myself then I'll suddenly scrap it and say 'well that's no flippin good' and start again.[22]

Although this may point to the importance of constructing a coherent story of the events leading up to a death and to the selectivity involved in so doing, it leaves open the questions of how the selections are made and how one story may be more readily recognizable than another as having a "nice story book finish."

Elsewhere,[23] I have attempted to show at some length how coroners and their officers select what they consider to be "relevant" evidence via a process very similar to that known to scientists as hypothesis testing. Thus, a preliminary analysis of the scene and circumstances of the death will provide a possible or probable description of the death as, say, a suicide or an accident. Depending on what is selected, different sorts of evidence will be actively sought after, or, in other words, the preliminary hypothesis will suggest the collection of particular kinds of data that will be relevant for testing the hypothesis. In cases where first appearances suggest an accident, for example, detailed questions about the deceased's domestic circumstances, psychological and emotional problems, past record of mental illness, history of making previous suicide attempts and threats, etc., are seldom asked and hence seldom appear in the official "stories" of how the death occurred. But, and this is an important point, if such data do emerge, they may lead to further questioning related to a suicidal hypothesis. In other words, just as a preliminary description of a death can be said to organize the inquiries and the resulting story, so also can the results of an inquiry be said to organize the description of the death as this or that kind of death. This can be clarified with reference to two kinds of evidence that seem to be very important in directing inquiries toward a suicide verdict, namely, mode of death and suicide notes.

Thus, I have suggested in an earlier paper[24] that some modes of dying, such as hanging, are much more likely to be identified as "suicidal" than others, such as deaths in road accidents. In other words, in British culture, it is very difficult to envision situations in which a death by hanging can occur other than in the course of committing suicide. Similarly, it is well known that persons who commit suicide often leave suicide notes, and, on the basis of these two rather obvious observations, I suggested that either could be regarded as an almost certain indicator that a suicide had taken place and hence that both would direct official inquiries toward the collection of evidence that would give added support to such a conclusion. But, although features such as death by hanging and suicide notes may be important pieces of evidence leading toward a suicide verdict, they are not sufficient in themselves in the sense that one can say if x then y. Thus, nonsuicidal stories that end in death by hanging can sometimes be constructed, as in the case of a young man who was found hanging from the stairs in his home shortly before embarking on a climbing holiday. That he was going on such a holiday, coupled with the report that a climbing instruction manual had been found lying open near to the scene, suggested that he might have been practicing and hence provided for the recognizability of "accident" as a more appropriate descriptor of how he met his death. Just as a preliminary descriptor may organize the inquiries and vice-versa, so the different pieces of evidence collected may organize one another. With regard to the view of suicide notes as "hard" evidence of a suicidal death, for example, a problem arises with respect to their identification as suicide notes in the first place, for they are often less than explicit in stating "clear" suicidal intent. Two such examples derived from my own research are:

> My darling poppet, My ticker isn't what it used to be and it's been getting worse lately.

> I'm sorry to everyone. I love my mum dad and Ken. Please look after my children.

As they stand, neither of these is "obviously" a suicide note, and one can readily imagine other situations in which they might have been written. But if a body were discovered hanging from a rope with one of these nearby, then it could immediately be recognized as a suicide note. Thus, the preliminary descriptor of "suicide" would be suggested by the death by hanging, and this in turn can provide for the designation of any note found near the body–however obscure or inexplicit its message–as a "suicide note." Once the note is indeed established as a suicide note, further "concrete" evidence for the appropriateness of the preliminary descriptor can be used to construct the grounds on which it becomes accepted as definite.

From the above, then, it would seem that members of British culture (and other similar ones) can use a description based on a preliminary analysis of a scene of death to find evidence that would enable a story to be written such that the descriptor can be seen as a culturally appropriate end to the story. That a process seems to be involved in which both the circumstances of the death and the person who has died are the principle foci of attention is of special interest in the light of the kinds of definitions of suicide typically found in English dictionaries, for these tend to distinguish clearly between the act of suicide and the person who commits suicide. The *Concise Oxford Dictionary* (1974 ed.), for example, includes the following:

> suicide, n. 1. Person who intentionally kills himself . . . 2. Intentional self-slaughter . . .

Insofar as dictionary definitions reflect common usage within the culture, it is hardly surprising that members engage in analyses of the person and the act in order to make sense of possibly suicidal deaths. It is arguable, however, that something stronger than this holds, in that, for all uncertainty and puzzlement to be removed, both kinds of analysis must be done and there must be some kind of consistency or "fit" between the two. In other words, some mystery will remain if the act appears to have been suicidal but the person appears not to have been, and vice-versa. These various points can be aptly illustrated with reference to the closing lines of Shakespeare's *Antony and Cleopatra.* The heroine and her maid have just died, and Dolabella and Caesar are about to discover the bodies:

(*Re-enter Dolabella*)
Dolabella: How goes it here?
2 Guard: All dead.
Dolabella: Caesar, thy thoughts
Touch their effects in this: thyself art coming
To see perform'd the dreaded act which thou
So sought'st to hinder.
Within: A way there, for Caesar!
(*Re-enter Caesar and his train*)
Dolabella: O, sir, you are too sure an augurer;
That you did fear is done.
Caesar: Bravest at the last,
She levell'd at our purposes, and, being royal,
Took her own way. –The manner of their deaths?
I do not see them bleed.
Dolabella: Who was last with them?
1 Guard: A simple countryman that brought her figs.
This was his basket.
Caesar: Poison'd then.
1 Guard: O Caesar,
This Charmian liv'd but now; she stood and spake:
I found her trimming up the diadem
On her dead mistress; trembling she stood,
And on the sudden dropped.
Caesar: O noble weakness!–
If they had swallow'd poison 'twould appear
By external swelling: but she looks like sleep,–
As she would catch another Antony
In her strong toil of grace.
Dolabella: Here on her breast
There is a vent of blood, and something blown:
The like is on her arm.
1 Guard: This is an aspic's trail: and these fig-leaves
Have slime upon them, such as the aspic leaves
Upon the caves of the Nile.
Caesar: Most probable
That so she died; for her physician tells me

> She hath pursu'd conclusions infinite
> Of easy ways to die . . .

What is noticeable about this extract in the context of the present discussion is that, on finding Cleopatra dead, neither Dolabella nor Caesar has any trouble in arriving at the preliminary conclusion that the death is a suicide. Given what they know about her and of the situation preceding the death, or, in other words, given their analysis of her as a person, they can readily conclude that this is a suicide. But, having used the results of that analysis to see the death as a suicide, Caesar realizes that there is a puzzle remaining: "The manner of their deaths?/I do not see them bleed." In a sense, one could say that here speaks the member of Roman culture, for whom normal ways of committing suicide (falling on swords, etc.) would involve a bloody mess. Then Dolabella instigates inquiries as to how they could have died, and the information about the figs suggests to them an alternative mode of death in the form of poisoning. Again, however, the analysis of the bodies produces an inconsistency with what members of Roman culture might expect a death by poisoning to look like, and it is not until a local Egyptian guard joins the analysis that the answer to the puzzle is provided. Once this character has used his local knowledge to locate a possible way in which they might have died, Caesar immediately accepts the answer and indeed renders this rather obscure method of committing suicide intelligible with reference to some "inside information" of his own which he had apparently gleaned from Cleopatra's doctor. By so doing, he accomplishes and displays a "fit" between the particular person who has died and this particular way of dying.

Although the discussion in this section has concentrated on the problem of how suicides get recognized as such by members of British culture, and hence may seem to be very narrow and limited in its scope, some general points can be made in conclusion. One is that suicide is an accountable matter in British culture. In other words, like other deaths it poses a puzzle for witnesses and others who hear of its occurrence with respect to how and why the person who has died could have died in this way. If the manner of the death were not apparently suicidal, or if the biography and circumstances of the deceased appear inconsistent with a suicidal end to his or her story, or if one of these holds without the other, then the plausibility of a definition of a death as a suicide will be in question. In using the word "suicide" in everyday life, then, members of British culture presuppose that the manner of the death was "suicidal" and that the person who died was the kind of person who might typically be expected to commit suicide, or at least that there were locatable antecedents that could be seen as possibly leading to a suicide. In other words, the use of the word to apply to certain deaths presupposes that there were recognizable patterns associated with it, so that talk about particular suicides typically involves questions about "why" and "how" this person could have died in this way, while newspaper reports address themselves to providing their readers with answers to such questions. The availability of so many possible plausible stories as to how a suicide might have come about, coupled with the uniqueness of individual biographies and circumstances preceding death, mean that an infinite list of possible patterns could be constructed. This is not least among the reasons for our earlier refusal to commit ourselves to any particular list of patterns as the most important or most significant ones. The contention is, in contrast with the kinds of generalized claims that might have been involved in such a venture, that the methods used in interpreting the infinite array of possible combinations do have a degree of generality. That this is so provides members with the means to construct and to recognize stories based on detailed and highly various contextual data.

Although members' analyses are conducted in particular contexts and addressed to particular contexts, the analyses of "expert" suicidologists for the most part have aimed at the production of purportedly "decontextualized" analyses and stories that are claimed to hold independently of the contexts in which ordinary members engage in practical reasoning about suicide. By failing to regard the ways in which members use methods and theories to understand suicide as a topic worthy of serious analysis, the experts have failed to notice both the close connection between these and their own theories and methods, and the significance of the fact that what they take to be "hard" or "objective" data is the product of members' methods of practical reasoning. Thus, in an interview with a coroner's officer, I inquired as to whether during the course of his work he had come up with any theories of suicide. He replied:

> Well, I did. But they're entirely personal and–um–and I think basically it's the inability of the individual to come to grips with a situation. *He finds himself totally isolated from his fellows, from his family, from his friends . . .* He can't see any way out of his dilemma and the only path open to him is through suicide, *generally brought about or preceded by depression.*[25] [My emphases]

Although sociologists and psychiatric researchers have "discovered" relationships between isolation and depression and suicide, their conclusions are apparently already known to this coroner's officer. Indeed, that such things are known provides a guarantee that the experts will discover them if they rely on data generated by persons who already know such things. The evidence of isolation and depression found in particular cases can be used to determine that the death was a suicide. And the finding that the death was a suicide then gets used by the "experts" in organizing their samples of cases on which to base their generalizations. Then they look for and find the same kinds of evidence as was initially used to categorize the death as a suicide in the first place.

This situation raises some very serious questions about conventional ways of arriving at causal statements about suicide and points to the need to analyze the ways in which ordinary persons go about explaining and understanding suicidal phenomena. They, like expert suicidologists, engage in the analysis of their culture, and to this end rely on cultural knowledge and conventions that normally remain unexplicated. As members of particular cultures, we are remarkably competent and resourceful in constructing descriptions, explanations, and stories about suicide which other members of our culture will recognize as plausible or "possibly correct," yet we know very little about the interpretive procedures that enable us to achieve this. By regarding such procedures as the central topic for analysis, rather than as unexplicated resources to be used in doing analyses, the ethnomethodologists have uncovered a new and exciting domain of study.

REFERENCES

1. Hume, D. 1789. *Essay on Suicide.* London.
2. Douglas, J. D. 1967. *Social Meanings of Suicide.* Princeton Univ. Press: Princeton, N.J.; Atkinson, J. M. 1969. Suicide and the Student. *Univ. Quart.* 23:213; and Atkinson, 1971. Social Reactions to Suicide: The Role of Coroners' Definitions. *In* S. Cohen (ed.), *Images of Deviance.* Penguin: Harmondsworth, Engl.
3. Durkheim, E. 1952. *Suicide.* Routledge & Kegan Paul: London.
4. Hansard: Published transcripts of parliamentary debates at Westminster, Engl.
5. Atkinson, J. M. *Suicide and the Social Organization of Sudden Death.* Collier Macmillan: London (in press).
6. Jervis, J. 1957. *The Office and Duties of Coroners* (9th Ed.). Sweet & Maxwell: London.
7. Stengel, E. 1966. *Suicide and Attempted Suicide.* Penguin: Harmondsworth, Engl.
8. Durkheim, E. 1952, *op. cit.*
9. Masaryk, T. 1970. *Suicide and the Meaning of Civilization.* Trans. by W. B. Weist and R. G. Baston. Univ. of Chicago Press: Chicago.
10. Stengel, E. 1966, *op. cit.*
11. Sacks, H. 1963. Sociological Description. *Berkeley J. Soc.* 8:1.
12. Garfinkel, H. 1967. *Studies in Ethnomethodology.* Prentice Hall: Englewood Cliffs: N.J.: Douglas, J. D. (Ed.). 1971. *Understanding Everyday Life.* Routledge & Kegan Paul: London.
13. Giddens, A. 1965. The Suicide Problem in French Sociology. *Brit. J. Soc.* 16:3.
14. Farberow, N. L., and E. S. Shneidman (Eds.). 1975. *The Cry for Help.* McGraw Hill: New York; Douglas, J. D. 1967, *op. cit.*
15. Henslin, J. 1970. Guilt and Guilt Neutralization: Response and Adjustment to Suicide. *In* J. D. Douglas (ed.), *Deviance and Respectability.* Basic Books: New York.
16. Varah, C. 1965. *The Samarians.* Constable: London.
17. An exception is Fox, R. 1970. The Samarians and the Medical Profession. *In* R. Fox (ed.), *Proc. 5th Intern. Confer. Suicide Prevent.* IASP: Vienna.
18. Walker, A. 1967. *Lifeline.* Fontana: London.
19. Sacks, H. 1968. *The Search for Help: No One to Turn to.* (Unpub. dissert.) Univ. Calif. at Berkeley; Sacks, H. 1972. An Initial Investigation of the Usability of Conversational Data for Doing Sociology. *In* D. Sudnow (ed.) *Studies in Social Interactions.* Free Press: New York.
20. Laing, R. D. 1967. *The Politics of Experience.* Penguin: Harmondsworth, Engl.; and other works. Also, Cohen, S. (Ed.), 1971, *op. cit.*
21. Garfinkel, H. 1967, *op. cit.* Quoted with permission.
22. Soc. Sci. Res. Council Grant HR 14961-1; Atkinson, J. M. 1973. Suicide Status Integration, and Pseudo-science. *Sociology* 7:441.
23. Atkinson, J. M. 1973, *ibid.*
24. Atkinson, J. M. 1971, *ibid.*
25. Atkinson, J. M. BBC/Open University program on suicide.

nine

THE ATTITUDE OF DUTCH SOCIETY TOWARD THE PHENOMENON OF SUICIDE

N. SPEIJER, M.D.

The Netherlands is a small country; one can drive by car from the west (*i.e.*, the North Sea) to the eastern border in 1.5 hours and from north to south in about 5 hours. On this flat land presently live about 12.5 million people. It is indeed the most densely populated country in the world, and because of its small size distances are negligible. This has certain repercussions on our general outlook.

In the Netherlands private agencies play a larger role in medical care and preventive medicine than in most other countries. In all countries there is, of course, an interplay between governmental and private agencies, but in Holland private initiative with regard to public health takes a very important place. Private organizations are on a *denominational basis*. There are Roman Catholic organizations, which cover about one-third of the population, as well as Protestant ones, covering a little less, and also general organizations that are nonsectarian.

The underlying principle is that family care should be provided, as much as possible, by medical and allied personnel of the same denomination as the family. This principle of organized life in the Netherlands holds not only in the field of medical care and preventive medicine but in all fields of social and cultural life. For instance, in education there are denominational schools as well as governmental schools. Trade unions follow the same pattern of organization, and so do employers' organizations.

The system of *zuilen* ("pillars") is deeply rooted in the population. It makes perhaps for a somewhat complex organization and it may not be the most economical and efficient one, but at least it means a lively interest of the citizens in various aspects of community life. (See for further information "Mental Health in the Netherlands," a brochure compiled by the Dutch Ministry of Social Affairs and Public Health.)

The Dutch are very individualistic, their general attitude being anti-authoritarian. They have a great spirit of liberty. *Caritas* is a general trait. Many times huge amounts of money are collected to help people somewhere in the world where a disaster has struck. On the whole the Dutch people are tolerant, and many are more or less religious. On the negative side, the Dutch are rather undisciplined. Grousing against everyone who is more or less in a position of authority is quite normal in daily conversations. Although quite tolerant in individual cases, the Dutch do not always accept situations in other countries that do not correspond to their way of thinking.

ATTITUDE OF DUTCH SOCIETY TOWARD THE PHENOMENON OF SUICIDE

Before 1945 the subject of suicide was virtually taboo. Suicides, except those of very famous people, were not mentioned in the press. Suicide generally was rejected on religious grounds. Since World War II, Holland has become rather progressive. Many taboos have been broken, as, for instance, the taboos on sex, homosexuality, pornography, etc. The same has applied to the taboo on suicide. The general public is kept informed in various ways. From time to time television and radio have programs on suicide.

Neither suicide nor suicide attempt has been punishable under Dutch law since 1809. The total number of suicides in the Netherlands is rather low (in 1966, 10.8 per 100,000 inhabitants of 15 years of age and over); together with Italy, Ireland, Scotland, and Spain it is among the countries with the lowest rate. For the last 80 years this rate has remained unchanged.

There is no difference in suicide rate between cities and countryside. There is also not much difference in suicide rates between men and women, as in other countries. At present the male-female ratio is 1.7 to 1.0 (1966 figures). In general, the suicide rate increases with age, with no decline in old age.

INDIVIDUAL EMOTIONAL REACTION TOWARD SUICIDAL BEHAVIOR

Most Dutch people will call an act of suicide either brave or cowardly, depending on the circumstances, but there is seldom a condemnation of the person involved. Many religious people who are basically against the act of suicide still do not condemn the suicide attempter.

Before 1945, a person who tried to take his own life was usually considered to be mentally ill or mentally unbalanced. Now, more and more, the Dutch are inclined to accept the so-called "balance suicide," especially when there is an incurable disease or such. There are many nowadays, especially among the young, who are in favor of euthanasia, and this will undoubtedly have repercussions on the attitude toward suicidal behavior in the near future.

ATTITUDE TOWARD AND HELP FOR SURVIVORS OF SUICIDE ATTEMPTS

The Dutch mostly feel sorry for the suicide attempter, sometimes believing that he was right to try and feeling that it would have been better for him to have succeeded. Sometimes there are feelings of guilt. But if the "cry for help" was not on an unconscious, but rather more or less on a conscious level, resulting in a kind of arranged suicide attempt, then the feelings for the suicide attempter are often negative.

One of the most dominant traits in the Dutch population is helping everyone who needs help: not only fugitives from other countries etc., but all handicapped persons, such as the mentally ill, mentally retarded, or physically handicapped. There are numerous organizations, many on a denominational basis, that try to help handicapped or nonhandicapped people who need help in some way or another. If necessary, the suicide attempter is helped too by a great variety of services or individual helpers. This concerns mostly the less serious cases.

There are no special suicide prevention centers, because a country with enough extramural facilities to help people has, in our opinion, no need for special centers for suicide attempters. Suicide attempters are considered as persons in a crisis situation or at the final stage of such a situation, who should be helped in the same way and by the same service as other people in crisis situations. Suicide centers perform excellent work all over the world, and if there are no other possibilities for help they are a "must."

There are in Holland SOS telephone services (16 at present) that work anonymously. Only about 3 percent of the calls originate from suicidal people, but the SOS services perform an excellent job by listening to everyone who calls. In doing so, they perform what we call *general suicide prevention*, for such callers can in the near future become potential suicidal persons.

Besides the SOS telephone organizations, most cities and rural areas of the country have community-centered, centralized, comprehensive social psychiatric services. Of course, not all of these services work efficiently, and many can be improved upon. In order to be effective, these centers have to be recognizable and accessible and have to work in cooperation with other centers. In major cities these centers have a service available around the clock and are staffed with psychiatrists, psychologists, social workers, and administrative personnel. The basic philosophy of these services, taking as a paradigm one functioning well in a big city, would be the following:

1. All physicians who wish to have their patients admitted to a hospital (inpatient clinic) because of psychic difficulties or mental disturbances require permission from the center that will screen the patient. After screening admission is allowed, the service arranges for transfer to a mental hospital and arranges for payment of the hospital charges. If admission is refused, the center takes charge of the patient.
2. When a patient is admitted to the hospital, one of the psychiatrists from the center has regular interviews with the doctors of the hospital during treatment and, as soon as possible, discharge of the patient is arranged. The center takes care of everything that has to be done for the resocialization of the patient.
3. Many individuals with difficulties do not need actual hospitalization. However, they will need help in other ways. Such cases can be reported to the center via family, physicians, ministers, city services, etc.
4. The same applies for the police. The moment a disturbed person is brought in, the police stations can call in a psychiatrist from the center, who is available day and night. This is also applicable to a policeman who encounters a distressed person on his beat.
5. Apart from psychotherapy, the service provides general help in solving housing problems, difficulties in getting a job, problems in spending leisure time, and financial problems.

The center has to provide help in some form or another for: a) persons discharged from a mental hospital; b) mentally disturbed persons who do not need admission to a mental hospital; c) persons referred to the center by all kinds of people, including the police; and d) distressed persons who need help without actual hospitalization. To give effective help, the center has to have at its disposal, in the community it covers, hostels and special boarding houses for those patients who cannot return to their family; sheltered workshops for those who cannot find normal work, or for those who are too defective to work in a normal job; and social clubs for those who cannot spend their free time without guidance. From a lack of these facilities many patients have to be admitted unnecessarily to hospitals or cannot be discharged when they are ready, or simply cannot be helped at all; this is against the basic Dutch philosophy of helping people.

The Dutch system differs from that applied in many other countries, because of a certain historical background with regard to the care of the distressed. In Holland, as mentioned earlier, there are no suicide prevention centers, but the social psychiatric services described herein have partly the same function. From the above, it should be clear that:

1. All suicide attempters needing hospitalization (in a general or in a mental hospital) are screened by the center (if, of course, the center works on a highly professional level), except for acute cases where immediate medical help is required. After admission and stay in the hospital—even if all thoughts of committing suicide have seemingly left the patient—the patient comes under the aftercare of the center. (Please keep in mind that distances are negligible in Holland.)
2. All suicide attempters not needing hospitalization or only requiring first aid (such as pumping out stomachs, applying stitches, etc.) also come under the aftercare of the center for the time required to effect better social adaptation.
3. Technical help (financial, housing, work) as well as interpersonal help (psychotherapy) is needed in most cases. For psychotherapy, help from other specialists in the field of psychotherapy is often sought.

All help is provided on a voluntary basis. If the person concerned refuses aftercare, there is little to be done. However, very few refusals are encountered.

All these forms of *inter*vention and *post*vention are at the same time forms of suicide *pre*vention. They not only prevent a *new* suicide attempt, but serve as a so-called psychohygienic prevention, their aim being to help those who attempted suicide to become better socially integrated.

Suicide *pre*vention is also applicable to those persons—referred to the center by physicians, ministers, and police officers for various problems—who may be *contemplating* suicide. By helping these people improve their social adaptation, the center hopes to avoid possible suicides. The success of the whole intervention lies in the number of distressed people referred to the center. Constant propaganda to all concerned (physicians, ministers, police, etc.) via radio, lectures, and the like is imperative.

Finally, I would like to point out that besides the *specific* pre-, inter-, and postvention, there is so-called *general suicide prevention*. Among the people with various problems who have been referred to the center are those who have not thought of committing suicide but who may contemplate it in the future if their problems are not solved. Thus, the center performs a kind of *general prevention*.

Often people ask whether a human being has a *right* to end his life. This question is incorrect. We should say rather that everyone has a right to live and *we* have the obligation to make it possible for everyone to live in such a way that he can be a socially integrated member of society to the maximum of his abilities. However, as long as we have not made society a place where everyone *can* live in a situation of physical and social well-being, we will have to go on helping suicide attempters.

ten

SUICIDE IN THE NETHERLANDS

PIETER NOOMEN, DRS. T.

The most remarkable aspect about suicide in the Netherlands is its low figure. The neighboring country in the south, Belgium, has twice as many suicides even though both countries are alike in their politics, economics, and their standard of living. Until the 16th century, their history was the same and the majority of Belgians speak the same language as the Dutch. Germany, too, which has the longest frontier with the Netherlands, has a rate that is almost three times as high. The Dutch suicide rate has remained the same, about 7 per 100,000, through many decades. It is only since 1970 that it has increased about 1 or 2 percent.

Why does the Netherlands have such a low suicide rate in comparison to its neighbors? In order to get a clear picture, one must look at the general standards of physical and mental health. As Speijer showed in his contribution to this book, the Netherlands has one of the best organized mental health programs in Europe. With concentrated efforts from both official and private sectors for optimal health care (in a country with a high, modern standard of living), it is not too surprising to find the Netherlands among the top in the rankings of life expectancy according to the United Nations World Health Organization figures for 1968. The average mortality age for men is 71 (fourth highest age in the world) and for women 76.6 (third highest). The Netherlands also have the lowest death rate for the newly born. Thus it seems reasonable to view the relatively low suicide rate in the Netherlands in part as a result of the genuine regard for health care in this country.

However, in this chapter we wish to focus upon other aspects of Dutch culture that are related to the suicide problem and that may account for the "low" rates in this country. What in its culture generates a suicide prevention outlook? First, we will provide some historical and geographical information as a general background for the subject in question. Then, we will look at some of the relevant characteristics of the attitudes the Dutch have toward each other. This will be followed by a discussion of the legal and religious attitudes toward suicide. Under the headings "Suicide and Church Membership" and "Suicide and Faith," the subject is examined in its relation to religious matters; this should not be surprising in a country that is said to be filled with real and semitheologians. Finally, we will discuss the tragic peculiarities of suicide during World War II.

HISTORICAL BACKGROUND AND GEOGRAPHIC FACTORS

History and geography are still very important in the everyday life of the Netherlands. A visitor from abroad might be surprised to see such a modern skyline: huge industrial areas, new housing projects with endless rows of high, flat buildings, a vast freeway system, etc. But soon he would discover two of the most typical Dutch characteristics: present-day landmarks of the country's history and a lifetime of accommodation to an abundance of water in sea, rivers, canals, ditches, and lakes.

The Netherlands has been an independent nation since the 16th century. The long war against the Spanish armies, and the cruelties of the Roman Catholic Inquisition which finally brought the Dutch freedom, has been regarded as primarily a religious one, even though many economic and political factors played a role. Many nationalistic hymns stemming from that period reveal a deep faith in the righteousness of the fight for freedom and express a profound trust in God's help to succeed. That focus prevented many martyrs of that time from becoming national heroes, among them the Prince of Orange, the leader of the liberation movement who was murdered in 1584. Rather, they were seen as examples of Christians who were faithful until the very end. The first stanza of the Dutch National Anthem, which is always sung at national ceremonies and before international soccer matches, has the Prince of Orange testify, "I am faithful to my Fatherland, unto death." However, in the only other stanza that is well known but sung only in churches, the Prince prays, "That I may be Thy loyal servant, O Lord, in the fight against this murderous tyranny." This kind of coloring of historic events with theological or religious concepts has had a long tradition in the Netherlands, contributing to the lack of hero worship or idolizing of martyrdom (with its possible association to certain kinds of suicidal behavior) in Dutch history.

In the 17th century the nation reached its economic and artistic peak. The Dutch possessed many strategic territories in all five continents. Their merchant navy sailed all oceans and brought the country enormous wealth. At home, it was the period of the world-famous Dutch school of painting (Rembrandt, Hals, Vermeer), and also of the expansion of the cities, with its delightful, rich, middle class architecture. That epoch, more than any other period in its history, gave the country its character, much of which is responsible for its outlook today.

While the achievements of that period were not particularly overwhelming, they did provide the Dutchman with a sense of proud accomplishment in his country's history. One can imagine that, for the average person, being a citizen of this country and, as such, being surrounded by this kind of heritage provided him with a safe and warm feeling. It gave him a sense of continuity with a peaceful past in which the events speak not of aggression or extraordinary achievements but rather of solid, down-to-earth accomplishments. The population has never seemed to care for extremes or melodramatics; rather, they have preferred to keep both feet solidly on the ground. This brings us to another characteristic that typifies the Netherlands and its population. In order to stand with both feet on the ground, that ground had to be regained from the water.

The escutcheon of 1 of the 11 Dutch provinces shows a lion with only the upper part of his body above the waves. The motto is, "Luctor et Emergo" ("I struggle and emerge"). Not surprisingly, this belongs to the typical delta province in the southwest (Zeeland). This area has been flooded twice in recent history, once in the last phase of World War II, and again in 1953, the result of a spring tide which caused the loss of almost 2,000 lives. Water is often the Dutchman's best friend, but more often his worst enemy. Very literally, the Dutch have had to fight the water, and all kinds of manmade constructions provide him with relative safety from it. "God created the world, but the Dutch made Holland" is a saying that hits close to the truth, because the land actually did have to be made dry in order to live on it. The reward has been great as most of the soil is very fertile; however, its existence can never be taken for granted. There was, and always is, the threat of nature destroying what men have accomplished. The "eternal enemy," the water, is always there.

This applies also to the individual citizen. There probably are very few Dutch children who have not played too near the water and gotten a dunking in a ditch or canal. For many of them this incident will have meant more than wet clothes; it may have been the first conscious experience of their being near death. In Dutch literature one can find many examples of the water being used symbolically for death. It represents both aspects of death: the enemy, who takes away, and the friend, who welcomes. The Dutchman knows about death, because he knows about the water.

It is therefore not surprising that drowning is a frequently used method for suicide. It was the most frequently used method for women until 1967, when barbiturates became number one. While the total figures for drowning continue to increase, the number using barbiturates has risen much more dramatically. Hanging or strangulation is the most frequently used means of suicide by men. In second place, we find that men who commit or attempt suicide use drowning and barbiturates almost equally (since 1967).

It is noteworthy that, as Kruijt (1960, p. 48) found, drowning is practiced most in the south, which is the driest part of the Netherlands. He connects this surprising phenomenon with the fact that the general attitude toward suicide in this Roman Catholic part of the country is one of concealment, and drowning can easily be made to look like an accident.

ATTITUDES TOWARD OTHERS

In his comprehensive sociological study about suicide in the Netherlands, Kruijt (1960) mentioned that, "The view . . . advanced in many foreign publications that living in a (large) city is harmful to the mental harmony of man and would be among the factors causing high suicide rates is not supported by the Netherlands data . . .." (p. 428). He found that, as a rule, the Dutch cities have suicide rates that are about the same as the rural areas. Like its neighbor, Belgium, the Netherlands has a long tradition of urban life. Trade and industry have flourished since medieval times. Towns never intimidated the farmers and rural residents. The proximity to each other in such a small country prevented any extensive alienation between the two sections of the population, the city-dwellers and the countrymen, neither spiritually nor in life style.

But the way Dutchmen tend to relate to one another is another factor worth noting. One of the most striking aspects of the nature of Dutch people, affecting also their way of living in a big city, is their display of a certain kind of "earnest curiosity." One Dutch writer, discussing suicide with his colleagues, expressed it this way, "The Netherlands has quite a few melancholic and pessimistic writers, but suicide does not occur often because the Dutchman is too curious about tomorrow and what he would miss by not living to see the next day." Labeling the Dutchman with this quality is of course a generalization. On the other hand, this trait can often be observed in his style of living. One example would be moving into an apartment building. In the Netherlands the chances are great that neighbors would come by under one pretext or another offering to take care of the children, or bringing coffee or food, as an attempt to come in contact with the newcomers. From these first contacts friendly relationships often develop. Wives have their morning coffee together and the children become playmates. There is no peace of mind until one knows exactly what kind of people the new neighbors are. Also, the neighborhood stays interested until all the old "secrets" are out or new ones come up. This may include help if a situation is discovered in which a neighbor actually needs help—which may also be another reason for the relatively low suicide rates in the Netherlands.

Of course, there is still much loneliness and social isolation in the large cities, and suicides and suicide attempts do occur. One may hypothesize, however, that the eagerness to intrude into the private lives of others and the willingness to be involved in his problems does prevent people from hurting themselves. In contrast, people in parts of Belgium have a popular phrase, "Everyone must find his own way" (*zijn plan trekken, tirer son plan*). This is not to say that there is no willingness to help in Belgium. However, help there is given much more "on request" and with a minimum of personal involvement. Privacy in Belgium is much more guarded than in the Netherlands.

The Dutchman's curiosity about others means that he always has to have an opinion about others and about the world around him. He is not satisfied until he can identify the outer world and incorporate it into his system of values. Then he can let it be known what he thinks about it. Passing judgments on other people and their habits has been called a Dutch "disease" and can surface in different ways. For example, people from the north and from the south mutually criticize each other's social attitudes. The south is considered to be too communicative and too easy going, thereby not revealing their real feelings. The northerners are blamed for their directness and laconic verbal expression, which leaves no room for superficial relationships. Each blames the other for being different and difficult. Being "judgmental" is second nature to a Dutchman. It makes him very conscious about who thinks the way he does and who does not.

A positive element in this general judgmental attitude is that it gives the Dutchman the opportunity to ventilate his negative feelings. It is also a way of letting other people know where he stands. The Dutch have a saying: "If a person has nothing to complain about, then his situation is really bad!" Understatements, or at least honesty, is more appreciated in social intercourse than optimism or bragging. On another level, this attitude toward honest realism is related to the establishment of personal identity. Caring about who and what the others are lessens the necessity to turn inward in order to be aware of his own uniqueness. Thus, he provides himself with a ready identity for social and personal use without having to dig too deeply into himself. It is said that the Dutchmen are very individualistic people. This is true only in the sense that the individualism does not stem from an inner independence, but much more from the degree to which he disagrees with others. This way of experiencing his self-identity, that is, by being so much aware of the position of others, may help slow down any dissolution of the "self" that occurs in some suicides. These characteristics of the nature of many Dutchmen are mentioned here to point to the unique way they tend to experience their relationship to the world surrounding them and its possible influence on the phenomenon of suicide.

LEGAL AND RELIGIOUS ATTITUDES TOWARD SUICIDE

Criminal law in the Netherlands does not forbid suicide or a suicide attempt, but it does provide for imprisonment, with a maximum of 12 years, for the person who takes someone's life on that person's explicit request. It also provides up to 3 years of imprisonment for the person who suggests suicide, helps to carry it out, or supplies the means for it, if suicide actually does occur. In his handbook about suicide, Speijer (1960, pp. 77–79) listed some early laws related to suicides and society. In the middle ages, the possessions of a suicide were confiscated unless it was a case of mental illness. Speijer also mentioned an old law that stipulated that the body of the suicide could not be carried out of the door, but had to be towed away through a hole in the wall. Sometimes the bodies were publicly hanged or burned. Still, the impression is that those punishments were not frequently applied. Speijer suggested that this might be a result of the influence of the Renaissance on legal practice.

The present law dates from 1886. A scientific study on the ethics of suicide by Den Hertog (1913) tried to enlist the government's aid in preventing suicide. Den Hertog said, ". . . that the Government with its legislature has a powerful weapon with which to fight the spread of suicide. Since the Government is God's servant . . . it should intervene to prevent suicide, which is an act that offends so horribly the order God has created." The author then urged the authorities to express publicly their condemnation of suicide in order to sharpen the public conscience. He concluded with the suggestion that ". . . to label it infamous is the most powerful method of fighting it!" (p. 282). His suggestion had little success. One of the country's most dynamic political and Protestant church leaders, Abraham Kuyper, who was once Prime Minister, had more influence at that time. In a theological study discussing the sixth commandment, he recognized the misery that often preceded suicide, but ended with a passionate warning: ". . . it is not true, that you are delivered from your suffering by committing suicide. Rather, as far as you are concerned, you throw yourself forever into much worse mortal fear and infernal agony, ten times more alarming and fearful than the most frightful agony you ever had to wrestle with on earth" (p. 113).

This brings us to the official attitude of the churches toward suicide. Kuyper was a representative of the solid Calvinistic tradition that has dominated Dutch theology and official moral standards since the Reformation. The Roman Catholic religion, which was, and still is, professed by about one-third of the Dutch population, was tolerated after the Reformation. Only after its emancipation movement in the 19th century did it gain influence upon Dutch public life.

The official attitude of the Roman Catholic church in the Netherlands toward suicide is the same as anywhere else. No burial in sacred ground is allowed unless there is repentance before death, or when the suicide can be considered as having occurred without any planning, or when the person was mentally disturbed. This last provision became a frequently used escape clause. In the famous Dutch *De Nieuwe Katechismus*, edited by the Dutch bishops in 1966, in which many religious items are presented in modern form, it is illicit to end a life deliberately, as in suicide. The reason for such an attitude is that we have received life from God and we cannot end it of our own free will. What is striking, however, is that they have added, "We cannot judge the guilt for others may be guilty too." The final decision thus rests with one's honest conscience (p. 496).

This has been more or less the attitude in the Protestant world too. Ultimately, the burden of finding an answer lies on the shoulders of the survivors. An elder of the author's first church once remarked, after having told with difficulty about the suicide some years ago of his mentally retarded brother, "We can only say that he is lost forever, because his sin cannot be forgiven, but we still trust that somehow God will be merciful to him."

From the standpoint of the Protestant church the option of committing suicide is not acceptable, but there is a variety of viewpoints on the subject which ranges in approach from the very humane and mild to the legalistic and prophetic. The main body of the Protestant churches in the Netherlands uses, in addition to the Bible, the *Heidelbergse Cathechismus* (1563) as its guidebook for Christian education and weekly sermons. The teachings of this small textbook have had an enormous impact upon the traditional thinking and life style of the Dutch population. Many know it by heart. It makes one direct reference to suicide in the context of the sixth commandment ("Thou shalt not kill"): ". . . that I harm not myself nor willfully expose myself to any danger." What is remarkable here is that the direct act and the "indirect" suicide are considered together. In all probability, this too has prevented too harsh an attitude toward suicide, since the nonsuicidal person is also recognized as being capable of transgressing the commandment by engaging in all sorts of life-endangering behavior.

One of the main issues dominating Calvinistic theology is never to play off against each other God's righteousness and his grace. This applies also in the attitude toward suicide, for example, in that it is no solution to regard the act as part of a mental illness. We, as human creatures, cannot change or modify the divine law. On the other hand, it would not be appropriate to reduce the absoluteness of God's love by saying that there is no forgiveness for someone who kills himself.

In more recent religious publications we find the factor of interpersonal relationships more strongly emphasized, especially in regard to the question of guilt. Critical notes about the established society are often added (Ammerlaan, 1970; Rothuizen, 1972). Except for the traditional Jewish religion, it is only in recent times that non-Christian movements have begun to pay attention to suicide as a problem. In their approach, humanistic and liberal thinking prevails.

SUICIDE AND CHURCH MEMBERSHIP

The churches have never accepted suicide as a positive act. However, it is an open question whether this is a factor that brings about the low suicide rates in the Netherlands. In the first place it is very hard to establish a relationship between official church doctrines and individual adaptation to them, especially since suicidal behavior often reflects irrational behavior. The general attitude of psychiatrists and other workers in the mental health field today is that religion is not a relevant issue in the actual suicidal crisis. In a recent nationwide survey to obtain data about suicide attempts in the Netherlands, it was decided not to ask for religious affiliation because it was likely that the data obtained would not be valid. Also, Dutch statistics about suicide frequency do not reveal a significant correlation between church members and non-church-affiliated persons. The label "church member" itself tells nothing about the level of personal involvement. However, Kruijt (1960), in his definitive study, concluded that it was the distribution of the various religious denominations in the population that exercised the greatest influence on the level of the regional Dutch rates. Also, some of the few Dutch studies about suicide indicate possible connections between religion and suicide (Bergsma, 1966;

Bloemsma, 1971). Although interest and participation in traditional church life has clearly decreased in recent decades, there is still a strong attachment to the various Christian denominations by at least 25 to 35 percent of the population. An equal number is not as involved but still identifies itself as church affiliated. Theological issues have always found a fertile ground in Dutch society, and Dutch society is still basically constructed on denominational orientations. Therefore, it seems appropriate to go somewhat deeper into this subject. First, we will examine the data and then we will explore the positive and negative influences of religious affiliation among the Dutch.

The general finding that Roman Catholics have lower suicide rates than the Protestants does not apply in the Netherlands. We even get a reversed picture when we separate the numbers for the two large Protestant churches, although both are very similar in structure and official doctrine. We see that the smallest church, Gereformeerde Kerken, which represents almost 8 percent of the population, has the lowest suicide rate, about half of the national average. The other Protestant church, Hervormde Kerk, known in the past as the "official" church, accommodates two rather extreme groups—a liberal and a pietistic one—as well as a very large, moderate, orthodox middle group. The liberals and the pious are far to the left and far to the right both in convictions and in life style from the middle group. We find the highest suicide rates in the regions where either of these two extreme groupings is dominant. Of course, this does not mean that the suicides there are necessarily "religious" or church related. It has not been determined whether the suicides in these regions are members of the dominant religious subgroup, or predominantly people from other church groups in the area, or those who live in opposition to the prevailing subgroups. But it is difficult to believe that the typical attitudes of the extreme subgroups, deviating from those of the majority of Dutch Protestantism, play no role in the suicides at all. It raises the question whether Dutch Protestantism has inherent in it direct or indirect connections, positive or negative, with the occurrence of suicide.

SUICIDE AND FAITH

One of the most significant differences between nonactive, or inactive, church members and those personally involved is that the latter are continuously exposed to a challenge to believe and to experience the truth of the Biblical message that influences their whole existence. An important part of this confrontation lies in the area of the meaning of life and the ways of considering death. Both are, of course, central themes in suicidal thinking. Children grow up with such concepts as human imperfection, sin, evil, punishment, eternity without God, on the one hand; and forgiveness, rewards, love, deliverance, and being with God, on the other hand. In other words, a topic such as death and dying and what comes after that is not concealed but is dealt with. Although suicide as such is not mentioned often, personal involvement in dying and death is difficult for a believer to experience without recourse to the religious tenets of redemption and meeting God. Bible verses, hymns, and traditional words of comfort and support are generally considered prophylactic in regard to suicidal behavior, but taken out of context, they can have an opposite effect. One of the characteristics of the so-called hyperorthodox preaching is a frequent heavy emphasis upon the damnation of sinful men and upon the wrath of God. Faith is not experienced as liberation, and the horrors of death are often used as illustrations of the fate for ungodly lives. In areas where these concepts prevail, suicide is above the national average. Apparently some persons who feel unable to fight their dark destiny prematurely surrender to it.

A similar symptom may be found in the actual act of believing, with its expressions of prayer, association with the Biblical world, and belief that one is God's child. It implies a continuous trust in divine guidance. Such experiences can contribute greatly to positive and mature conduct in life and serve the person well when he encounters suicidal situations. However, in some depressive states, a failure to trust and an inability to pray can be easily experienced as a double burden. The emphasis that some religious circles put upon being one of God's chosen can give way easily to the feeling of being rejected, resulting in an acting out of that idea. The verses in the Bible about the only sin that is not forgivable, the sin against the Holy Ghost (Matthew 12:31, 32; I John 5:16, 17) darken sometimes the minds of some church members. (Den Hertog, p. 259, even claimed that many suicides are the result of this sin against the Holy Ghost.) It seems that legalistic and rigid teachings have almost always contributed negatively to deeper desperation of depressed (suicidal) persons.

In addition to the teachings of the church about death and personal beliefs, there is another attitude that might have implications for suicidal behavior. This is an awareness of religious law: the Ten Commandments, the double law of love, and the rules of the New Testament. Especially important are the Ten Commandments, read in many Sunday morning worship services. Their negative influence can be easily understood, as a legalistic approach prevails. Unresolved hate feelings toward parents or sexual frustrations, for example, can become unbearable burdens under weekly confrontations with the divine law of the Ten Commandments.

Guilt feelings and lessened self-respect are easily awakened. Young people with suicidal problems are readily affected. On the other hand, knowing clearly what is expected of a person, the possibility of forgiveness, and working toward real happiness can have an enormous positive influence. It provides a solid base for ethical thinking and for common sense functioning in family and social life.

Finally, we might mention the social impacts of being involved in church life. Durkheim and many others stressed the positive value of the integration factor as related to suicide. As far as the Dutch Roman Catholics and Protestants are concerned, this factor plays an important role. Close family ties, an intense domestic life, and participation in social activities are all highly valued. In the past, a dropping out of the denominational circle could even mean complete abandonment by the family or group.

In many Protestant churches it is the custom that every member or family belonging to the church is visited at least once a year by one or two elders, in order to keep track of each other's spiritual life and for mutual Christian encouragement. This is an excellent opportunity to detect tendencies that might lead to self-destructive behavior. In the church with the lowest suicide rates mentioned previously, this is a firmly maintained tradition. In some churches the Holy Communion, a solemn occasion, is celebrated four or six times a year. It is well known that several suicides are committed on that day, and it is believed that suicidal thoughts increase markedly in the period preceding that special celebration.

In the regions where the more liberal church members dominate, it is much more difficult to relate the higher suicide rates with religion. One can generally say that there is not much "social control" within the liberal churches and group activities as well as group morals are not so strictly supervised. Identification as a group and as a religious body in the traditional sense is much more vague.

WORLD WAR II AND SUICIDE

In this section, we change abruptly from an analysis of the religious influences on Dutch suicide to discussion of factual incidents of the past. The Dutch suicide rate increased by 50 percent during the period of the invasion of the Netherlands by Nazi German troops in the spring of 1940. About 380 persons took their own lives, many of them in suicide pacts; entire families often died. Anticipating the horrors of the German occupation, they chose death by their own hand. About 230 of them were Jews, some of whom had fled from Germany as the Nazis took over. The misery they (correctly) foresaw, provoked the tragedy of these decisions. Among the non-Jewish Dutchmen who killed themselves, some wanted to protest the treacherous invasion. Van Duinkerken (1972) wrote of his friend, Ter Braak, a famous writer who committed suicide, "He didn't commit suicide, he murdered Hitler in his body. He didn't want to see that man, and the only way he could do that was by closing his own eyes!" (p. 72). Another colleague, Roland Holst, wrote about him and a friend who died the same day, "Life knighted them to men; death enlarged them to humans" (p. 49).

Still, suicide was not only a tragedy of war. Kruijt (1960) analyzed the Dutch statistics and found in 1945, the year the Netherlands were liberated, a "surplus" of about 300 suicides above the average number (pp. 202–209). He came to the conclusion that a considerable proportion of those suicides were former members of the pro-German Nationalist Socialist Party in the Netherlands, considered as traitors by the rest of the population.

A third comment about suicide and war is that, contrary to what happened in most other countries, the suicide rate in the Netherlands did not decline during the war. Kruijt, who gave considerable attention to this fact, felt that the answer lay in the weakening of the usual suicide preventive influences during the war, such as marriage and family life. He also found support for his hypothesis in the variety of family patterns, stating that "the unfavorable influence of war on family life varies with the prevailing family pattern. The traditional pattern is more vulnerable than the modern one due to, among other things, the larger size of the family" (p. 423).

FINAL REMARKS

As already mentioned, the suicide rates seem to have increased quite markedly since 1970, and there are unofficial reports that suicide attempts by young people have also increased considerably. If this trend is correct and if it continues, the question arises as to how much cultural changes are contributing to this. It is widely accepted that there is a change in thinking and in many traditional attitudes in the Netherlands. Taboos are being broken, and, apart from a diminishing influence of the institutionalized churches, there seems to be an authority (or identity) crisis on many levels. Whether these changes are strong enough to affect the factors preventing suicide found in the Dutch culture today remains to be seen. Of course, new ones may appear. Den Hertog in 1913 predicted an increase of suicide frequency for the Netherlands, an increase that never occurred. As for us: who wants to be a prophet of the future, when the present in an ever rejuvenating country offers so many challenges and chances to participate positively in the process?

REFERENCES

Ammerlaan, J. 1970. Ethische vragen von Zelfmoord. Unpublished paper.

Bergsma, J. 1966. Suicide en Suicidepoging, speciaal bij Jongeren. Nederlands Tijdschrift voor de Psychologie en haar Grensgebieden, deel XXI.

Bloemsma, F. 1971. *Zelfmoordpoging: een poging om te leven.* Nat. Fed. voor de Geestelijke Volksgezondheid, Amsterdam.

Den Hertog, M. M. 1913. *De Zedelijke Waardering van den Zelfmoord.* De Swart en Zoon, 'sGravenhage.

Holst, A. R. In. Berijind verzet (no date).

Kruijt, C. S. 1960. *Zelfmoord; statistisch-sociologische verkenningen.* Van Gorcum, Assen.

Kuyper, A. *E Voto Dordraceno; toelichting op den Heidelbergschen Catechismus.* Kok, Kampen (no year).

De Nieuwe Katechismus. 1966. Geloofsverkondiging voor volwassenen. In opdracht van de bisschoppen van Nederland. Brand, Hilversum.

Rothuizen, G. T. 1972. *Afspraak met de Dood; gedachten over ethiek en suicide.* Kok, Kampen.

Speijer, N. 1969. *Het Zelfmoordvraagstuk; een samenvattend overzicht van de verschillende aspecten van de zelfmoord.* Van Loghum Slaterus, Arnhem.

Van Duinkerken, A. 1972. In: G. T. Rothuizen, *Afspraak met de Dood; gedachten over ethiek en suicide.* Kok, Kampen.

eleven

PSYCHOCULTURAL VARIABLES IN ITALIAN SUICIDE

MAURICE L. FARBER, PH.D.

The cultures of modern, technologically developed nations are heterogeneous, often characterized by conflicting and contradictory forces. Thus, observations of the Italian culture reveal a complex interaction of influences bearing upon suicide, some impelling individuals toward suicide and others acting to prevent it.

One of the most immediately salient facts about Italy is that it is a Catholic country, with suicide regarded as a grave sin. Suicide is more severely disapproved and regarded with more horror than in many other countries. A suicide cannot be buried in sacred ground; the family is grievously shamed. On a practical level, for example, an applicant will be rejected by the police force if there has been a suicide in the family. It is understandable, therefore, that a sympathetic doctor, priest, or police official will collaborate in having a suicide reported as a death from some other cause. Such behavior is widely acceptable in the Italian culture, in which family loyalty outweighs the value of civic responsibility.

This is illustrated by the attitude of an outstanding Italian suicide expert, who, although regretting the resulting inaccuracy of the statistics, stated to me that if a colleague of his were to commit suicide he would go to great lengths to protect the family by covering up the event. The officially reported rate of about 4 per 100,000 is, doubtlessly, understated.

The same cultural value is responsible for a severe distortion of official statistics on the reasons for suicide. Overwhelmingly, the reason given is tal illness." Again, a covering-up process is involved. In the eyes of Church only suicide by a sane person, who is responsible for his sion, is a sin. The label of mental illness allows for normal, religious burial and provides a shield for the family. Since many suicides are indeed depressed, anguished, and agitated, there is a sufficient aura of ambiguity to allow for the diagnosis of "mental illness" with little strain on the conscience. It is clear that official Italian statistics, not only with regard to the frequency of suicide but also concerning its reasons, must be treated with caution.

More important, however, is the fact that the strong moral and religious condemnation of suicide in Italy doubtlessly does tend to discourage it, in contrast to the situation in a country like Denmark, where the cultural attitude is much more tolerant of suicide.

One feature of Italian life about which there is wide agreement among observers is the importance of the family in the life of the individual and the availability of succorance from members of one's family. Although loyalty to society, the state, or government may well be weak, loyalty to the family remains deep-seated in the Italian culture. A troubled individual may well expect to receive large supplies of love, help, protection, and solace. All of these will act to soften life's blows, to dull the sharp edge of desperation, and thus to reduce the likelihood of suicide.

It may be noted that with increased industrialization and urbanization the Italian family might well be losing some of its cohesiveness. Should this trend develop, it might be expected that the family will lose influence as a mitigating factor in Italian suicide.

Possibly related to feelings about family is what might be called "social accountability." People may be held responsible for encouraging an antisocial act, or even for not intervening to prevent one from happening. People are apt to stop their cars to break up a youthful fist fight. It is actually illegal to encourage a suicidal act, and one is expected to bend all efforts to prevent a potential suicide from committing it. Such attitudes, even if only haphazardly effective, must be seen as countersuicidal.

As one observes the Italian culture, one is struck by a widespread characteristic: the tendency, in the face of difficult conditions, of Italians, at least of certain classes, to use the expression *pazienza*. This means more than "patience." It involves acceptance that one cannot do anything about much of the world, that many conditions of man are like the events of nature: storms, volcanic eruptions, the movements of the planets.

This tactic of folk wisdom may well have powerful consequences for survival. A low but viable level of hope is maintained; hardships are tolerated and seen as acceptable life conditions that might throw other nationals into despair. Moreover, difficulties are not attributed to failings in oneself, and so the basic sense of competence is not attacked. The attitudes underlying the posture of *pazienza* must be seen as countersuicidal.

The Italian writer Luigi Barzini has ascribed to the Italians a genius for making the surfaces of life attractive, for erecting beautiful and dramatic facades in front of the dismal facts of life. Thus the stress upon beautiful clothes, personal appearance, sparkling displays in Italian life. This can be seen as a kind of mechanism of defense against anxiety and despair, developed through the experience of centuries by the wisdom of the people to counteract these feelings in the face of the threats of starvation, slaughter in war, and oppression.

If we assume the validity of Barzini's observation—and it does appear to have considerable support—then such a mechanism would seem clearly to possess countersuicidal properties. Attention is diverted from dismal reality to the attractive surfaces; it is possible to enjoy life. And yet it can be seen that such a mechanism is limited in effectiveness. One cannot live on surfaces only; the grim facts lurk behind the sparkling surfaces to crash through and plunge one into desperation, depression, and despair. Overall, then, the mechanism may well be countersuicidal, but its effectiveness seems limited.

It might be fair to say that the Italians are extrapunitive rather than intrapunitive, *i.e.*, tending to blame others rather than themselves for difficulties. Rather than search oneself for flaws, the tendency is to blame, often with great heat, officials, the government, other segments of the population, other countries. Since the failure is not in oneself, the sense of competence is left intact and depression is avoided. Again we have a characteristic that must be seen as countersuicidal.

Conceptually closely related to the foregoing formulation is, of course, the problem of the management of aggression, which plays an important role in the psychodynamics of suicide. Orthodox psychoanalytic theories tend to see aggression turned inward as a central explanation of suicide. I myself prefer a formulation that sees the frustration that follows from thwarted aggression as attacking the basic sense of competence and thus rendering one helpless and more susceptible to suicide. In any case, externalization of aggression tends to be countersuicidal, and this is what we appear to find among the Italians. There is an emotional lability, an ease in expressing aggression, rather than a suppression and a hoarding of it. Auto accidents on the road are often followed by violent arguments between the participants, but the aggression remains verbal and is usually discharged quickly without bodily injury to an adversary.

Part of the same dynamic constellation is the role of guilt, which attacks the sense of competence and thus contributes to suicidal behavior.

One receives the impression that guilt is relatively unimportant in the Italian personality structure. One notes, for example, in contrast to the situation in England, where one-third of all homicides are followed by suicide, that homicide in Italy is rarely followed by suicide.

One contributor to the low level of guilt may be, as suggested by Franco Ferracuti and others, the institution of the confessional in the Catholic Church. The confessional may act as a periodic discharger of guilt as sins are accumulated and then absolved. It might be noted, however, that this mechanism presumably would be more powerfully effective for the devout, which many Italians no longer are. But among those who are not devout, confession might well provide emotional catharsis as well as, for some, an excuse for divesting oneself of punishing guilt.

One gains the impression in many Italian men of an apparent self-confidence in their manner. It is difficult to say whether this reflects merely the expected social role behavior for males in Italian culture, or possibly a certain narcissism, or, on the other hand, a more deep-seated sense of competence, a high degree of ego strength. If it is the latter, it would of course, represent a force in the personality resistant to suicide.

The influences discussed thus far are countersuicidal in their effects. What influences in Italian culture promote suicide? An important one can be called "demands upon interpersonal giving." It is the other side of the coin of the "availability of succorance" discussed in connection with the Italian family. That is, those who provide the succorance may have demands put upon them that are unbearable but which they feel obligated in the closely knit Italian family to fulfill. The sense of competence is attacked; the situation becomes insufferable.

Moreover, the family quarrels that result from disagreements about these demands are apt to have a special poignance and even violence when they occur among those who have close emotional ties to each other. Some appear actually to become sick from the pent-up rage and frustration. In some other countries such conflicts might be handled with greater coolness. It is out of such heated conflicts that a proportion of Italian suicides occurs.

It might be noted here that there is a certain histrionic, operatic quality in Italian life. Suicide, a severely forbidden act in this Catholic culture, consequently has a heightened, dramatic quality, an act that demonstrates with operatic *éclat* the desperation of the perpetrator before an audience that will be profoundly horrified. Thus, this quality may serve to impart to suicide, or at least to threats of suicide and spectacular attempts, a garish attraction for those who might wish to make a dramatic appeal or a smashing exit.

There is one kind of suicide that, while not uniquely Italian, is nevertheless characteristic of traditional Italian culture. *Suicidio per motivi di onore*, suicide for reasons of honor, is recognized as an established type. Typically, for example, a business man may find his affairs in disastrous condition, unable to repay his debts, and threatened with bankruptcy. Such a development would bring shame and dishonor upon himself and his family. His suicide is seen as precluding this dishonor. It is, moreover, often followed by a rescue operation by relatives and associates in the making available of credit and other help to the business so that the creditors can be paid and the dishonor avoided. To be sure, the family now suffers, in addition to the personal grief, certain social penalties because of the suicide, such as the closing off of employment as a police or military officer, but honor has been maintained. The basic psychodynamics of this type of suicide are not essentially different from those in other types of suicide, but in its details and emotional nuances it is characteristically Italian. With recent rapid changes in Italian life, suicide for reasons of honor may well be dwindling in frequency.

Beyond demands of the family there are many other demands upon the individual in contemporary Italian society. Despite recent sharp rises in the gross national product, there are a variety of gross dysfunctions in Italian economic life. There is still much grinding poverty and unemployment, especially in the south. Many Italian workers must leave home and seek work in other parts of Europe. Huge numbers of backward south Italian peasants have moved to northern cities, such as Turin and Milan, to find work, where they live under miserable conditions of social disruption and anomie. These are fertile conditions for suicide, and indeed the suicide rate for these groups has been shown to be relatively high. Competition for jobs and in business can be cutthroat. Government is rife with inefficiences and is distrusted by the population. Having to deal with a governmental bureaucracy can be interminable, unjust, unspeakably frustrating. The educational system is antiquated and inadequate, producing hardship and disappointment for many students. Daily life, even for the relatively well-to-do, can involve extreme irritations and frustrations. Strikes in essential services have been frequent, involving transportation, mail, and the removal of garbage. Vast areas of Rome are without water for periods of each year when the ancient aqueducts are cleaned. Awesome traffic jams develop as hordes of modern automobiles try to make their way through streets built for pedestrians and medieval carts. The effects of pollution of the environment have in some parts of the country become highly destructive and obnoxious.

The fact is that, although there is much of the sweetness of life to be found in Italy, and similar difficulties may be found in other countries, there is nonetheless an unusually wide assortment of frustrations that require, to survive them, extensive giving of oneself and struggles with impotent rage, that can, in those whose personalities are vulnerable, contribute to suicide. Some of these may not be basic causes, but they add to life's burdens.

Italian statistics on methods of suicide reveal hanging to be the most frequent method, in 1961 to 1962 constituting about 32 percent of all suicides. Firearms and drowning are each about half as frequent as hanging. These relative frequencies are not dissimilar to those of a number of other countries, and it is doubtful that any uniquely Italian psychological inferences can be made from them. In all probability, they reflect the availability of various means of self-destruction and perhaps traditions regarding such acts. There is, to be sure, a contrast with the situation in the United States, in which the use of firearms has been by far the most frequent method, reflecting, one would assume, the easy availability of firearms in the United States as well as a tradition of violence. There are in Italy, as in many other countries, differences in frequency of methods of suicide between men and women, with men tending to favor more violent methods, such as firearms and hanging, and with women tending to favor more passive, less bloody methods, such as drowning, jumping, poisoning, and gas. In general, with regard to the frequency of methods of suicide, we may expect, as is happening throughout the world, that in Italy, too, the relative frequencies of method will change with changes in the ways of life of the Italian people. For example, it is not improbable that the use of pills, such as barbiturates and tranquilizers, will increase.

It is perhaps impossible to perceive in its entirety a complex culture. But it does seem possible to disentangle something of the living web and expose some of the relevant variables. Elsewhere, in my book *Theory of Suicide*, I have attempted to develop the relationships among some of these variables more formally into a general theory of suicide.

REFERENCES

Amministrazione Provinciale Di Milano, Centro Nationale Di Prevenzione E Difesa Sociale. 1968. *Suicidio e tentato suicidio in Italia*.

Barzini, L. 1964. *The Italians*. Atheneum, New York.

Farber, M. L. 1968. *Theory of Suicide*. Funk and Wagnalls, New York.

Ferracuti, F. 1957. Suicide in a Catholic country. In: E. S. Shneidman and N. L. Farberow (Eds.), *Clues to Suicide*. McGraw-Hill, New York.

twelve

SUICIDE IN LOS ANGELES AND VIENNA

NORMAN L. FARBEROW, PH.D., and
MARIA D. SIMON, PH.D.

Suicide has been with us as long as humanity (Dublin, 1963), and yet our understanding of this complex phenomenon is fragmentary. Its roots are both intrapsychic and environmental, with social aspects relating to the wider cultural setting as well as to the private sphere with its unique web of family, work, and interpersonal relationships. While Durkheim's classic *Le Suicide* (1951) laid its major stress on the generalized societal factors, modern researchers have, on the whole, tended to turn their attention to the variables that stem from the suicidal individual's personality and his nuclear social setting.

Comparative studies of suicide in more than one culture are few (Hendin, 1964; Ohara, 1961), and the conclusions are tentative rather than definitive. Clearly more research is needed to help distinguish between the intrapersonal, the interpersonal, and the societal causes of suicide so that the appropriate remedies may be applied. It has been found, for example, that in the United States the modal suicide will be a white, Protestant man, 45 to 55 years of age, who has recently suffered the loss of a loved one or whose health has deteriorated to the point where he can no longer work effectively (Farberow, 1968). Does this finding also hold in other Western industrial cultures or in less developed cultures?

This chapter compares data gathered by identical methods on suicides in two different settings. The subjects of the study were from Vienna,

Reprinted with permission of the publishers of *Health Services Reports*, formerly known as *Public Health Reports*, 1969, 84(5):389–403. The tables in the original report have been deleted.

Austria, and Los Angeles, California. Suicide rates in the two cities are roughly comparable, namely 17 per 100,000 population in Vienna (1966 police records) and 18 per 100,000 in Los Angeles (1967 coroner's statistics). There is no need for this chapter to dwell on the flaws in suicide statistics; however, both localities undoubtedly have high suicide rates and have had them for many decades. This report is the first of a series planned from the extensive data obtained about suicides in the two cities.

PROCEDURES

The data from both localities were obtained by the "psychological autopsy" method, a technique first employed by Farberow and Shneidman (1961). An "autopsy" goes beyond the usual data supplied by police records and coroners' reports; intensive interviews are conducted with family, relatives, and significant friends of the deceased to uncover as much as possible about the dynamics that led to the final lethal step.

Each national group in this study consisted of all the suicides that became known through public records in either city over periods of time. The period in Vienna was October 1, 1965 to April 29, 1966, and in Los Angeles from January 1 to May 16, 1967. The Viennese cases were gathered consecutively, while the Los Angeles cases were collected in two periods, approximately half in January and half in May. (Case collection was interrupted when the time interval between the death and interview began to exceed 1 month. The Los Angeles case data were gathered within a shorter time span than the Vienna data because Los Angeles County is a "catchment area" of approximately 7 million people (about 1,100 suicides occur there each year).

The interviews in Vienna were conducted by social workers for Lebensmuedenfuersorge, the Vienna Suicide Prevention Service, a departlent of Caritas, the Catholic Welfare Service Organization.

The Los Angeles interviewers were research assistants at the Suicide Prevention Center and the Central Research Unit, Veterans Administration Center, Los Angeles.

For each suicide, a member of the investigating teams contacted a survivor and enlisted his cooperation for an interview that lasted an average of 2 hours. If the contact refused to be interviewed or if no contact could be found, the case was recorded as an "incomplete data case." In Vienna, attempts to investigate 149 cases were necessary in order to accumulate the desired 50 "complete data cases." In Los Angeles, attempts to investigate 94 cases were necessary before reaching the goal of 50 complete data cases. In an extensive investigation of suicides in Vienna in 1961, Ringel had to examine 382 cases to obtain full data on 50.

The reasons why complete interviews could not be obtained in this study were noted. The number of refusals was about the same in both localities (24 Viennese, 20 Los Angelinos), but in Vienna many fewer contacts with close knowledge of the deceased could be found. No contact was located in 21 suicides in Vienna and in 15 in Los Angeles. Cooperative but uninformed contacts were found in 41 cases in Vienna and in three Los Angeles cases.

A partial reason may be that in Los Angeles the initial contact with survivors was always by telephone and an interview arranged then. In Vienna few people have a telephone, and interviewers had to take their chances and make unannounced home visits, usually during the evening. When no one could be found, the interviewer returned at least twice and left messages in the mailbox before abandoning attempts to find an informed contact. Even allowing for this factor, there is evidence that those committing suicide in Vienna simply had fewer close contacts. Also, in Vienna six contacts denied that the deaths were suicides; no Los Angeles contacts made such denials.

The amount of information about the incomplete cases varies from the barest identification data obtained from Vienna police records and the Los Angeles coroner's office to fairly detailed histories—if of dubious validity—supplied by neighbors, janitors, or even the mailman. For the complete data groups most informants in both cities were women, 82 percent in Vienna and 64 percent in Los Angeles. That most informants were women is a logical consequence; men committed 80 percent of the complete data suicides in Vienna and 54 percent of the suicides in Los Angeles. The median age of informants in Vienna was 50 years, with 38 percent age 44 or less, 50 percent age 45 to 64, and 12 percent age 65 or older. For Los Angeles, the median age of informants was 45, with 50 percent age 44 or less, 34 percent 45 to 65, and 16 percent age 65 or older. Approximately half the informants in each city were spouses (58 percent Vienna, 48 percent Los Angeles); 24 percent of the Viennese informants were children, parents, or siblings compared with 38 percent of the Los Angeles informants. The rest, 18 percent in Vienna and 14 percent in Los Angeles, were in-laws, fiance(e)s, or very close friends. In both groups about 72 percent of the informants knew the decedents 10 years or more.

Some of the hard data from the incomplete records could be meaningfully pooled with data from the complete cases, thus providing us with a larger sample for some variables. Subsequently in the text, "total sample" refers to pooled data from both complete and incomplete records; "complete data cases" refers to the group for whom complete interviews were possible. The interview was semistructured; that is, questions concerned each of the following topics, but the interviewer was not limited in order and format in conducting the interview: 1) identifying information about the deceased; 2) details of suicide act; 3) communication about suicidal intent; 4) reactions to presuicide communication; 5) previous suicide attempts and motivation; 6) syndromes; 7) lethal intent; 8) personal and background information (medical, psychiatric, marital, social, occupational and financial, residential, and developmental).

The first seven categories mainly relate to the act itself and the situation immediately leading up to it: the personal and background information refers to the deceased's personality, interpersonal situation, and history. The same amount of information could not always be obtained for all subjects. However, apart from the individual differences, some noticeable national characteristics in type and amount of information obtained from different items emerged. These characteristics are discussed subsequently.

Information from the protocols was coded and tabulated according to a special coding procedure. The coding procedure allowed the more than 500 variables to be analyzed by computer. Approximately 75 percent of the variables were factual (age, sex, number of previous attempts, and so forth), but for the remaining 25 percent, the coder was required to make a judgment about the respondents' statements. Reliability of coding was tested by selecting five cases at random from the 50 complete data cases and having another interviewer code them. Agreement on factual items ranged from 91 to 94 percent; on the judgmental items, from 82 to 92 percent.

RESULTS

Unless specifically noted, results are based on the complete data records for 50 cases from each city. Some information is missing for some subjects, and consequently the findings are related to smaller numbers for some items. Unless otherwise noted, all statistical comparisons in the "Results" section were computed by the chi-square test.

Identity Information about the Deceased

In both total samples, slightly more men than women killed themselves. In Vienna 55 percent of the decedents were men, and in Los Angeles, 53 percent. The differences by sex were not significant. A significant difference in sex composition did emerge when complete and incomplete cases were considered separately.

In Vienna there were four complete records for men for each complete record for a woman, whereas the 57 women outnumbered the 42 men among the incomplete cases. In Los Angeles, by contrast, the proportion of men to women was about the same for both complete and incomplete cases—23 men, 21 women in the incomplete cases; and 27 men, 23 women in the complete cases. Possible reasons for these findings are considered in the discussion.

The mean age for the total sample of those committing suicide in Vienna was 53 years and for Los Angeles it was 48 years. The difference was not significant. The mean for men was 50 in Vienna and 45 in Los Angeles; and for the women, it was 56 in Vienna and 51 in Los Angeles. None of the differences between mean ages for sexes between or within cities was significant. Likewise, none of the differences between or within cities for mean age or age by sex comparisons for the incomplete data cases was significant.

When the mean ages of the complete data cases were compared, the Vienna group tended to be older than the Los Angeles group (52 and 46 years, $p < 0.05$) as were Viennese men (52 and 42 years, $p < 0.05$). The differences between the women were not significant, either between or within cities.

The marital status for the complete cases did not differ significantly between Viennese and Los Angeles decedents. In Vienna, 56 percent were married, 14 percent were single, 18 percent separated or divorced, and 12 percent widowed. In Los Angeles, 46 percent were married, 12 percent single, 22 percent separated or divorced, and 20 percent widowed.

Details of the Suicide Act

In the total sample no suicides occurred significantly more often on any day in either city. Although it seems curious in this sample that most suicides in Vienna (37 percent) and fewest suicides in Los Angeles (21 percent) occurred on Friday and Saturday, the difference is still nonsignificant.

For both the total sample and complete data groups, there were two significant differences in the method of suicide. In Vienna, 38 percent of the total sample used domestic gas; none of the Los Angeles suicides died using gas, since the gas in that city is nonlethal ($p < 0.01$). Guns were used in 39 percent of all Los Angeles suicides, but in only 4 percent of those in Vienna ($p < 0.01$). The differences between the two cities in use of any of the other methods are insignificant. No Viennese killed himself using motor exhaust gas. In Los Angeles, a city infamous for its high ratio of cars per population, 6 percent of the total group used this method. No significant differences occurred between methods for the total sample and methods for the complete data groups.

Where did subject die? Was he likely to be seen at the place of suicide? Who found the body? Was there indication that the suicide was planned? These questions were posed to determine the chances of rescue. No significant differences were found between Vienna and Los Angeles in the answers to the first three questions for the complete data groups. However, 54 percent of respondents in Vienna denied the act was planned, while 93 percent of the Los Angeles contacts felt there had been some planning ($p < 0.05$).

Approximately the same number of subjects in both samples (41 percent in Vienna and 32 percent in Los Angeles) were reported to have been drinking at the time of the act.

Communication about Suicidal Intention

As findings from systematic suicide research accumulate, it has become increasingly apparent that many, if not most, persons who become suicidal give ample warning of their intentions and, in a sense, plead to be rescued. To what extent have these forewarnings been comprehended, heeded, and responded to in our samples?

Did the subject leave a suicide note? Had he been writing regularly to anyone? Both these questions seek the extent of communication between the person and society preceding the act. Respondents' answers to both questions indicated that the Los Angeles subjects had significantly greater communication. Forty-six percent of them left suicide notes; only 18 percent of the Viennese did so ($p < 0.01$). Thirty percent of the Angelinos, compared with 9 percent of the Viennese, had been writing regularly to someone ($p < 0.05$).

To the straightforward question whether the subject had talked about killing himself on last contact, nearly all the respondents replied no or evaded the answer. Only four of 43 Viennese and two out of 43 Angelinos said yes. When the question was framed more subtly by asking whether the deceased had behaved in an unusual manner at the last contact, that is, did he communicate nonverbally, 32 percent of the Angelinos and 12 percent of the Viennese remembered he had ($p < 0.05$).

To whom had the subject talked about his intention to commit suicide? Answers to this question were categorized as "significant others," a heading that combined spouse, relatives, fiance(e), lover, and friends or as "to no one or don't know." Communication between subjects and significant others on the impending suicide was markedly higher in Los Angeles than in Vienna (72 percent compared with 27 percent ($p < 0.01$).

Did the subject act as if he would not be around any longer? Although the deceased did not seem to talk about killing himself, more Los Angelinos seemed to act as if they would not be around long (by taking out insurance, writing a will, putting their affairs in order, giving away personal belongings). The percentages were 25 in Los Angeles, 2 in Vienna ($p < 0.01$).

The respondents were asked what problems the subject spoke about. Most often the problems were physical health (about 35 percent), feeling unwanted (about 32 percent), and interpersonal difficulties (about 17 percent). Differences were not significant between the samples.

How did significant others react? Communications were more often ignored in Vienna, 56 percent compared with 34 percent in Los Angeles ($p < 0.05$). Help seemed more frequently extended in Los Angeles (30 percent versus 10 percent, $p < 0.05$).

Past Attempts, Motive for the Suicide

More previous attempts were reported for the Los Angeles group than the Viennese (50 percent versus 29 percent, $p < 0.05$). Three or more previous attempts were reported for six persons from Los Angeles and one person from Vienna. Either would-be suicides in Vienna succeed more often on their first attempt or prior attempts are more often denied.

Respondents' reasons for the deceased taking his life are likely to be surface ones, but are interesting as indications of "acceptability" within each culture. The Viennese ascribed the cause most often to physical illness (39 percent) while the Los Angelinos most often thought of interpersonal difficulties (36 percent, $p < 0.05$).

Many attempts are not meant to end in death. The act is a plea for help, a gesture, an effort to manipulate the environment, rather than an act to terminate life (Farberow and Shneidman, 1961; Shneidman and Farberow, 1957). How many subjects seemed to have a high degree of lethal intent in their actions? While generally difficult to evaluate from our respondents' information, one measure used was the response to the question posed directly to the informant. These responses showed that about two-thirds of the suicidal acts in both groups seemed intended to be lethal. There were no significant differences between the groups.

Syndromes

Continuing research at the Los Angeles Suicide Prevention Center and Veterans' Administration Central Research Unit has indicated that certain types of personality and certain environmental constellations seem to appear often in suicidal events. Some of these "syndromes" have been described in connection with children by Schrut (1964), adolescents by Peck (1967), middle-aged men by Pretzel (1967), "discarded women" by Wold (1967), and object loss by Farberow and McEvoy (1966). We devised a tentative classification of the patients into several syndrome types drawn principally from behavioral aspects and descriptively categorized. The taxonomy was applied to all complete data cases and to the incomplete data for Vienna to 114 (64 men and 50 women) and to 82 for Los Angeles (42 men and 40 women).

1. Down-and-out or alcoholic subjects were so classified if they had a history of downward social and occupational mobility or a major alcohol or addiction problem, or both. They were socially isolated except for drinking companions and had reached "the end of the rope." In both samples men greatly outnumbered women, but the difference between cities was not significant for either sex.

2. The typical person with the middle-aged depression syndrome is over 40 years of age and has had a stable work and marital history. A crisis, such as a financial setback or rejction, may trigger severe depressive feelings and a suicidal act, although in many instances no obvious precipitating event can be found. Our samples showed equal proportions of men and women, and no statistically significant differences between the cities.

3. Cases included in the reactive depression category were those in which there was a direct and clear connection between a grievous event and the suicide, and the subject had no known history of recurrent depressions. The causal event in our cases was in all instances either the death of a loved person or a terminal disease. The differences between male subjects were significant (20 percent Vienna, 8.5 percent Los Angeles, $p < 0.01$); but not for women (15 percent Vienna, 12.2 percent Los Angeles).

4. The classification of emotional instability was used for subjects with a variety of histories of social maladjustment and neurotic or psychotic episodes. There were significantly fewer decedents in this category in Vienna than in Los Angeles. This observation held true for both sexes. For men, the percents were 3.5 for Vienna, 41.6 for Los Angeles ($p < 0.01$); for women, 4.4 for Vienna, 13.4 for Los Angeles ($p < 0.05$).

However, the criteria for inclusion in this category are unreliable, and no conclusions should be drawn about the mental status of the populations from which these samples were derived. It may be that more people have a history of treatment and hospitalization for mental illness in the United States than in Austria simply because more treatment facilities are available.

5. Those with the "old and alone" syndrome were persons who had minimal social contacts, were in precarious financial circumstances, and who felt that they had outlived the usefulness of their lives. They contributed the bulk of the cases in which no close contact could be located. The largest group with this syndrome was Viennese women, 15.0 percent compared with 6.1 percent of the Los Angeles women ($p < 0.05$). The difference for men in the two cities was nonsignificant.

6. The interpersonal relationship difficulty category refers to symbiotic relationships between partners in heterosexual or homosexual liaisons or

between parent and child that have come to an end. No significant differences between national samples were found for this category.

Not infrequently the suicide of the "discarded partner" is coupled with homicide of the other partner or someone dear to the partner. It is of interest that while no case of attempted or completed homicide in connection with suicide occurred among the Austrian subjects, there were three completed homicides and one attempted one in the Los Angeles group.

7. There were two men in each city that fitted the "violent man" type. Violent men are young, irascible, and masculine. They run around with the boys and drink fairly heavily without being alcoholics. Although outwardly very virile, they generally have deep-seated doubts about their masculinity. Their preoccupation with guns may be seen as a reaction formation. These men often use guns and sometimes play Russian roulette. No differences were evident between our sample populations.

In 21 of the 196 cases the dynamics were too obscure or the circumstances too unusual to allow categorization.

Background Information

This section summarizes only the salient findings on the subjects' physical and mental health, their interpersonal and occupational situations, and their developmental histories. Since many questions sought information not readily revealed to strangers or not known to the respondents, the data tend to be less complete. Some of the information was undoubtedly distorted, consciously or unconsciously, by the informants. However, even the fact that information on certain topics seems to be more readily divulged in one culture than another is in itself of interest.

Thirty-six or 72 percent of the Austrians were reported to have been in poor health as compared to 22 or 44 percent of the Los Angelinos ($p < 0.01$). Twenty-seven or 54 percent of the Vienna subjects, compared to 8 or 16 percent in Los Angeles, were said to have been getting worse in recent months ($p < 0.05$). A little over one-fourth of each group was reported to have undergone surgery in the past 5 years, and approximately half in each group used barbiturates habitually before the suicide. Opiates were reported to have been used by two Viennese and nine Angelinos.

When did the subject last visit a physician? Answers to this question indicated that about a fourth of each group had been seen by a physician within 1 week, 44 percent within 1 month, and 66 percent within 6 months before the suicide act. Only three Viennese and one Angelino were reported as not having seen a physician recently. No significant differences appeared between the groups. However, they differed significantly ($p < 0.01$) in reasons for visiting the physicians. The greatest difference was that the Viennese seem practically never to have regular health checkups, 2 percent compared with 27 percent of the Los Angeles subjects.

The Los Angeles respondents specified 15 instances (30 percent) of hospitalization for mental disorders among the victims as compared with eight (16 percent) among the Vienna group. Thirty-one or 62 percent of the Los Angeles subjects were reportedly advised at one time or another to seek psychiatric help, but only 16 or 32 percent of the Viennese were so told ($p < 0.01$). Information on the type of psychiatric treatment the subjects had received in and out of hospitals proved too vague to be useful.

The role of alcoholism was determined. Many of the "down-and-out" subjects were alcoholics, but for others alcoholism was not the central feature in the suicide although it seemed to be a major contributing factor to their problems of living. Thus a drinking problem was reported for 20 or 40 percent of the Viennese subjects (two of them women) and for 18 or 36 percent of the Los Angeles subjects (four women). Alcohol seemed to be a serious difficulty for at least a third of the suicidal persons in both groups.

At the time of the suicide 28 (56 percent) of the Viennese and 23 (46 percent) of the Los Angeles subjects were married. Sex appears to be more of a taboo topic in Vienna, as evidenced by replies to the question, "Did he (she) discuss sexual matters with you?" Eighty-five percent of the Viennese said no, compared with 47 percent of those in Los Angeles ($p < 0.01$).

Other areas of conflict within the families in both groups centered around the problem of drinking (28 percent in Vienna and 32 percent in Los Angeles); sharing no activities with their partners (50 percent of the Viennese and 60 percent of the Los Angelinos); and rarely sharing leisure time (24 percent of the Viennese and 14 percent of the Los Angelinos). There were no significant differences between the samples.

The marked differences in social life between the samples no doubt extend to the societies from which samples were drawn. Club activities, for example, are reported for seven Vienna subjects or 17 percent, as compared to 38 Los Angeles subjects or 56 percent ($p < 0.01$). Sixty-seven percent of the Los Angeles sample had three or more close friends, but that was true of only 37 percent of the Viennese ($p < 0.01$).

All socioeconomic strata are represented in both samples, roughly proportionate to the general populations of the two cities. In line with the age distribution of the Viennese population, there was a preponderance of retired subjects in the Vienna group.

When the personal incomes of the two groups were compared by grading income as average, below average, and above average by local standards, no significant differences were found between the samples. Two Viennese and seven Los Angeles subjects were reported as having had no income at all, and three persons in each group had above average income.

In reference to occupation two items of information stand out; differences in occupational stability were significant ($p < 0.01$), with the Los Angeles subjects having held many more positions, and with the Viennese tending to be more satisfied with their last job ($p < 0.01$). Increased monetary pressures during the last year were reported for 20 percent of both groups.

Housing conditions are not strictly comparable between the two cities. About half of the Los Angeles sample lived in one-family dwellings and the other half in apartments; all except three Viennese lived in apartments. The Los Angeles group was not only occupationally but also residentially mobile, as indicated by the number who had moved within the 1 year preceding the suicide. Forty-four percent of those in Los Angeles had moved, but only 8 percent of those in Vienna ($p < 0.01$) had moved.

Many informants could give only minimal replies to questions about the family and developmental history of the subjects. One question concerned the causes of death of the subjects' parents. Twelve percent of the Viennese had both parents living; 58 percent had both parents dead. Twenty-four percent of the Los Angeles sample had both parents living, and 38 percent had both parents dead. In both samples three parents each ended their lives by suicide. If we take the suicide rate for persons over age 40 to be about 34 in 100,000, based on the average of age-adjusted rates for decades after 40 in Los Angeles County, then the parents of our subjects killed themselves at a rate more than 88 times the expected rate. Alcohol seemed to be a common factor, with 40 percent of the parents of Viennese and Los Angeles subjects reported as either being alcoholics or as having a drinking problem.

Little that was useful could be learned about the subjects' early home life and development. Los Angeles subjects left home slightly younger than Viennese (modal age 19 as compared to 22), and 60 percent of the mothers in both samples were reported to have worked outside the home.

While school systems in the two countries are not comparable, it can be said that most subjects completed public school, which in Austria ends after 8 years and in California after 12 years of attendance. Respondents reported that 5 or 10 percent of the Viennese and 20 or 40 percent of the Angelinos had been dissatisfied with the amount of schooling they had received ($p < 0.01$).

DISCUSSION

This study, reporting on a few of the salient points investigated, reveals many similarities in the suicides committed in the two cities as well as differences. Some differences, it was felt, were due to cultural influences, local conditions, mores, values, and so forth. One caution must be borne in mind. The proportion of men to women in both total samples is about 55 to 45 percent, which approximates the sex ratios for those committing suicide previously reported for the two cities, 52 percent men to 48 percent women (1966 Vienna police records) and 61 percent men to 39 percent women (1965 Los Angeles coroner's office records). However, in our study, men who committed suicide were easier to investigate in Vienna than women because female informants were easier to contact. Eighty-two percent of the informants were female; 18 percent were male. Thus, there were 57 incomplete data cases for Viennese women and 42 for men, but the complete data cases contain many more men (40 versus 10). The information in depth for the Vienna cases is, therefore, more likely to be about men, and conclusions or inferences must be viewed with caution, especially if they refer to sex differences.

Some general comments can be made about suicide in the two cultures which seem appropriate to the significant differences. Perhaps one can usefully distinguish between avoidable and unavoidable misery. Some of the stresses leading to suicide seem to be more or less universal (for example, loss of loved one, serious illness, and physical and emotional exhaustion), and they are perhaps part and parcel of life in all places and at all times. There are, however, particular stresses that seem amenable to mitigation if members of a society are sufficiently aware of them and willing to look for remedies. In Vienna, the primary impression about those who commit suicide is that they are very alienated and isolated. This observation emerges from the apparently greater difficulties in communication and the prevalence of syndromes indicative of interpersonal detachment. For example, one of the syndromes found most often for Viennese women was "old and alone." About 21 percent of the men and 27 percent of the women now living in Vienna are over 60 years of age (1961 census). The women live for the most part on very small pensions, all alone in small, dreary, constricted apartments in large apartment blocks. There are few social clubs or similar facilities for oldsters, there is no visiting nurses' service for the ailing, and there traditionally is little social interaction between tenants in apartment buildings.

The generally lower level of social group cohesion and communication seemed to extend even into the family sphere. It was striking to note how little spouses knew about the thoughts, hopes, aspirations, and problems of their partners. Only 27 percent of the Viennese were reported to have voiced their depressive feelings and self-destructive intentions directly to significant others. This observation is consistent with the 32 percent reported by Ringel in 1961, and it contrasts with the Los Angeles cases, in which 72 percent of the deceased were reported to have indicated their intentions. The impression was that the Austrian informants were not so much unwilling to give such information but that they were often unable to comprehend questions that related to problems of interpersonal communication. The Viennese did not share activities or leisure time with their mates and, in addition, showed great reluctance to discuss any facet of their sex life. In Los Angeles communication seemed not only to occur more often, but also to be more verbal; more of this group were writing regularly or had left a note or had talked about suicide.

Related to the lower sensitivity concerning emotional states is the apparent tendency of Viennese informants to discount psychologial causation. Thus, in Vienna the victim's ills were in many more instances attributed to poor and worsening health than to emotional or interpersonal causes than among the Los Angeles victims. Another finding was that the Viennese were in mental hospitals or used psychiatric help less often than the Angelinos. Paradoxically, the second most frequent cause of the act, as attributed by the Viennese respondents, was mental illness. In predominantly Catholic Austria the identification of mental illness as the cause of suicide is more acceptable to survivors than other causes and helps them tolerate the event, as well as to facilitate burial arrangements. In Los Angeles, the syndrome of emotional instability was found more often than in Vienna, and interpersonal difficulties were identified as the primary cause of the suicide in at least one-third of the cases. The greater proportion of mental disorders found in the Los Angeles sample probably reflects both a greater awareness of and acceptance of mental health problems as factors in everyday living than in Vienna. Thus, for the Los Angeles cases, most suicides were attributed to an interpersonal crisis in the family sphere with environmental factors playing a minor role. In fact, it is striking in how few Los Angeles cases the suicide was attributed to bad living conditions or financial troubles, and how much more often to breakdowns in interpersonal relations.

We recognize that the interviewers' biases and varying diagnostic criteria may well have affected the results of the study. The Los Angeles interviewers may have been more alert to interpersonal factors because of their background, training, and clinical experience. Using the same protocol in both cities may not have been enough to obviate these biases. However, all interviewers were given extensive training and participated in pilot sessions in an effort to standardize approaches.

Other stresses specific to the Los Angeles sample were the greater reported pressures to advance educationally and occupationally. Related to these pressures were the subjects' frequent moves to new locations and dwellings. Physical and social mobility was more frequent in Los Angeles that in Viennese subjects, and the Californians seemed to derive less satisfaction from education or position. This discontent may be related to the American emphasis on position, prestige, and wealth, an ethos that encourages the American to dream that, if not he, then his son can become President (Henry, 1963).

Differences between the two cities in the suicidal act itself are of interest. Although Vienna and Los Angeles have about the same over-all rate of suicide, the preferred method was domestic gas in Vienna and guns in Los Angeles. Gas was lethal in Vienna until 1965 and not in Los Angeles; guns are readily accessible to Americans and not to Austrians. It is not clear how much accessibility of methods to kill oneself has to do with the over-all rate of suicide in a given area. However, knowing that most people have second thoughts about dying if given half a chance, it is probable that readily available means increase suicide rates. It is also worth noting that all of the completed or attempted homicides in connection with suicide were perpetrated in Los Angeles, and all were committed with guns. The three methods that account for 87 percent of the suicides in Los Angeles were: shooting, 39 percent; barbiturates, 32 percent; and hanging, 16 percent. In Vienna, 84 percent was accounted for by: gas, 38 percent; hanging, 25 percent; and barbiturates, 21 percent. Barbiturates have been used increasingly more frequently in Los Angeles, accounting for 39 percent of the certified suicide deaths in 1962, compared with 26 percent in 1953 (Curphey *et al.*, 1970). Ringel's study in 1961 indicated that in 20 percent of his 50 cases barbiturates were the cause of death.

As noted, the largest group with the syndrome "old and alone" was Viennese women. Do they contribute more than would be expected to the population of older persons who commit suicide in Vienna? How does this proportion compare with age-sex-specific rates in the two cities? A comparison was made between suicide and population statistics for elderly persons over 60 for the two cities. The suicides are those reported by the Vienna police for 1966, and the population totals are from the 1961 census. For Los Angeles, the coroner's 1966 statistics and 1960 census totals were used.

For both Vienna and Los Angeles the number of women who killed themselves was still considerably lower than the number that could be expected from their representation in the general population ($p < 0.02$ for Vienna, $p < 0.001$ for Los Angeles). The discrepancy between suicides of men and women was larger in Los Angeles than in Vienna (17.9 versus 10.7, respectively), which reflects the relatively higher suicide rates among the elderly men in Los Angeles, as shown by the age-sex-specific suicide rates for persons 60 years or older: Los Angeles—men 47.8, women 23.2; Vienna—men 37.1; women 23.8. Apparently, old men in both cultures continue to be the main source of disproportionate contributions to the suicide problem. However, the "old and alone" women in Vienna constitute a group of special high risk. An intensive study seems called for to explore conditions and contributing factors that might yield an effective preventive program.

Two points of similarity are of interest. With alcoholism noted as a prominent problem in the histories of one-third of those committing the suicides in both Vienna and Los Angeles, it is apparent that preventive procedures could be profitably applied in another readily identified high risk group. Trained personnel in alcoholism clinics as well as in outpatient mental hygiene clinics and mental hospitals could be alerted to look for suicidal tendencies. The supposition that alcoholism may actually provide a substitute outlet for anxieties and tensions for many people, thus obviating overt suicidal activities, apparently does not apply to all persons with the alcoholism syndrome.

An effort was made to determine the lethal intention of the deceased, a significant point in view of the established ambivalence in suicidal behavior (Farberow and Shneidman, 1961). The question is not easy to assess, for information on the relevant factors is often difficult to obtain from survivor informants close to the deceased and often reacting with their own dynamics of guilt, anxiety, shame, and denial. Nevertheless, the rough estimate was that about 70 percent of the two groups had been serious in their intention to die. Even if one makes the most extreme assumption—that none was preventable—presumably interventive activity would have been both feasible and effective for the other 30 percent. A 30 percent reduction in the number of suicides would make a considerable dent in the suicide rates.

Many of the larger social problems mentioned as factors in suicidal behavior are not amenable to reform in the short run. Also, of course, these factors affect many others who do not react with a self-inflicted fatal consequence. Laws specifically against the act of suicide seem to have little impact on the suicide rate and practically no deterrent effect. Austrian statutes make suicide a crime, yet the rate has been high since the turn of the century in that country. England, with a rate in the middle ranges, between 10 and 11 per 100,000, repealed the law against suicide in 1961, after it had been in effect for at least a century. The suicide rate in England has not varied significantly since repeal. Seven of the 50 states in the United States have laws against suicide that are rarely, if ever, enforced. Yet preservation of life and social regulation are society's responsibility, and laws to control the availability of some common methods, such as acquisition of guns in the United States and the ease of obtaining barbiturates in both countries, seem socially justifiable. It is uncertain if such steps would affect the suicide rate.

However, depoisoning the gas in Vienna has had considerable impact. The carbon monoxide content in domestic gas has been progressively reduced from 9.2 percent in 1965 to 6.8 percent in 1966 to between 4.5 and 2.5 percent in 1967. Even at the lowest level, the gas is still lethal if a person goes to extraordinary lengths. The following table shows the total number of suicides and the number and percent committed using household gas in the city from 1961 to 1967 (Jorde, 1967):

		Suicides by Gas	
Year	All Suicides	Number	Percent
1961	347	199	57.3
1962	321	181	56.4
1963	308	202	65.6
1964	288	194	67.4
1965	349	175	50.1
1966	264	130	49.2
1967	246	80	32.5

Not only was the proportion of suicides by gas to total suicides radically reduced but also the over-all rate has dropped by 30 percent since 1965, a reduction that far exceeds expectations from the long range trend. In view of these results, it seems worthwhile to attempt external controls for some of the other common methods.

Primary prevention (antevention, that is, detecting the suicide-prone person before he becomes suicidal) is beset with difficulties. Not the least difficult task is to predict accurately a rare event even with the best screening procedures (Rosen, 1945). However, there seems to be ample support in this study for the view that we need not seek out the individual person contemplating suicide; he will let us know of his plight, if we are willing to perceive the message. Many suicidal persons distribute clues to their preoccupations, but our study also shows that the clues are often ignored. With 23 percent of the group visiting their physicians within 1 week and 43 percent within 1 month before they acted, it is apparent that physicians especially have an excellent opportunity for identification and intervention. Ringel (1961) reported that in half of his cases the person had seen a physician just before he acted. The need for training general practitioners in sensitivity to suicide prodromes has been recognized (Litman, 1966) and to some extent followed through in Los Angeles; few medical men in Austria are aware that suicide prevention and allied mental health tasks fall within the province of the general practitioner (Ringel, 1961; Strotzka and Leitner, 1964).

However, most efforts in suicide prevention must at present be carried out in specialized services, such as the Suicide Prevention Center in Los Angeles and the Vienna Suicide Prevention Service, agencies mentioned by the interviewers in the study. When asked, 82 percent of the respondents in Vienna and 62 percent in Los Angeles stated that they had never heard of the agencies, an impressively high percentage in the light of the 2 and 1 decades, respectively, of their existence in the communities. There is an obvious need for more suicide prevention and crisis centers with trained staffs that can be reached around the clock, along with informational publicity and extensive public education about suicide.

But greatest of all is the need to dispel the taboos (Farberow, 1968; Ringel, 1961; Shneidman, 1963) and permit both intervention and antevention processes to operate. Suicide prevention services will be of little value until the cry for help is allowed to be heard.

SUMMARY

Cross-cultural differences and similarities in suicide were investigated by examining 50 suicides committed in Vienna and 50 in Los Angeles. Through in-depth interviews with family and other informed survivors, information was sought on details of the suicide act, communication given and received about suicidal intent, previous history of suicide attempts, estimation of lethal intent, personality syndromes, and personal and background information about the deceased. Comparable data for the two cities were obtained by using a protocol with similar items.

In general, the Viennese seemed socially alienated and isolated and in poor communication with spouses, relatives, and close friends. Those committing suicide in Los Angeles were more often in strained or broken interpersonal relationships and under great social and occupational pressures. Communication of feelings seemed to occur more often among the Los Angeles cases than in the Viennese cases. The results showed no significant differences in age, sex, and marital status for the two groups.

The Viennese used domestic gas primarily to kill himself while the Los Angelino most often used a gun. For the Viennese, the cause of the suicide was more often attributed to physical illness; for the Los Angelinos, most often to interpersonal difficulties. About two-thirds of the suicidal acts in both groups seemed intended to be lethal.

More Viennese men showed reactive depressions, more Viennese women were old and alone, and more Los Angeles men and women showed emotional instability. Alcohol was a serious problem for at least one-third of the decedents in both groups. Those in Los Angeles were occupationally and residentially more mobile than the Viennese.

Ways of decreasing the suicide rate in both cities are discussed, including legal, social, and professional action. At present, increased direct intervention capabilities through more suicide prevention centers are needed. For the future, primary prevention programs to improve early identification of the suicide-prone and also to provide public education that dispels taboos hold most promise.

REFERENCES

Curphey, T. J., Shneidman, E. S., and Farberow, N. L. 1970. Drugs, death and suicide. In: W. G. Clark and J. del Giudice (Eds.), *Principles of Psychopharmacology*, Academic Press, New York.

Dublin, L. 1963. *Suicide: A Sociological and Statistical Study*. Ronald Press Co., New York.

Durkheim, E. 1951. *Le Suicide, Etude de Sociologie* (Suicide, A Sociological Study). Alcan, Paris, 1897. Translated by J. A. Spaulding and G. Simpson. Free Press, Glencoe, Ill.

Farberow, N. L. 1968. The psychology of suicide. *International Encyclopedia of the Social Sciences*. Crowell, Collier & MacMillan, New York.

Farberow, N. L., and McEvoy, T. L. 1966. Suicide among patients with diagnosis of anxiety reaction or depressive reaction in general medical and surgical hospitals. *Journal of Abnormal Psychology,* 71:287–299.

Farberow, N. L., and Shneidman, E. S. (Eds.) 1961. *The Cry for Help*. McGraw-Hill, New York.

Hendin, H. 1964. *Suicide and Scandinavia*. Grune & Stratton, New York.

Henry, J. 1963. *Culture against Man*. Random House, New York.

Jorde, W. 1967. *Ueber die Engiftung des Wiener Stadtgases* (On the Depoisoning of Municipal Gas in Vienna). *Oesterreichische Gemeindezeitung*, 12:274–277.

Litman, R. E. 1966. Acutely Suicidal Patients: Management in General Medical Practice. *California Medicine,* 104:168–174, March.

Ohara, K. 1961. Suicide of the aged (Suicide among aged Japanese, translated by D. Reynolds and K. Ohara). *Psychiatria et Neurologia Japonica*, 63:1253–1268.

Peck, M. 1967. *Suicide and Youth*. Paper read at the Suicide Intervention Workshop, sponsored by the Mental Health Association of Fresno, California, Fresno State College, March 11.

Pretzel, P. W. 1967. *The Quiet Crisis–The Suicide of the Apparently Successful Man.* Paper read at the California State Psychological Association, San Diego, January.

Ringel, E. 1961. *Neue Untersuchungen zum Selbstmordproblem* (New Investigations into the Problem of Suicide). Brueder Hollinek, Vienna.

Rosen, A. 1954. Detection of suicidal patients: An example of some limitations in the prediction of infrequent events. *Journal of Consulting Psychology,* 18:397–403.

Schrut, A. 1964. Suicidal adolescents and children. *Journal of the American Medical Association*, 188:1103–1107.

Shneidman, E. S. 1963. Suicide, a taboo topic. In: N. L. Farberow (Ed.), *Taboo Topics*. Atherton Press, New York.

Shneidman, E. S., and Farberow, N. L. 1957. *Clues to Suicide*. McGraw-Hill, New York.

Strotzka, H., and Leitner, L. 1964. *Arbeitszeitanalyse in der Aertzlichen Praxis* (Worktime analysis of medical practice). *Weiner Medizinische Wochenschrift*, 114:421–424.

U.S. Bureau of the census. 1962. *U.S. Censuses of Population and Housing*; 1960. Census Tracts, Final Report PHC (1)-82, U.S. Government Printing Office, Washington D.C.

Wold, C. 1967. *Evaluating Suicidal Personality*. Paper presented at the San Francisco State College Symposium on Suicide, October.

thirteen

SELF-DESTRUCTION IN BULGARIAN FOLK SONGS

N. SCHIPKOWENSKY, M.D., K. MILENKOV, and A. BOGDANOVA

Man is the only living being capable of destroying its own body. This capacity is rooted in evolution: man evolved from an organism, which is a biological category, into a personality, which is a social category. The three principal parameters of his personality are self-consciousness, self-cognition, and self-determination of behavior. It is precisely these that enable him to make a choice between life and death.

This choice, however, does not consist in a refusal to exist or in a relapse to nonexistence, as one may be tempted to regard at first glance. Man destroys his body because this act is a necessary prerequisite for making his personality immortal, be it as a spirit in the "yonder world" or as an ideal value in "this world." In certain extreme cases the destruction is done with a view to preserving one's own dignity. True enough, man may repudiate his bodily presence in the world when it is incompatible with his vital aspirations or when it has become unbearable because of external pressures, internal collisions, somatic or mental disease, economic ruin, or moral distress. These are the fields of force within which self-destruction takes place. Its motive powers, notwithstanding their variety, have nevertheless been subordinate to certain common intrinsic principles throughout the millenia of man's history. The all-human characteristics of motivations for suicide undergo specific reflection in the social experience of various tribes and nations in one and the same era or in one and the same nation during various transitional periods of history.

The transcultural aspects of self-destruction—as is the case with other individual actions, such as dependence among individuals with social relations—reveal the specific mental makeup of a particular nation. A nation's mental makeup is directly reflected in its folklore as well. This fact prompted us to survey the images of self-destruction in Bulgarian folk songs. We would like to point out in advance that self-destruction is not depicted by other types of folklore, such as tales, fables, proverbs, and sayings. This indicates that people resorting to self-destruction, no matter how different they may have been as personalities and regardless of the diversity of their motives, have always been construed as lyric heroes. The imagination of the singer proved very susceptible to their tragic fate, which, on the other hand, was not used by storytellers as the subject of their narration.

The epidemiology of self-destruction cannot be studied through folk songs. Nevertheless, the number of songs referring to various suicides can give a good idea about the frequency and the motivational structure of the act of suicide.

Self-destruction obviously must have been a rare phenomenon, for we found reference to it in only 200 out of the several thousand folk songs published in folklore collections within almost a century (between 1889 and 1963) and in the books written by S. Berkovich, by the Miladinov brothers, and by others.

In the first place, there are many songs that are variants of one and the same story. There can be no doubt that it is quite possible for one particular drama to take place in approximately the same way among people of various nations. It may also happen within one and the same nation at consecutive periods or even at one and the same time. Significant, too, is the psychogenic induction of motives generated by the conduct of people who have already committed suicide—those starting along their path used to identify their own lot with the fate of the suicides. Under such conditions the behavior of others suggests a decision to follow their example. Certain variants have obviously appeared after the folk singer had heard a song depicting a certain kind of self-destruction. He adopted the general line of the plot, introducing some changes in it as well as in the names of the characters. The aim of the folk singer was, in all probability, to try to produce a certain effect on particular persons in his audience by picturing to them their moral responsibility and eventual guilt if they should oppose the union between the young couple. In some cases this was the folk singer himself and his or her beloved.

MOTIVATIONS TOWARD SELF-DESTRUCTION

Love

In the motivational dynamics of self-destruction, the broadest field is that of love relations. It is true that erotism stems from the sexual drive and that generally it is directed toward satisfaction of the sexual drive. However, it undergoes many transformations in man, such as the transformation into creative inspiration. It may even succeed in gaining the upper hand over his instincts, including the most powerful instinct of all, that of self-preservation.

Two Lovers United in Death because of Affection There are many songs that very picturesquely depict self-destruction as the result of love uniting in death those who could not unite in life. The most frequent case is the suicide of two lovers. As a rule, it is the maiden who dies first, followed by her beloved. In these songs the inseparability of the lovers after death is expressed by the poetic symbol of trees or vines growing over the common grave and entwining their branches into one another. The recourse to death is not determined by any impossibility in satisfying the sexual drive, but rather by the love and affection existing between the two lovers. Affection thus has nothing in common with sexuality, be it in its unconditioned reflex basis or in its essence. It is rooted in the instinct for the preservation of the genus. It rises to the level of readiness for self-sacrifice for one's child or friend and for supraindividual values, religious or political ideas, whether organization, nation, or mankind. The two young people who unite through the grave make the truly "divine" hermaphrodite, the united man-woman whose indivisibility continues beyond life. They have had no other way open to them of overcoming the hatred of the parents but to unite in their common death. The most intransigent bearer of this hatred is usually the mother.

Life Loses Its Meaning The act of following one's beloved in death is rooted both in the love and in the affection toward the person who has committed self-destruction, the person without whom life has become meaningless. That is why we see it occurring also in cases of death resulting from disease or accident. This theme as a motivation category accounts for the second largest group of folk songs. There are 25 songs in which the death of the beloved man is followed by self-destruction, and 10 more songs in which this is done after the death of the beloved woman, accounting for about one-sixth of the total number of songs depicting self-destruction. Two songs belong here in which married women commit suicide after the death of their husbands. An additional reason to believe that both love and affection are present in such cases is found in the fairly large number of songs (eight in all) in which suicide is perpetrated as a result of the death of many or all other members of the family. In five of these songs the sister takes her life after the death of her brother.

Unshared Love Unshared love drives the young man toward self-destruction in four songs.

Deceitful Love Deceitful love is a still more frequent motive for self-destruction. Thirteen songs, or one-fifteenth of the total number of songs examined, had this motive. The lesson that the folk singer tries to convey to his listeners is that it is not always a case of actual abandonment. He is apparently anxious to prevent the women he sings to from making too rash decisions when they find that they have been abandoned.

Ambivalent Love: Disgust, Hatred, Murder Love in folk songs may turn into disgust, and affection may turn into hatred, although reversals are quite possible in such cases owing to the ambivalence of attachment and repulsion. Love and affection are sometimes apt to appear in the husband even after the murder of his own wife. For example, a husband resorts to self-punishment when he hears coming from his wife's cut-off head a voice that speaks with tenderness and care about the murderer (psychogenic auditory hallucination that reincarnates his own feelings).

Incest relations are referred to in a small number of songs and they all end in death. Self-destruction prevents the commitment of incest proper (blood incest) in four songs. Incest among relatives results in a tendency to kill the offspring, and there is only one song in which there is unconscious incest.

Preservation of National or Personal Dignity

Women prefer self-destruction to violent love. Those abducted prefer to die rather than to satisfy the sexual passion of an enslaver, such as a Turk, a Tatar, or a chieftain. All the women who commit self-destruction in the songs repudiate the infringement of their human dignity and denounce their physical existence when it has to be purchased at the price of losing their national or personal liberty. The desecration of human dignity may also be committed by humiliating labor: the wife who had been harnessed by her husband to the plough during the day takes her life by hanging herself in the evening. Her decision is additionally motivated by the fact that her child had died of hunger during the day. Preservation of national or personal dignity is the motive toward self-destruction in 15 people, one-thirteenth of the total number of characters covered by the study.

Insult

Personal dignity can be affected not only by violence in the field of sexual relations or labor but by words as well, words of either abuse or derision (7 songs). There are two cases that may be classified in the category of self-destruction prompted by insult. They tell of two people who could not put up with the infringement on their dignity.

Deceit or Disappointment

Similar to the motivation of insult is that of people who commit suicide because they cannot reconcile themselves to having been deceived or disappointed. Foremost in this category are the hostile relations between wife and mother-in-law, constituting the theme of the largest number of songs (36 in all). Hatred of the mother-in-law for the wife and vice-versa seems to be the rule in Bulgarian folklore, although it does not reach the status of an omnipresent phenomenon. In some cases the mother-in-law succeeds in inducing her son to kill his wife. However, upon learning the truth about the exemplary conduct of his wife, the credulous husband commits suicide in self-punishment for his acts.

Impasse

Self-destruction resulting from impasse is perpetrated under conditions of real or imaginary impossibility of finding a way out of an agonizing situation, such as insurmountable financial difficulties, moral quandaries, etc. It is contained in the plots of four songs. We would like to add to this category the tragic plight of the two village belles whose beauty was so great it upset the normal life of their respective communities. They were therefore denounced by their fellow villagers and by their own relatives.

Physical Suffering

Serious illness accounts for only one case of motivation for putting an end to the suffering of the body.

Jokes

Even a joke may lead to self-destruction when it is taken at its face value (3 songs). In this case the folk singer probably wants to warn his listeners against light-minded entertainment with words that may turn out to be fatally significant to some credulous people.

Inheritance

The division of inherited property or of a trophy may spark off a case of murder. However, it constitutes a case for self-destruction in only one song.

Self-punishment

In all the categories of self-destruction examined above, the act takes place within the fields of force of relationships among individuals or in society. Notwithstanding the great variety of these categories, they have one feature in common, namely, the blamelessness of the perpetrators. Other people invariably bear the moral responsibility for their lot. However, there are also cases of self-punishment for the perpetration of avowed crimes.

Guilt Suicide in self-punishment follows two principal patterns. The first one involves the murder of the wife whom the husband suspects of infidelity but who is actually in a state of narcosis. The perpetrator follows his victim in death as soon as he realizes that his motives had been groundless.

Childlessness The second pattern centers around the impossibility of satisfying the human desire for producing progeny. There are songs in which the husband kills his childless wife, but his act of destruction is promptly punished by his finding that in actual fact his wife would have given him a child. He then punishes himself in despair. In some variations of this plot, the child itself, taken out of the uterus of its mother, denounces her assassin (psychogenic hallucination incorporating the conscience of the doer in a paradoxical manner). It must be further pointed out that in most cases the husband cannot bring himself to perpetrate the murder of the childless wife and asks a paid assassin (a butcher) to do so instead.

Termination of one's life by way of self-punishment is depicted in 23 songs—one-ninth of the total number studied. The folk singer attaches responsibility to the acts of the drunkard, and on that account he justifies the need for self-punishment.

Aiding or Abetting Suicide

Incitement to suicide is a crime. This theme occurs only twice in the 200 songs dealing with self-destruction. On one occasion the husband told his wife, who was seriously ill and wanted him to bring her mother to her, that her mother was far away while "the black earth was nearer." On another occasion the brother advises his sister, whose beauty has played havoc with the world, to commit suicide so that peace may come to the world again.

As a rule, the motivation for self-destruction stems from understandable relations among individuals and within society. It takes its source from experiences connected with the senselessness of existence, from a preference of death to servitude and sexual violence, from the impossibility of putting up with a humiliation of human dignity, and from an expiation of moral guilt connected with the perpetration of a crime. Although suicide is usually committed without any conflict of countermotives, it is not an act of impulse, a "short circuit" of feelings, or a pathological affect. Those who commit self-destruction are individuals who are thinking and reasoning clearly.

Melancholia

A melancholy tendency or state leading to self-destruction is found in only one song. Beautiful Yana is wringing her hands and shedding tears because she wants to die young and unmarried. Her mother tells her in jest to eat the fruit of the juniper tree if she wants to die. Beautiful Yana does so and is poisoned.

Incomplete Suicide

There are only two songs depicting self-destruction that has failed to materialize. In the first case the girl abandons her attempt at suicide when she learns that she will not be buried with the usual religious rites. In the second case, the attempt by the wife to hang herself in despair over the criminal activities of her husband is foiled by her relatives who bring her down from the rope.

Bulgarian folklore makes no mention of attempts at self-destruction and of their various motives. Such attempts have either not been perpetrated in the past, or, what is much more probable, they were not considered acts worthy of being depicted in a tale.

DISCUSSION

One characteristic feature of self-destruction in Bulgarian folk songs is that it usually appears within the triad consisting of the young man (husband), the woman (the wife), and the mother (the mother-in-law). The sex of the principal character has a certain bearing on the choice of the means of self-destruction. For instance, 96 out of the total number of 101 men referred to in the songs of the present study resort to the use of a knife, while only one-half of the women committing suicide use knives (44 out of 90). On the other hand, one-third (31) of the women hang themselves, while this method is very rarely depicted among men (3). Women also drown themselves 10 times more frequently than men.

As each case of self-destruction became a known tragic event, it was apt to catch the imagination of its contemporaries. It was described with due imagery and has come down from one generation to the next without losing its impact or emotional charge on the listeners. The lofty moral standards of the folk song are conveyed by the deeds of its lyrical heroes, not by way of a verbal sermon. The song shows love to be stronger than any kind of death, as when the two dead lovers are described as becoming plants that embrace forever. The folk singers also resort to the poetic image of two trees with intertwined branches in order to demonstrate the all-pervading power of love. Folk songs also depict the affection for the family as a whole, or for the husband or brother whose loss the wife or sister finds it impossible to survive. It extols the self-sacrifice made for one's country. It fortifies the will of man to resist his nation's subjugation and makes immortal the idea of safeguarding one's dignity even when the preservation of these vital values means the destruction of one's own body.

The folk singer strongly condemns the vicious mother-in-law who drives her daughter-in-law toward self-destruction. He also condemns those parents who are opposed to the union between the young man and the young woman, as well as husbands who humiliate or kill their wives. The moral lesson contained in these songs is one that protects people against self-destruction. There is no excessive verbiage in the teaching of these moral standards; it takes only several simple but expressive words to attach the responsibility for the death of innocent victims to the guilty survivors. The social condemnation of the act is usually found in the words uttered by the suicide just before his death.

Folk songs have depicted a great number and variety of cases of self-destruction. Portraying brilliant images of the triumph of love and affection over death, they have fortified the resolve of the bold to renounce physical existence when it comes to safeguarding their personality, to prefer death to servitude, to uphold their human dignity and national ideas, and to punish themselves for a crime, regardless of whether it had been perpetrated in a state of drunkenness or whether it had been prompted by motives which seemed justifiable (infidelity, childlessness, etc.). Whenever the preservation of the body had to be purchased at the price of renouncing individual or popular ideals, the heroes of the Bulgarian folk songs have preferred to die. As we know, those who commit suicide usually do not believe in the annihilation of the ego upon the destruction of the body.

The folk songs attribute immortality both to the victim and to the person responsible for the untimely death. They extol the person committing self-destruction for his readiness to sacrifice his body in order to preserve his personality, and they condemn those who are responsible, directly or indirectly, for the crime perpetrated.

The impact of the songs is not confined to the environment in which the events take place or to the time of their occurrence. By their imagery, their content, their tragic conflicts, and their whole atmosphere, the Bulgarian folk songs describing self-destruction have remained close to the people until the present day. Their spirit is still in conformity with the attitudes and with the aesthetic ideals of the people.

fourteen

JEWISH SUICIDE IN ISRAEL

LEE HEADLEY, PH.D.

Although Israel as a state came into existence in 1948, the Jews as a group have maintained an identity for almost 2,000 years without benefit of territorial unity. This is a remarkable fact in itself and could not have been accomplished without the cohesive force of religion and a core of traditional customs and beliefs. Widely scattered throughout the world and often existing as small minorities in hostile host nations, the Jewish people had a common enough identity so that Jews from one side of the world could migrate to a Jewish community on the other side and manage to fit.

The question as to whether Jewishness should be defined as a religion or as a nationality is often debated by Jews as well as Gentiles. Historians agree that the unity of the Jewish people was preserved throughout the Diaspora by religious beliefs; traditional customs and rituals; historical memories; a common expectation of future redemption and return to Zion (although not literally expected in past centuries); a common educated language of Hebrew; continuing community institutions; and a super-comprehensive body of laws which minutely regulated the actions of everyday life in religion, business, and personal and family life. The commonality of these factors stems from the religion and its elaboration, particularly after the Diaspora (dispersion).

The Jewish community in exile after the Roman Conquest continued in Babylonia under the leadership of a descendant of the House of David until about 100 A.D. During that time and after the center of influence had shifted to Spain and Eastern Europe, questions of law and procedure were sent by Jews of all lands to the center and answered by Responsa.

There was constant interchange between exile groups and the maintenance of homogeneity of belief and custom.

Today Israel has a strong group identity, a sense of family and close kinship with all the Jews in Israel, and also with all the Jews of the world. The state is founded upon the basic premise that immigration is open to any Jew—an ingathering of the exiles. The population has grown from 650,000 in 1948 to approximately 3 million. They come from more than 100 countries and speak 70 languages. Between 1949 and 1951 refugees arrived at the rate of 18,000 to 30,000 a month. After 1957 immigration diminished, and today perhaps 30,000 to 35,000 arrive annually. The present population consists of Western and Eastern European Jews (Ashkenazim), Oriental Jews from Asia and Africa, sabras or native-born Israelis, and a small Arab minority. Oriental Jews comprise more than half the population, and it is estimated they may predominate by two-thirds by 1975 owing to a high birth rate and continued immigration.

The impact of such a varied set of peoples and cultures cannot be underestimated. It created an intolerable economic strain on a fledging country. Jobs and housing were scarce; refugee camps, in which people lived for years, had to be erected. Housing is still extremely tight in Israel, and only those who can afford it purchase their own homes or apartments at very high prices. European or Western Jews were apt to have education, skills, and possibly some capital and family connections. Oriental Jews were less fitted for Western life, which was and is the prevailing style in Israel. The Oriental Jews were largely uneducated, lived in primitive style, and came from agricultural backgrounds so that they could not compete in skilled trades. Besides these actual handicaps, there were prestige rankings that put them at the bottom of the scale. Yemenite, Morrocan, Kurd, and Rumanian Jews were looked down upon for their backwardness.

Israel's Central Bureau of Statistics has calculated Jewish suicide rates and compared them with those of other countries. The rate is above that of Norway and the Netherlands and below that of the United States. These figures are higher than those reported by the World Health Organization. Incidence rises with age; a relatively large percent are widows and widowers; twice as many married persons commit suicide as single and divorced.

Female rates are high in contrast to Western data. During the period 1949 to 1966, male suicides averaged 1.3 times that of females. Male and female rates rose in the order of African born, native born or sabra, Asian, and European. In the last decade suicide rates for persons born in Europe, especially Eastern Europe, were 2.5 times higher than those of African birth. This order is reversed in attempted suicide and may reflect age incidence, inasmuch as native and Oriental Jews make up the more youthful group. Reported reasons are primarily insanity or depression, with family quarrels higher for Oriental Jews.

The most frequently used methods for males are hanging, poisoning, and jumping. Female suicides are most frequently committed by poisoning, hanging, and burning oneself to death. The latter means is used by Oriental Jewish females (African and Asian born). Attempts are most often by drugs and poisoning, cutting and stabbing, and burning (females 8 percent, males 6 percent).

There is a noticeably abrupt decline in suicides and attempted suicides on Friday, the Sabbath eve, and deaths are at their lowest point on Saturday, the Sabbath. The incidence then begins to climb on Sunday, which compares to an American Monday, and remains approximately the same through Thursday.

The outstanding features of Israel's suicides are, therefore, the almost equal proportion of female to male deaths, the high rate among Eastern European Jews, and the method of burning employed by women.

LAWS AND RITUALS

At this point it may be appropriate to consider the laws concerning suicide. Sacred writings mention suicides without condemnation. King Saul killed himself when defeated in battle; Abimelech, son of Gideon, ordered himself killed because he had been injured by a woman; Razi of Maccabean times killed himself before capture; two traitors, Ahitophel and Judas, were suicides. However, Josephus, the historian of the Jews, mentions a custom of leaving bodies of suicides exposed until sunset and sometimes burying the bodies away from the regular line of graves.

The *Code of Jewish Law* (Ganzfried-Golden, 1961, p. 108) states:

> There is none so wicked as the one who commits suicide. He who destroys one human life is considered as though he had destroyed a whole world. Therefore, one should not rend his garments or observe mourning for a suicide nor should a eulogy be delivered for him. He should, however, be ritually cleansed, dressed in shrouds and buried. The rule is, whatever is done in deference to the living should be done for him. If a man is found asphyxiated or hanged, if it is a possible murder he should not be considered a suicide. A minor who commits suicide is considered as one who took his life accidentally. If he is an adult and the act was prompted by madness or fear of torture, treat it as a natural death. . . . Whereas relatives observe all rules of mourning for one executed, since he was killed by man, he had an atonement for sins.

From this it appears that a criminal is accorded more honor than a suicide, and also that if there is any way that the suicide might be considered within the rules, the attempt is in that direction. Emphasis is on proper attention to the family, attention to the living, not to the suicide.

Rules regarding burial are no small matter in Israel. The burial societies are run by religious groups and not by secular businesses as elsewhere. A family could, therefore, be put in a difficult position trying to arrange burial for a suicide. The personal shame and notice drawn to the family are significant.

Although there is specific exception made in the case of torture, Jewish history abounds with examples of martyrs who refused to take the route of suicide and were killed for their religious beliefs. In recent times with the rise of the Nazis, there was a wave of suicide, particularly in the Low Countries, before the Nazi invasion. Throughout history persecution of Jews has produced similar waves of suicides–Mainz and Cologne in Germany (11th century); York, England (12th century); Ukraine, Russian (1648 to 1649).

Secular and legal codes of law for the State of Israel are derived from English law, in part because of the existence of the British Mandate prior to the establishment of the State. However, even before the revisions of suicide law in England (1961), there were no laws in Israel making committed suicide a crime. Under 5.225(1) of the Criminal Code Ordinance, a person *attempting* suicide was guilty of a misdemeanor punishable by 3 years imprisonment, a fine, or both. Since the establishment of the State in 1948 there had been no prosecutions for attempted suicide, in spite of this legislation. The law was changed in 1966.

Laws regarding suicide pacts or aiding and abetting are more severe. Abetment is considered in the class of murder and Criminal Code Ordinance 5.225(2) states that "any person who: (a) procures another to kill himself; or (b) counsels another to kill himself and thereby induces him to do so; or (c) aids another in killing himself is guilty of felony and imprisonment for life" (Drapkin, 1965).

Thus, the religious and social laws of the Jews against suicide are uncompromisingly condemnatory, but legal prohibitions are less strict. From the religious point of view, if a suicide is "considered as though he had destroyed a whole world," such a person on the judgment day of resurrection is not likely to enter the Promised Land.

CUSTOMS AND ATTITUDES

The attitude above toward suicide is seemingly one of the facets of the Jewish ethos that has continued in force throughout the centuries. It remains an unacceptable act that Israelis do not even like to discuss. The paucity of articles on suicide is one reflection of this attitude. Psychiatric patients indicate fear of shaming their relatives should they commit suicide, and of the problems of burial they would visit on the family since religious groups control services and arrangements.

Other rules for conformity are prohibitions against conversion, violence or aggression toward peers, marrying outside of the religion, obligations to give to charity, and a common commitment to a Jewish image because the disgraceful act of one Jew besmirches the whole group. Embodied in the idea of the Covenant with God is that Jews consider themselves a special people who must endure adversity and maintain the faith and practices for eventual reward. Suffering can become almost a religious act. Customs have been preserved by adherence to the explicit laws and regulations of Judaism, notably by ceremonies of the life cycle. These observances involving family participation are circumcision, coming of age (*bar mitzvah*), marriage, and death rites. Further family fulfillment of tradition lies in religious calendar observances such as Passover and Yom Kippur.

Adherance to these ethical ideals and ritual practices does not mean, however, that Israel has a common culture. On the contrary, there is a mixture of differing cultures that are often in conflict and are further complicated by the large population of young people who have different goals from those of their parents. Family types generally fall into three groups: Kibbutzim; Ashkenazim, especially Eastern European; and Oriental Jews from North Africa and Asia. Israel, which employs a State anthropologist, is very much interested in cultural variants. Most attention has been paid to Oriental Jews.

Kibbutzim

The Kibbutz family is widely known and hardly warrants lengthy description. The basic orientations of the Kibbutz are equality, cooperative endeavor, and encouragement of independence and initiative. The Kibbutzim have been so widely publicized and researched by various professional groups that they assume far more importance than their numbers warrant. There are about 230 Kibbutzim comprising about 4 percent of Israel's population. Originally they were based on a theory of community living in which the parents would not have a dominant role. Marriages were of free choice, and partners were not economically dependent on each other but each participated in the community effort. Marriages were based on love relationships with an ideal of equality between the partners. Children were raised in groups attended by child care attendants or nurses (*metapelet*) and a network of responsible adults. They saw their parents briefly for the most part. Reciprocal sharing and influence of peers was important, and emphasis was on manual labor, together building and sharing the Kibbutz activities cooperatively.

Although originally the parents were not to be the major focus of the children's emotional life, tendencies have been toward more parental time and participation with children. In some Kibbutzim, children now stay with their parents at night. The first Kibbutzim families were of nuclear parents, but now older members of the family remain so that there are three generation groups to be seen. As a result Kibbutzim are becoming more family-oriented. There have been dissatisfactions on the part of women in these groups, however, who feel that, in spite of the ideal of male-female equality, women have not been given equal authority and that the major share of child rearing still evolves upon the woman.

In some Kibbutzim teenagers live coeducationally and are encouraged to regard each other somewhat as brothers and sisters, seeking marriages outside of their own Kibbutzim. Other Kibbutzims do not have this rule and the children do tend to intermarry. Younger members feel that their elders are too rigid in matters of education, for older Kibbutzim tend to discourage higher education and often do not send their children to schools that will prepare them for universities. Nevertheless, younger members are insisting on going to universities and may not return to the Kibbutz with its limited opportunities for the college trained.

The Kibbutz system seems to produce an independent, active, confident child. Army service records of Kibbutz members have been outstanding in initiative and competence and show a high percentage of officer ratings.

As to suicide rates, 4 percent of the suicides in the period 1962 to 1966 were from veteran Kibbutzim and 1.3 percent from younger members. Moshavim had a lower rate, however, 2.1 percent. Moshavim are collective enterprises where the individuals own land but cooperatively buy equipment and sell produce. They have existed as long as Kibbutzim but do not draw as much attention.

Eastern Europeans

The largest group of suicides came from Eastern European families, particularly Polish and Rumanian. Israel has not been as interested in the cultural patterns of this group, but there are considerable data from literature and various studies. An extensive description of the Eastern European *shtetl* or community indicates how closely the community life kept to the rules of the *Shulhan Aruk* or *Jewish Code of Law* (Zborowski and Herzog, 1962). This code is incredibly detailed and supervises the most minute everyday functions. There are specific directions as to how and when one should wash his hands, what fruits and grains may be eaten, how one may enter or sit in a room, exact rules for making of a prayer shawl—materials permitted, number of fringes, how the edges can and cannot be sewn, etc.—personal and sexual regulations between husband and wife, etc. For the Orthodox every action of life is completely regimented. The traditional life of the *shtetl* continued until very recent times, as late as the 1930's (by one estimate) and even as late as World War II (Zborowski and Herzog, 1962). These Eastern European groups rigidly observed the religious rituals. Community life proceeded as it had for centuries, emphasizing study of the sacred writings, observing ceremonial days, and maintaining charitable institutions. There was close supervision by each community member of the other to see that they stayed within their obligations. A recent study of first and second generation Jews in the United States—90 percent of whom came from Eastern Europe originally—found that the cultural elements are still very important (Zborowski and Landes, 1967). The ultraorthodox groups in Israel continue to maintain these religious and cultural rules.

Males were considered superior and the religious and social authority. The ideal man was a scholar, well versed in the sacred writings and willing and able to help all those who were not so learned. His manner was restrained and decorous, and he did not show excesses of emotion in any direction, except perhaps in eloquent religious debate. He must not smile or laugh excessively over a joke, but briefly acknowledge it with a smile. He must be a man of honor and integrity, who helps the poor and unfortunate, sees to the community welfare, advises, instructs, inspires; all this commanded a certain authority and sense of distance. However, the members of the community were keenly aware of how well the requirements were being met, and the individual's rating on the social register grew or diminished as he met expectations with regard to social, economic, and ethical behavior. Constant attention must be paid to winning or maintaining status, a demanding task, ever so precisely evaluated by one's neighbors.

Marriage was for procreation. A person only attained full adulthood when he married and could carry on God's injunction to increase and multiply. Bright scholars were married as early as possible, at the age of fourteen at times, in order that the young scholar might not be distracted by thoughts of sex and so that this necessary obligation be put behind him. Usually marriages were arranged via a marriage broker, the *shadkhen*, with the mother having choice of the daughter-in-law and the father choice of the son-in-law. However, marriage involved the status of the entire family so that all factors of learning, money, appearance, and social standing were critically evaluated. Learning could be balanced by money, however. Personal preferences had little to do with the decision; one might learn to love the spouse later. However, young people were seldom forced to marry against their will. Neither party was given any instruction or information about sexual matters, except the rules of the *Shulhan Aruk*. If the marriage was unsatisfactory, divorce was possible, but all the advantage was to the man. In cases of childlessness, it was automatically the woman's fault and after 10 years of childless marriage, the man was required to divorce her.

A wife was expected to be submissive and subordinate and to remain in her domain of household and children. She lived in the real world of household responsibilities, child care, and economic management while he concerned himself with the spiritual and the intellectual. Ideally, he was inept to cope with the physical environment and so must be treated like another child in the family. She was viewed as an expediter of things but also as a potentially dangerous distraction to him.

The position of women, as outlined in the *Shulhan Aruk*, or *Code of Laws*, is inferior to men. The attitude of the Law is that women are inherently sinful. The first prayer a man says on arising is to thank God that he was not made a woman. Women have not been allowed to join men in the same section of orthodox congregations but have had separate quarters. Today there is a strict separation of the sexes at the Wailing Wall in Jerusalem. Women were not encouraged to study the Torah and Talmud, a male preoccupation. They did not become Rabbis although there is an exception historically in Eastern Europe and nowadays an occasional woman is admitted to study for the Rabbinate. A truly orthodox married woman must shave her head and forever after wear a wig or keep her hair covered. "And the hair of a married woman which must always be covered, is treated as part of her body" (and so if exposed is considered nakedness). "The singing of a woman is akin to nakedness," "A man must not pass between two women, two dogs, or two swine," "A man cannot be alone with a woman, or a child more than three years old," "A man cannot hear the voice of woman singer or look at her hair" (Ganzfried-Golden, 1961, p. 11). During menstruation a woman is ritually impure and cannot touch her husband, hand him anything, or even throw him an object from a distance. The *Shulhan Aruk* says that it is mandatory to divorce a quarrelsome woman. A divorced husband is permitted but not required to support a divorced wife. Even rumors of infidelity on the part of a wife requires that a Rabbi must be consulted as to whether the husband should or should not return to her.

Owing to the sinful and distracting nature of women, there was a strict separation of the sexes in everyday life, except in the market place. Men avoided looking at women whenever they met and managed when possible not to speak to them directly. At social functions men and women sat apart. These rules are still observed today in Israel by the ultraorthodox.

The main function of the woman was childbearing, and she exerted considerable power as the mother, the hub of family life that is so essential to the Jewish ethos. Boys were preferred, of course, to girls, and the woman was ritually unclean for a shorter period of time after the birth of a boy than of a girl. While the economic support of the family was the responsibility of the husband, he was relieved of this responsibility if he was a scholar, and the wife, aided perhaps by the relatives, supported the family. This meant she ran the household, took care of the children, and also had a business or some occupation. Whatever control and power she exerted in the family had to be covert and cloaked with modesty.

The mother's main interest was in the son, for in him lay her potential for status and emotional satisfactions. She indulged him, anticipated his wants, and worried over his health. He was plied with food, his clothing was carefully supervised, and his wishes were promptly satisfied. Mothers offered their sons warmth, intimacy, unconditional love, security, and practical aid. Although demonstrativeness was discouraged between spouses, there was no lack of it between mother and son. Zborowski and Landes (1967), in their study of American Jews of Eastern European origin, reported the practice in Eastern Europe for the son to sleep with the mother until fairly advanced ages. They state: "It seems to us that though the marital obligations are fulfilled with the husband, the romance exists with the son." When a son married (a woman acceptable to the mother) the mother soon started criticism of his wife as not taking adequate care of him. "When a son marries he gives the wife a contract and the mother a divorce," was a common folk saying.

Daughters were possible competitors for status and therefore were nagged and criticized. Fathers were more able to have a positive relationship with their daughters than with their sons, who had preempted the mother's attention. Paternal love could be more openly directed to daughters than could affection between husband and wife. However, the demands of distance, restraint, and authority often led fathers to cold, distant relationships with their daughters.

An American Jewess (Stern, 1969) wrote in an autobiography of the distance and coldness existing between her and her religious father, so much so that as she looked at him in his coffin she felt that at last she was free. Their relationship was one in which his word was law, and she as a woman had had practically nothing to say about her life. Even though she repudiated Judaism for some years, she still was psychologically bound by the restrictions upon women. Her descriptions bring to life some of the starkness of the *Shulhan Aruk* in its attitudes toward women.

There is a description by a psychoanalyst of a female character type who results from such Eastern European families. (Grinstein, 1967). This type is narcissistic, superficial, overly concerned with dress and appearance, frigid, and seeks psychiatric help for vague anxiety symptoms. The husbands, generally well to do, are passive in home relations but preoccupied with business. Mothers of these patients were aggressive, loud, and ambitious for their daughters to marry well. The patients felt that psychologically they had been married to the highest bidder. They seemed lost and childlike, seeking a love relationship with which they could identify themselves because love had been denied in their relationship with their mothers. The mothers' preference for the sons caused the daughters to repress aggression and to feel self-critical and envious of men. Fathers had done little to provide a positive image for these women. The outward, overdressed appearance attempted to create a positive image of a desired attractive person in order to conceal the inner fright and loneliness.

Fathers in this family system would be more able to relate to sons-in-law than to their sons, for at home respect and distance must be maintained from the son. The whole household seems to worry about sexual interest and contact. Brothers and sisters avoid one another; brothers maintain distance from each other. Family balance often may be threatened by the tensions between father-son, mother-daughter, and sister-brother, as well as between mother and daughter-in-law. A state of tension between all these groups leads to shifts in balance of power.

From this family pattern it would be possible to postulate some stressful situations: the dependency of husband and sons upon mothers and vulnerability to loss; the resentments of daughters who might find it difficult to form satisfactory identifications with critical mothers and who find themselves with poor self-images; competitive relationships with siblings and with peers.

Orientals

Oriental Jews had the lowest completed suicide rates but the highest attempt rate, particularly around family quarrels.

Oriental Jews from the African and Asian areas tended to be the most religious and most traditional. These families were characterized by status by ascription; heirarchial power centered in males and elders; an extended family; frequent cohabitation; orientation toward the past; stress on large families; early marriage ages; especially for women; and subservience of women. Marriages were arranged with wealth, education, and moral reputation in mind. A woman's value lay in bride price (*mohar*) and in bearing children, which is in keeping with the past economic life of Oriental Jews based on agricultural pursuits. Chastity was extremely important so that her movements in the community were severely curtailed. Rules were close to the *Shulhan Aruk*; marriages were at puberty and earlier, before sexual maturity. In Yemen, where polygamy existed, child brides were forced to marry relatively elderly men. Israel has passed laws against both child brides and polygamy, to the annoyance of Yemenite Rabbis.

Marriage customs included proof of virginity by the bride's family on the wedding night and anxious supervision by the clan over each marriage ritual (Palgi, 1970). Since discussion of sexual matters was taboo, neither party to the marriage came psychologically prepared. Once married, the woman was subordinate to all her male relatives—father, father-in-law, husband, brothers, and brothers-in-law.

Children were seen as economically useful, as well as visible evidence of the status of the father as a male and a ratification of the function of the mother as a female. Children were breast fed for long periods—up to 2 to 3 years—on demand, then sharply and quickly weaned by sending the child away to a relative or smearing a bitter substance on the breast. Toilet training was nondemanding. However, children were early expected to conform to well defined hierarchical lines of power exercised through males and elders. Patriarchical authority was not to be questioned, no matter what its quality. Habit training was done by threats and physical punishment, ususally at the mood of the parents, who did not feel the need to be consistent. Praise and rewards for good behavior were not given. Total obedience to the father placed little responsibility on the child to know by himself what was considered right or wrong. The whole trend of the rearing was such that it did not develop in the personality the capacity to stand frustration in the present for greater rewards and satisfaction in the future. Children obtained their way by temper tantrums if they outlasted the punishment. This training led not to personal independence but to group dependence and conformity. This child training would be useful only in static, nondemanding environments but would not be helpful in a changing industrial society where one must adjust to circumstances with some initiative and independence. Oriental Jewish families came ill equipped psychologically, educationally, and vocationally to adjust to Israeli life. The men were not able to find jobs as rapidly as European-born Jews, but often wives found domestic work easily. The Oriental Jews live in groups without much upward mobility. Their status change led to increased expression of hostility. The only riots that occurred in Israel were by Moroccans who were physically aggressive in their demands.

Such family dynamics should lead to angry submissiveness on the part of women and hostility turned back upon themselves in depression or somatic disorders. Men would tend to become anxious if their status were questioned, would tend to be depressed by discrepancies in ego ideals, and would tend to overcompensate by aggressiveness.

The lower suicide rate might be explained by the fact that there is a large proportion of young people among Oriental Jews, but there is evidence that stress is expressed significantly more frequently in this group with delinquent behavior, somatic symptoms, and work habit disturbances. Neurotic syndromes often include belief that the individual is under the power of the evil eye or someone with supernatural powers. Symptoms most often are fatigue, vague body pains, and hysterical reactions.

A study in 1966 showed the rate of juvenile delinquency for those of African-Asian origin to be 30 times as great as the rate for those of European-American origin (Amir and Hovav, 1970).

CONCLUSIONS

Shuval (1970) investigated the possibility that utilizing Israeli public health clinics was a significant means of relieving social needs for support, catharsis, and status. She found that the traditional nonacculturated Oriental Jews were the most frequent users of the clinics, doctors, or nurses, particularly the Kurdish, Morroccan, and Rumanian. They were older, female, non-Hebrew-speaking, more religious, more traditional, and less educated. Thus, the public clinics did meet some of these sociopsychiatric needs of the most traditional and least integrated sections of the population. This outlet for stress might diminish the likelihood of suicide.

Eastern European suicides may involve other factors besides the fact that they are in the older age groups of the population. Most importantly, they had focused their standards and well being on a strongly knit family and community life that was now broken since so many families were decimated or scattered. Their normal reference points of status and human satisfactions were seriously askew. Dependency loss may account for male suicides, while for females it was the loss of family and of purpose. This group suffered markedly from war and Nazi terrorism.

Oriental Jews, on the contrary, were often moved en masse and whole communities and clans continued together. If separated into housing developments they tended to drift back together. Therefore, their ethos and community standards continued more intact although in conflict with the trend of Israeli life. Their inclination toward dependence as taught in the family might well incline them either to delinquent gangs, to dependence on illness behavior, or to aggressive opposition and demonstrations against Israeli organizations.

In reference to the high female rate of suicide, it would seem that the low position of women in the Eastern European and Oriental groups would be a cause for suicide stemming from depression or hostility.

The anxious overprotective mother, of "how-to-be-a-Jewish-mother" fame, is familiar. The connotation is that she is generous with time, attention, affection, and food, and inclined to be a martyr. Goodness and giving are part of the ideal but self-abnegation sets up stresses of hostility if the relationship is not reciprocal. A Jewish psychoanalyst stated that traditional Jewish women have a self-image that they are instruments to be used by man, that men do not really admire their beauty or see their personalities or their mental abilities as desirable qualities. They often feel that men need them only for sexual relief (Van Den Haag, 1968).

Even though Israel has passed laws of equality for women, cultural patterns do not change rapidly. In matters of marriage and divorce, Rabbinical courts are still in charge and rulings are weighted in favor of men. Women are admitted to schools of higher education, but university education is viewed as a means for the woman to advance her husband's status and comfort. Fewer women work as compared to women in other modern industrialized countries (Palgi, 1970).

The method of suicide by burning used by Asian-African women seems to be an acculturation to the host nation's styles. Asian suicides have frequently been by fire and continue so today. Statistics for the non-Jewish (mostly Arab) population of Israel show that most female suicides were by fire, used as a retaliatory hostile gesture by lighting kerosene poured over one's body while in the center of a village crowd. Women in this Oriental Jewish group are probably subject to more disadvantages in living and probably would have fewer means of alleviating a distressing situation. While choice of this means is revolting to a Westerner, it may not appear so to one raised in a surrounding culture with such a prevailing mode.

Collective identity of the Jews seems to lead to apprehensiveness about personal maintenance of the group ideal. Failure reflects not only on individual self-esteem but on the status of the group as a whole. This is reflected in child-rearing practices that emphasize the necessity of conforming to the ideal as a matter of normalcy. If the child does well, it is only to be expected; therefore praise is not extended. Disciplinary attitudes emphasize what the child has not done. This may lead to high expectations and easily aroused guilt feelings.

Aggression is hedged about by various rules. One is not to be aggressive toward one's peers. (Leviticus is frequently quoted in the injunction to treat others as one's brother.) Since there are inevitable frictions, however, the problem is complicated by prohibitions against certain popular outlets such as alcoholism, violence, or sexual immorality. A combination of high expectation of ego ideals with restrictions on expression would likely lead to suppression of aggression with consequent depression. Martyr-like suffering may be endured because of the special position of the Jews as a chosen people. Passivity therefore may become a positive adjustment mechanism. Dependency on wives, which appears particularly marked, could lead to anxiety and depression when there is object loss.

Whatever the origin of stress, whether from external realities or from intrafamily and intragroup frictions, there are some approved and characteristic means of relieving the stress. Verbalization is frequent, and it is expected that others will share in the contemplation of the problem. Verbalization is accompanied by graphic gestures or expressions to portray fully the feelings of the person. Furthermore, one may feel free to ask for and depend upon others for actual help, for it is the obligation of others to help in times of distress. This principle of mutual help has been in existence for centuries. Diaspora communities helped Jewish communities throughout the whole history of the Jewish people, sometimes from great distances. However, people living in a community consider it their duty and a *mitzvah* ("Commandment") to be helpful to others. Dependence and asking for help, therefore, is not decried but is a mutually accepted responsibility. From its very beginnings, Jewish community life has had organized charitable institutions. In countries of adoption they have as a group been active in benevolent institutions.

Another attitude of great antiquity is to consider no question or problem as closed. No authority is too awesome to challenge, even the Torah and Talmud itself. Resourcefulness is a positive asset and energetic seeking of ways out lead to initiative and independence. Combined with the emphasis in Judaism on the goodness of life and the enjoyment of its offerings, such open-mindedness offers an escape hatch to feelings of failure and depression.

Physical illness is an acceptable means of dealing with stress. Although emphasis on maintaining health is an important and integral part of Judaism, the presence of illness is a cause for concern by all members of the family and for self-indulgence by the patient. In *People in Pain*, Zborowski (1969) investigated the attitude toward pain of four different ethnic groups in the United States. He found that cultural attitudes of

Anglo-Saxons and Irish forbade much expression of pain or giving in to illness. Italians and Jews, however, allowed themselves the gamut of vocalization about their feelings accompanied by gestures, moans and groans, and facial expressions of great descriptive quality. Jews allowed themselves indulgences in their illness and whatever comfort and attention the illness brought. Not only did they vividly describe their feelings and experiences in superlative terms to their hospital personnel, but they tended to draw in other persons and members of the family. An illness mobilized the whole family group, so that everyone including the children worried about the patient and paid attention to him.

> Thus, the Jewish patient has a very definite and clear concept of complaining. His complaining is just as rational as the noncomplaining of the old American patient. Complaining fulfills several important functions: it gives relief through its cathartic function; it is an effective medium of communication; it mobilizes the assistance of the environment; and finally, it affirms the kind of family solidarity that is the basis of Jewish family organization (Zborowski, p. 108).

At the same time that these patients were demanding assistance and attention, they were also critical and questioning of their doctors and deciding for themselves whether or not they would go along with the medical regime, for "the patient knows best." Although dependent and craving attention, they also reserved the privilege of an individual making up his own mind about the surrounding power structure. In the study previously mentioned on clinic service in Israel, Shuval (1970) found that rates of clinic usage are among the highest in the world, indicating that Jews have a readiness to see themselves in a sick role. One study (Mechanic, 1963) found that among college students, Jewish students, whether religiously observant or not, were much more prone to illness behavior than non-Jews.

Food is a most popular and pervasive means of emotional outlet. It embodies the positives of Judaism such as enjoyment of family affairs, religious observances, and performance of "mitzvahs." Mothers can use food offering as love, coaxing, indulgences, or rewards to their children. Food tends to be a center of family and group activities. Furthermore, indulgence in food is permissible whereas the use of liquor to a similar degree is forbidden, as is sexual expression with anyone but a spouse, and violent or aggressive acts are not culturally allowed. Although homes in Eastern Europe were often poor enough so that villagers themselves had scarcely enough to eat, a traveller or stranger who arrived in the community on the Sabbath was always invited to a home for the Sabbath meal.

Humor, particularly wry and self-deprecatory, is a means of anticipating pain from the world and blunting its impact, or taking the sting out of suffering. Jewish humor is seldom aggressive toward non-Jews, rather the aggression is turned back upon oneself. "In nothing is Jewish psychology so vividly revealed as in Jewish jokes—we need not be surprised to find countless Jewish jokes mocking the Jews themselves. Self-awareness, pushed into self-analysis, turns to self-criticism" (Rosten, 1970). While this turns frustrations and hostilities back upon the self, the manner is cathartic.

REFERENCES

Amir and Hovav. 1970. Juvenile delinquency in Israel. In: *Children and Families in Israel*. Gordon and Breach Science Publishers, New York.

Drapkin, I. S. 1965. Aspects of suicide in Israel. *Israel Annals of Psychiatry and Related Disciplines,* 3(1).

Ganzfried-Golden. 1961. *Code of Jewish Law*. Hebrew Publishing Co., New York.

Grinstein, A. 1967. Profile of a doll. In: N. Kiel (Ed.), *Psychodynamics of American Jewish Life*. Twayne Publishers, New York.

Mechanic, D. 1963. Religion, religiosity, and illness behavior—The special case of the Jews. *Human Organization*, 22:3.

Palgi, P. 1970. Family types. In: *Children and Families in Israel*. Gordon and Breach Science Publishers, New York.

Rosten, L. 1970. *The Joys of Yiddish*. Pocket Books, New York.

Shuval, J. 1970. *Social Functions of Medical Practice*. Jossey-Bass, San Francisco.

Stern, E. 1969. *I Am a Woman—and a Jew*. Arno Press and New York Times, New York.

Van Den Haag, E. 1968. *The Jewish Mystique*. Stein and Day, New York.

Zborowski, M. 1969. *People in Pain*. Jossey-Bass, San Francisco.

Zborowski, M. and Herzog, E. 1962. *Life is with People*. Schocken Books, New York.

Zborowski, M. and Landes, R. 1967. The Eastern European family. In: N. Kiel (Ed.), *The Psychodynamics of American Jewish Life*. Twayne Publishers, New York.

fifteen

SUICIDE IN INDIA

A. VENKOBA RAO, M.D., PH.D., D.P.M., F.R.C.P.

The prevalent attitude of a society to suicide among its members is shaped and fashioned from time to time by the beliefs of its people in the different periods of its history. In India, for example, Vedic, Upanishadic, and other ancient Indian writings and her religions and philosophies have held certain views on such a mode of dying. The Vedic age, predominantly one of rituals, permitted suicide on religious grounds. The best sacrifice was man's life itself. To give up everything and to wander about in the forests was recommended in the Vedic period, and this amounted almost to suicide. A few passages from the Vedas support this statement: "To them the Lord of the creatures gave himself. He became their sacrifice. He, having given himself up to them, made a reflection of himself which is sacrifice. Therefore, they say that the Lord of creatures is a sacrifice for he made it a reflection of himself. By means of this sacrifice, he redeemed himself from them." Again, "With sacrifice the Gods worshipped the sacrifice." "These were the first institutions. These great beings attained the heaven where the Gods, the ancient Sadhyas reside." Although the Vedic commentators are divided on the point whether Vedic injunction allowed self-destruction, there is definite evidence from the hymns that human sacrifice was considered the best, and that other forms were poor substitutes.

On the other hand, the Upanishads, with their posture of revolt against the Vedas, condemned suicide. The Upanishadic seers were not favorably disposed to the rituals of the Vedic people but stressed philosophizing and "looking inwards," to realize the greater Truth. A verse from *Isavasya Upanishad* is condemnatory toward suicide: "He who takes his self reaches after death the sunless regions covered by impenetrable darkness." However, some later Upanishads show certain leniency toward the act: "A *sanyasin* who has acquired full insight may enter upon the great journey or choose death by voluntary starvation, by fire or by a hero's fate or drowning." The literature on *tirtha* ("pilgrimage") recommends suicide at places of religious importance, e.g., confluence of rivers. It also permitted hanging from a particular tree called *Vata* ("the tree of death"). The perennial question whether man has the right to shed his mortal coil has been discussed in the *Dharmashastra* of India. The question was approached from a moral point of view. According to these works, those who commit suicide by poisoning, fire, hanging, drowning, or falling from a cliff or a tree are to be classed with those who commit cardinal sins. Such persons are denied cremation and funeral rites. However, such condemnation did not apply to religious suicides, *e.g.*, *sati*, drowning at confluence of sacred rivers, and also suicides by the ascetics and those suffering from intractable diseases. Kautilya, the ancient lawgiver of India, prescribed severe penalties to the bodies of the suicides, and also to their relations if they performed the last rites. Certain Brahmanical texts recommended that he who resolved to kill himself should fast for 3 days, and if the suicide attempt failed he was liable for severe penances. The *Bhagavad-Gita* admonishes self-torture and self-killing.

Hindu philosophy holds that life in its broadest terms does not end with death. According to the ancient Indian thinking, death opens the door to the next life whose type is determined by the way the preceding one was utilized. This is the law of *Karma*, or cosmic justice, or the theory of reincarnation that occupies the central place in the Vedantic philosophy. The Vedantic view admits only to the death of the physical or gross body while attributing immortality to the "soul"–a collective term for the psychic qualities. Life is not viewed as a term, but in series. A well known Upanishadic verse says; "It is the body that dies when left by the self; the self does not die." The *Bhagavad-Gita* declares; "Even as a man casts off his worn-out bodies and enters into others that are new." Such was the attitude toward death, and its cheerful acceptance was enjoined to the aged and those enfeebled by incurable disease. When a person has gone through successive stages of life he reaches a state of asceticism. The ancient Indian social system held that none can reach asceticism without crossing the preceding stages of life and carrying out one's obligation that life demands, such as that of a student, householder, and retired individual. "The blossom cannot deny the leaf; the leaf cannot deny the stalk nor the stalk the root" (Radhakrishnan, 1960).

Although there are many elders in India who take a philosophical view of the approaching death, naturally there are others who fear death. Fear of death as a symptom among the anxiety neurotics is not uncommon.

Similarly, the aged depressives are afraid of sleeping lest they may die while asleep. In a survey carried out in Madras on the attitude toward death, Ramamurti (personal communication) found that poorly adjusted individuals had considerably greater degree of negative attitudes toward death. Another study of his revealed that with increasing age (levels between 20 and 70 years) the attitude toward death became negative. The attitude toward death was brought out in an interesting manner in the Indian epic, *Mahabharata*. In the chapter on "Enchanted Pool," answering the voice of his divine father, who commanded him to speak out on the greatest wonder in the world, Yudhisthira replied, "Every day, men see creatures depart to Yama's (God of death) abode and yet those who remain seek to live forever. This verily is the greatest wonder." The same thought was re-echoed in the twentieth century by Freud (1915): "Our own death is indeed unimaginable, and whenever we make the attempt to imagine it we can conceive that we really survive as spectators. Hence, the psychoanalytical school could venture on the assertion that at bottom no one believes in his own death, or to put the thing in another way, in the unconscious, everyone of us is convinced of his own immortality." Further systematic work needs to be done on this facet of the suicide problem, namely, one's attitude toward his own death from the Indian cultural point of view.

In the history of suicide in India, *sati* has occupied an important place. It consisted of self-immolation of a woman over the funeral pyre of her husband. The custom was not indigenous to India; rather, it was definitely an importation. Herodotus has drawn attention to it among the Scythians and Thracians. The *Atharva-Veda* of India, literally a compendium of demonology, refers to the practice as ancient. The attitude softened during the Vedic period when the woman was required to lie for a few moments on the pyre before the cremation. Being buried alive in a pit or burnt alive were the alternatives to cremation with the husband. Gradually, the practice degenerated into a social evil with many a woman being fed to the flames against her wish. It was Raja Ram Mohan Roy, the Indian social worker, who waged a relentless battle against *sati*, and, during the vice-regal tenure of Lord Bentinck in 1892, the custom was declared a legal offense. In ancient times, the Kathaei, a Punjabi tribe, had made *sati* a law to prevent the wife poisoning her husband. Next to *sati*, a passing mention should be made to *jauhar*, which consisted literally of mass suicide by women of the Rajput clan to avoid molestation by the invading victors. Instances have been recorded of *jauhar* when Akbar invaded Marwar and Allauddin seized Chitore. There have been epidemics of suicide recorded in India's epic *Ramayana*, Harshacharita and Rajatharangini. The Jaina religion of India enjoins termination of life by self-denial of food, a practice called *sallekhana*. However, this was permissible only to the ascetics. Several aspects of suicide in India have been dealt with by Thakur (1963).

The religious and philosophical views have tended to color the popular ideas on and toward suicide. For example, it is held that for a soul whose body has been destroyed by suicide there is no liberation or salvation. Prejudices, fears, censure, condemnation, and shame are some of the attitudes displayed by society toward the act of suicide, the suicide attempters, and the survivors. There is always a section of the press wherein are published news items of suicide as sensational headlines, and these read more as murder stories and help little to foster a helpful attitude among the public. Since the Indian penal code at present holds attempted suicide to be a legal offense, fear of the law drives people to avoid notification, punishment, and consequent involvement in legal and police matters. Family members seem concerned more with the legal consequences on social grounds rather than with the outcome of the attempted suicide. Except in rare instances, the survivors are looked down upon as if they were "tainted members." Marriages in such families become difficult. Naturally, the occurrence of suicide is suppressed in these circumstances. In general, there is a failure to perceive the psychological and social factors that lie behind the suicidal acts and also to recognize that mental dysfunction could account for many of them.

That the theme of suicide is invested with fear can be supported by several instances. It is not uncommon for some (probably the predisposed) to develop severe neurotic or even psychotic reactions either after seeing the body of the suicide, living in the house where a suicide has taken place, or even by frequenting places where suicides have occurred. In India some houses, localities, wells, etc. are feared as haunted and hence avoided by people lest the spirits of the dead may seize and possess them. There are religious ceremonies that are practiced to purify these places. The author knows many patients who developed severe neurotic or psychotic reactions after pulling out suicide corpses from the wells. These situations may well offer support to the concept of "contagion effect" in suicidology.

The common mode of attempting or committing suicide in India is by gulping down an insecticide (organophosphorus compound) preparation. They are cheap and easily available. This method does not appear to bear any cultural characteristic. This agent has been the choice in both planned and impulsive suicides and irrespective of the strength of motivation for self-killing. Of course, there are many other methods: ingestion of Oleander and sleeping pills, hanging, drowning, burning, stab injuries, getting run over by automobile or train, jumping from heights, etc.

The attitude of the survivors toward the suicidally dead is one of pity, sadness, and consideration. Also, survivors suppress the fact if a suicide has occurred in their own family and condemn, criticize, and censure if it has occurred in other families. It is this dissociation between the in-group and the out-group attitude that appears interesting. On the other hand, the survivors of attempted suicide or those in the family where suicide has taken place are the victims of an unhelpful attitude by the public. There is also occasionally a mixed attitude toward the suicide among his family members. I have heard parents saying after their son's suicide, "We are terribly sorry and grieved over his death. But we can never reconcile ourselves to the fact of his suicide." In such an attitude, one can discern the blending of the reaction of bereavement and the fear of public opinion. They were apprehensive of the future prospects of children of the suicides, especially their marriage and employment. Sometimes deaths from suicide are attributed to acute illness, heart attack, accidents, and the like.

Among the Indian cultural factors of psychodynamic import, we shall deal briefly with two important areas, namely, marriage and family. Marriages in India continue to be solemnized on traditional lines and are generally arranged by the parents within the caste. Hence, personal choice of marital partner against parental wish, or selection from another caste without parental approval, or forced marriages are sometimes the etiological factors in cases of attempted and completed suicides. Some girls who remain unmarried for long because their parents have not been able to procure a suitable match for them consider themselves as a burden to their family and put an end to themselves in an altruistic fashion. Indian culture lays a great stress on the sanctity of married life. The woman is considered an equal partner in the commerce of life and is expected to raise children, especially a son, and be dutiful to her husband. The author knows many women who have either attempted suicide or killed themselves as a result of their husband's paranoidal delusions of marital infidelity. Suicide prophylaxis among the wives of such deluded husbands assumes importance in the Indian setting. Schwartz (1958) remarked on the traditional system of matrimony, "That it is not passionate love that decides the success or failure of marriage is proved abundantly by those marriages which are contracted without love in a completely impersonal manner. I refer to those marriages in earlier centuries in the West or nowadays over almost the whole of the East, when the parents or councils of elders decided who should marry whom. These marriages were the best and the happiest ever known." Nevertheless, there are reports in newspapers of double suicide of lovers who could not get married owing to the disapproval of their parents. Forced marriages have resulted in suicides of several young persons. These indicate that in spite of modernism, the authority of the parents or the elders prevails in matters matrimonial in India.

Sex plays as important a part in the life of an Indian as perhaps in any other part of the world. A high value is attached to semen as a source of robust health. Its loss through emission and spermatorrhoea causes a great concern and constitutes important features of anxiety neurosis in Indian patients. These and also fear and guilt over masturbation may form the nucleus for sexual difficulties during pre- and postmarital years. Psychogenic impotence is a common hazard of such a progress of events, and the individual may be driven to suicide under the feeling that he lacks the most important quality of manliness. Impotence either from physical or psychological causes is not an infrequent cause of suicide in India.

In India childless couples are viewed as unlucky and a sterile woman as inauspicious. The family is considered as blessed only if a son is born. Female children are not so much prized as male children. For example, asked about the number of children he has, the average Indian male replies with a figure which invariably excludes daughters. Similarly, he includes only brothers when questioned about his siblings. A son is called a *puthra* because he prevents entry into a specific type of hell called *puth*. It is not uncommon for the childless couple to adopt children of their relatives with a view to having their obsequies performed by the adopted sons and also for purpose of inheritance of property. Sterility can often be the motive for suicide among women in India.

Much has been written about the joint family system of living in India, characterized by "generation depth." Owing to the possible pathological interpersonal relationship among its members, hysterical reactions tend to occur as a means of escapism from the authoritative figureheads of the family. In such a family, the mother-in-law usually reigns supreme over the rest of the family and the daughters-in-law (especially the younger ones) are most vulnerable to psychological illness. They suffer from hysterical reactions that vary from paralysis to possession, from tremors to trance, and from dermatitis to deafness. The mother-in-law invariably comes under criticism especially from the bride's people. The daughter-in-law, unable to suffer any more torments from her superior, may commit suicide. Such is the familiar trend in some parts of India. The daughter-in-law secures all the commiseration while the mother-in-law is declared the villian. With Westernization and migration to cities consequent to industrialization, joint family living is becoming less common, and with the emerging nuclear and the extended type of living, mother-in-law and daughter-in-law confrontation is becoming less frequent.

As both the life span and the number of psychiatric disorders among the aged in the country have gradually increased, one can anticipate a growing number of suicides in this age group in the next decades. The aged continue to receive the reverence and respect in the family and only rarely do they experience a state of isolation to force them to an anomic suicide. The author in his recent research has come across quite a few aged with suicidal tendencies, but the association between the loss of status and respect in the family and a suicidal tendency is difficult to establish. Suicidal behavior appears to be less often an outcome of family factors, and more often attributable to mental illness that has occurred in the aged members of joint family living.

It is generally held that economic poverty is a less powerful predisposer to suicide than affluence. An undernourished Asiatic is believed to cling to life at all costs. This is quite contrary to the real situation in India. Poverty and unemployment are definite causes of suicide and suicidal attempts. Often entire families have put an end to themselves by poisoning or by other means because of being unable to live in poverty. There was a wave of suicide a few years ago among the goldsmiths in India when they found themselves suddenly unemployed as a result of the promulgation of the Gold Control Order by the Government of India.

Finally, while discussing suicide in Indian culture, reference needs to be made to fasting. Suicide by starvation, called *sallekhana*, sanctioned by the Jain religion in India and prescribed for ascetics, has already been referred to. Starvation as a political weapon was developed by Mr. Gandhi with a spiritual basis and was intended as a strong moral force against the British rule. He undertook fasting several times and on more than one occasion it was started as a fast unto death. Subsequently, fasting was undertaken by several other political leaders for various reasons. Notable persons in recent history whose fasts ended fatally are Mr. Potti Sriramulu, who starved for the creation of Andhra Pradesh on a linguistic basis, and Mr. Pheruman, whose fast was aimed, albeit unsuccessfully, toward getting the city of Chandigarh included in the state of Punjab. Acts and threats of self-immolation for political reasons are not uncommon in India today.

REFERENCES

Freud, S. 1925. Thoughts for the times on war and death (1915). In: *Collected Papers,* Translated by J. Riviera, Vol. 4, pp. 288–317. Hogarth, London.

Radhakrishnan, S. 1960. *The Hindu View of Life,* p. 65. Allen and Unwin Ltd., London.

Radhakrishnan, S. 1967. *The Bhagavad-Gita,* Ed. 8, p. 108. Allen and Unwin Ltd., London.

Rajagopalachari, C. 1958. *Mahabharata.* K. M. Munshi and R. R. Diwakar (Eds.) p. 139. Bharatiya Vidyabhavan, Bombay.

Ramamurti, P. V. Personal Communication.

Sarma, D. S. 1961. *The Upanishads–An Anthology,* K. M. Munshi and R. K. Diwakar (Eds.). Bharatiya Vidyabhavan, Bombay.

Schwartz, O. 1958. *The Psychology of Sex*, p. 228. Penguin Books, Middlessex, England.

Thakur, U. 1963. *The History of Suicide in India*, p. 6. Munshi Ram Manoharlal, Delhi.

Venkoba Rao, A. 1965. Attempted suicide: An analysis of 114 medical admissions. *Indian Journal of Psychiatry*, 7:253–264.

Venkoba Rao, A. 1968. Depression in Southern India. In: L. Ibor (Ed.), *Proceedings IV World Congress of Psychiatry*, Vol. III p. 1882–1885.

Venkoba Rao, A. 1970. A study of depression as prevalent in South India (abstract of Ph.D. thesis). *Transcultural Psychiatric Research Review*, 7:166–167.

sixteen

SUICIDE IN TAIWAN

HSIEN RIN, M.D.

Little has been written about suicide in Taiwan by social scientists or psychiatrists. One of the few articles that appeared in a medical journal was Okumura's study in 1943 on suicide among aboriginal tribes[1] (Kato, 1970). Another article by the author (1972) dealt with attempted suicides among Chinese psychiatric inpatients. In the past several years the author has also engaged in a suicide study with the staff of Mackay Memorial Hospital of Taipei in which a suicide prevention center and life-line programs were successfully established.[2] From experience in the suicide prevention center service and from ongoing epidemiological studies of suicide and suicide attempts, the author describes suicide in Taiwan from a

---

[1] Formosan aborigines are of Malayopolynesian stock, which has had a semi-primitive culture until fairly recent days. Okumura's report is, so far, the only article on suicide of natives of Taiwan during the war period. His data, based on police report files on several mountain aborigine tribes, reported a heightened rate of successful suicides among them. It was suggested that the aborigines had a higher risk of suicide whenever they met with greater life stresses (from the modern standpoint), such as frustrated marriage, difficulty in earning a livelihood, or the administrative movement of a village to a nearby plain area. Okumura also suggested that the aborigines were highly suggestible and impulsive. The major methods of suicide were hanging and poisoning with fish-cane powder. An unusual finding was the frequently reported suicide pacts occurring among young boys and girls who met objections to their marriage by observing the rules set by their taboos, suicide. The present author also reported suicide pacts among Atayal youngsters (Rin, 1961). Villagers were sympathetic to those youngsters and buried them face-to-face in order that they could marry in their afterlife world. Sorrowful melodies written for those deceased pairs were played by young men with bamboo harmonicas, called *habuns*.

[2] A Canadian missionary physician, Mackay (1842 to 1901), devoted his whole life to offering medical service to native Taiwanese, mostly during the *Ch'in* dynasty. His memorial hospital, located in the north-central part of Taipei, was noted for its fine emergency and clinical services. It had a fairly large service area covering the

psychocultural viewpoint, with emphasis on changes that have occurred in the mode, attitude toward, and pattern of suicide from the past until the present.

Researchers, such as Kato (1970), have pointed out that in almost every area of the world there is considerable variation in the data over time. This means that many of the general statements concerning cause of suicidal death must be suspect. Articles about Chinese suicide, such as Yap's study in Hong Kong (1958), and Bourne's report from San Francisco (1970), for example, deal with one area within a given period of time. Since it seems to be universal that suicidal behavior is socioculturally affected and that its pattern changes rapidly, a cross-cultural epidemiology of suicide presents great difficulties in terms of methodology. The main focus of discussion in the present paper is on the mode and pattern of suicide of the Chinese, contrasting suicides in the traditional culture with those in the contemporary culture in Taiwan. Of course, this paper cannot apply to the suicide of those Chinese who live in other parts of the world.

In order to clarify how suicide is closely related to loyalty and close family ties, both of which are emphasized in Chinese society, it is necessary first to look into the history of China. To do this, the author will describe the Chinese attitude toward suicide, presenting both Confucian and Buddhist ideas about suicide. Changes occurring in the pattern of suicide will then be discussed, and data obtained in a series of suicide studies in Taipei will be presented.

PATTERNS OF SUICIDE IN THE HISTORY OF CHINA

From excavations of the prehistoric Shan culture, it was learned that numerous slaves, as many as 2,000, were sacrificed for a dead emperor.

---

northern half of Taipei city and suburbs. With thousands of emergency patients per month, it is the second largest clinic next to the university hospital. Superintendent Dr. M. S. Noordhoff, Vice-Superintendent Mr. C. W. Chang, and Rev. R. S. Lin had started, with missionary enthusiasm, pastoral counselling of suicide cases in 1968 with the assistance of a neuropsychiatrist, Dr. J. T. Liu. In March, 1968, the first Suicide Prevention Center was established in this hospital and a committee for a Suicide Prevention Center was organized, having members of interdisciplinary consultants, including ministers, psychiatrists, psychologists, and other allied field experts. Six case workers with backgrounds in nursing and the social worker fields have engaged in extensive intake and followup of suicide cases under supervision of the staff consultants. In the same year, the Taipei North Rotary Club donated two telephones to assist in the establishment of a life-line program. Presently, nearly a hundred volunteers with different professional backgrounds operate the telephone counselling service. In the following year, a second life-line program was established by religious groups in Kaohsung of southern Taiwan.

Anthropologists have not yet reached agreement as to whether those buried belonged to the clan people or were captured slaves. Most of the scholars discussed the possibility of a slave system used during the Shan dynasty on the basis of the discovery of such a huge scale of burial. Those sacrificed were probably forced to take poison and to be buried in the tomb of the emperor. It was believed that one way to assure the longevity and prosperity of the emperor in his afterworld was to bury a person who had committed suicide with him. This is a form of culturally imposed suicide.

To review the suicides of a country with such a long history as China is an exhaustive task and also beyond the purpose of this chapter. Nevertheless, several representative stories of suicide written in the history of China appear to be characteristic of legends and therefore reflect the cultural influence. The stories can be categorized into three forms of suicide patterns: 1) politics and/or war; 2) loyalty to nation, emperor, or master; and 3) family affiliation, such as wives' loyalty to their dead husband.

Early Ch'in Dynasty

During the absence of Ch'in's first emperor, Su-hong-teh, a political strategy took place in the emperor's palace around 210 B.C. The people had not been informed of the death of the emperor while he was on a mission of conquest eastward. The emperor's iced coffin was still on its way back to the home country. Without being aware of this event, Tsaukao and Lee-su secretly planned a coup for Fu-hai, one of the emperor's sons, by sending false letters allegedly signed by the emperor. One of these letters indicated the crimes and declared a death sentence for Fu-su, the emperor's first son and his successor, and for Mon-tien, the emperor's most trusted general, the Commander of War-Affairs with northern savages. Both of them killed themselves under the pressure of this threat.

Downfall of Ch'in Dynasty

Both Liu-pang and Hsian-yu were outstanding generals who defeated the Ch'in government troops. Later, however, competition between the two generals sharpened, and they used many tricks to conquer each other. Hsian-yu had several opportunities to kill Liu-pang but failed each time. In 202 B.C. Liu-pang, in the name of the first Han emperor, attacked the country of Tsu where Hsian-hu governed and defeated him in the battle of Hai-hsia. On the last night Hsian-yu escaped from the battlefield with 800 calvalry. Only 28 of them survived when he finally reached Wu-chian on the Yang-tze river. The place was near his native land but he refused to go all the way and instead killed himself with his sword. Before he committed suicide he said that he had lost face with his countrymen and elders and that he was ashamed of his failure. He was only 31.

Mass Suicide

Tien-hung, king of the Chi country, was defeated by Quang-yin, a general of Han, prior to the reunion of China by Han's emperor, Liu-pang. At that time, Tsu country had already been destroyed by Han. Tien-hung retreated to a coastal island with his 500 men where they continued to defend themselves against Han's conquest. The Han emperor invited him to come to Luo-yang city to negotiate his status. Tien-hung traveled to Luo-yang with two of his men, but he committed suicide just 30 miles before reaching his final destination. His two men buried him and killed themselves too. His 500 men on the island heard about Tien-hung's act, and all of them committed suicide to follow their king.

A Patriotic Poet–Chu-yuan

After a number of failures in political crises in Tsu, which, during the era of Chan-kuo, was under pressure from the Ch'in regimen in the north, the Tsu politician-poet, Chu-yuan, was finally dismissed by Tsu king Tze-lan. Chu-yuan wandered on the Yang-tze river with tremendous desperation and resentment. He continuously sang his sorrowful poems and became extremely disturbed and exhausted. A fisherman who met him asked, "Why are you wandering here?" He replied, "I was thrown away because I was the only pure person in this turbulent world and I was the only sober one among drunken people." The fisherman said, "A saint would disregard the trouble of the world, and he might follow the waves of the stream. Why should you destroy yourself having such a talent?" Chu-yuan replied, "One will brush dust from his hat and clothes after bathing. If I cannot remove dust from my cleansed body, I would rather drown in a great river and be buried in the stomach of a fish." He continued to wander and to compose his poems, completing nine chapters of poems. Finally, on May 5, 278 B.C., at the age of 67, he drowned himself in the river Mi-lo when he was informed that the Tsu country was entirely conquered by Ch'in. Later, in memory of Chu-yuan, people would throw glutinous rice dumplings to the fishes in the river Mi-lo in order to prevent them from eating the drowned body of the sorrowful poet.

Suicides were often brought about by the downfall of a dynasty. For instance, at end of the Song dynasty the following took place. After Yen's troops captured Kong, emperor of Song, premier Lu Shiu-fu and Chang

Su-chich supported Wei-wang as the emperor, who relocated at Ya-shan. Yen's general Chang Hong-fan surrounded Ya-shan with battle ships. Lu Shiu-fu then took the emperor on his own back and walked with him to his death into the sea. Chang Su-chich followed them. Another instance of suicide occurred at the end of the Ming dynasty. Before Ch'in took over the country, Lee Tsu-chen, a local militant, defeated the Ming troops and invaded most of the cities in the North. The Ming emperor, Su-chong, killed himself. Before he died, he commanded that all of his relatives commit suicide. When his daughter refused to do so, he killed her and then hanged himself.

As is written in our history, during turbulent times when a crisis arose it became necessary to choose between loyalty to the country (*chung*), loyalty to the husband (*tseng*), or loyalty to the father (*hsiao*). Many women bravely followed this culturally emphasized behavior. These women have been praised throughout history with the name of loyal women (*lieh-nü*). Some examples are presented below.

Captured Mother

At the end of the Han dynasty, China was divided into three countries (San-kuo). A brave and scholarly man, named Hsu-su, was a loyal subject of Liu-pei, the ruler of Shu country. However, Tsau-tsao of Wei country captured Hsu-su's mother and then sent him a false letter allegedly signed by his mother, asking him to join Tsau-tsao. Hsu-su then accepted Tsau-tsao's invitation to become an official of high rank. His mother, however, hanged herself, giving the reason that she would not ask her son to go against his loyalty to Liu-pei even though she had been captured by the opponent, and that she was ashamed of seeing her son because he was disloyal. Hsu-su never actively helped Tsau-tsao after this.

Ten Women's Grave

Several years after the establishment of the Ming dynasty by Tai-tsu, the emperor, the following story was recorded. Yueh-o was the daughter of a Yuen official, Ma Tin-lu, and was married to one of the Lu family. She was an extremely clever, learned, and loyal woman, and all the women of the clan families were taught by her. On one occasion, a group of mobile militants attacked the area where they lived, which was near the Yang-tze river. The women were evacuated to Tai-peng in order to obtain the protection of their strong army. However, when the town was defeated, Yueh-o took her young daughter in her arms and drowned herself and her daughter for her family's honor. Nine women followed Yueh-o and jumped into the water. It was said that because it was midsummer, their bodies did not float up for seven days, and when they were recovered from the waters of the river, their faces did not have the look of death on them—they seemed alive. People buried them together and built a 10-woman grave.

There are numerous tales of women who died because of loyalty to their families, appearing especially in the history of Ming and Ch'in. Chien Su-shen, the daughter of a Ming official, hanged herself at Yang-chou when Ch'in's troops defeated her country. At the end of the Ming dynasty when Yan-chou was defeated, all the family members of governor Len Ming-yu jumped into a well because of their loyalty to him. Several stories tell us about women and their performances of *tseng*, which is committing suicide out of loyalty to a dead husband. Again during the Ming dynasty a beautiful lady, Su Ko-tso, committed suicide when she was forced to marry an official named Nieh-shan after her husband's death. Another girl, named Kong at the age of 17 married a man of the Liu-wang family. The family was poor and her mother-in-law and her husband died successively in quick succession. A man who wanted her for her beauty tried to help her to buy coffins. She refused but he insisted. She sent her 6-year-old son and 3-year-old daughter to her mother, and that night she burned the house and died with her husband's body. During the Ch'in dynasty, Pong-Ta-su was a young native of Foo-nan. The military group of Lee Tsu-chen conquered the country and captured Pong's mother in order to rob her. Pon Ta-su deceived them saying that the money was concealed in the well, and led them away from his mother. He jumped into the well, and his wife also jumped in to follow him. Pong was only 18 and the couple had just been married 20 days before.

The legend of Tsao-o was written in the latter Han period, an earlier time in history. Fourteen-year-old Tsao-o's father drowned in the river on May 5th of that year. His body was never found. She cried at the riverside for 17 days and nights. Finally, she ended her own life by drowning herself in the same place. People built a memorial for her and named the river as well as the town Tsao-o. Although this story is only a legend, it illustrates the intense devotion felt by this girl for her father and is an example of the closeness of family ties in Taiwan. The last story is a rather complicated one in which mother-in-law and daughter conflict is interwoven. It was written in a long sorrowful poem (writer unknown), the famous *Kon-che Ton-nan-huei* ("flying peacock east-southward") during the Nan-pei dynasty.

The Sorrowful Life

There was a very clever woman named Liu Lan-tse, whose husband was a civil worker. She could weave white silk at the age of 13, could make dresses at 14, could play music at 15, and also could memorize numerous poems. She married her husband at 17, but her mother-in-law neither appreciated nor accepted her capable work. Although the couple loved each other, she was finally forced by the mother-in-law to divorce. Ten days later she returned to her maiden home, and a remarriage contract was arranged by a matchmaker. The second proposal came from a man of a good family. She accepted the marriage proposal only because her elder brother insisted, but 1 day before the wedding ceremony, she jumped in a pond and drowned herself. Her ex-husband heard about her suicide and hanged himself on a tree in the garden. Both of them were buried together in Hwa-shan.

Similar stories are found in the history of the same dynasty. A wife named Hsung-tsai married to the Yin family at age 17, had a baby girl at age 19. Her husband died shortly thereafter. She hanged herself when she was forced into remarriage by her father. Another story illustrates again the widow's refusal of remarriage. The wife of Liu Chang-chin had a baby boy, but lost her husband during the 5th year of their marriage. She refused to go back to her maiden home in order to avoid the possibility of remarriage. When her son died at age 15, she even cut her ears off to refuse forcible remarriage. She believed that a woman who was brought up in a Confucian family had to be loyal to her spouse. Premier Wan-chi of Pei country reported this matter to the Emperor to praise her.

PUBLIC ATTITUDE TOWARD SUICIDE

A ghost house on Ping-chian Street of Taipei is well known by the inhabitants of the city. Because the area in which the house is located is on the direct path of the Taipei Airport, there are not many buildings, it is especially dark at night, and the house is in ruins. It is built in the old colonial style, a thick-walled, concrete, white mansion. During World War II, the family of a Japanese naval officer resided in the house, and his wife committed suicide, allegedly by hanging, for reasons that are unknown. Because people often heard the woman's weeping voice thereafter, the house was considered haunted. It was abandoned by the owner after the war, and nobody has lived in it for nearly 30 years. Fear of the ghost has kept it empty.

A few years ago, a shrewd merchant invested in the house, added some new construction, and introduced it as a possible building to be used as a mental hospital. However, so much fuss was made about the woman's ghost that there was no possibility of establishing a mental hospital in that house. The merchant insisted that mentally sick persons would not fear a ghost, so why not use the house as a treatment center?

This story illustrates the Chinese attitude toward suicide. If a suicide occurs out of loyalty to the family or in order to save face, then the suicide is accepted, but when suicide occurs because of deep unhappiness or mental illness then people respond with the deepest fear. It is a fear so strong that one avoids hearing or going close to the place where a person committed suicide.

It would be correct to say that, in general, fear and avoidance of talk about suicide is the attitude of most people in Taiwan. However, it does not explain the attitudes of all Chinese. Also, to say that people consider the immediate surroundings of the suicide to be haunted is not a sufficient explanation either. In spite of the above story, the Chinese do not think that every soul of a suicide becomes a ghost and creates fear among people. Buddhists believe that the soul of a man who killed himself remains in hell where it receives eternal punishment and is not allowed to reincarnate into a future life. In the history of China, numerous stories of loyal women's suicide have been written. Those women chose to die when they lost their husband, often when they were being forced to remarry. Tales of such loyal women's suicide (*lieh-nu tsuang*) stressed the greatness of women's loyalty to the family, even at the price of death. Hence the spirit was culturally praised and encouraged. Suicide in Chinese culture from ancient times to the present seems to involve complex aspects of change. However, there is a tendency for suicide to be closely bound up with the cultural attitudes toward the family, as DeVos (1962) found in Japan, and it seems to occur most frequently in those who hold onto the cultural traditions most tightly.

Confucianism stressed the virtue of family affiliation with the teaching that one should not injure his own body, even his hair and skin, because it is given to him by his parents. In the Chinese mind, with such structurized doctrines of family duty, self-mutilative or self-destructive behavior is unacceptable. Although there is no exact dictum that one should not attempt suicide, suicide is prohibited within the framework of Confucius' teachings, except for the occasion when one would indicate his loyalty to an organization to which he or she belongs.

An interesting epilogue can be presented from the author's experience in a psychiatric examination of a case of patricide. A 19-year-old schizophrenic boy killed his father under the delusion that his father was trying to poison him by putting pills in a glass of cider. He strangled his father with a necktie when he became upset about his father's refusal to give him pocket money. The psychiatric examination concluded that the patient was overtly schizophrenic and suggested that criminal responsibility must be exempted. However, the judge gave him a death sentence. There was a strong reaction to the judge's ignorance of criminal responsibility. Some scholars agreed with the judge's decision because to them the killing of one's father is the greatest crime in the Chinese culture. Thus, destroying one's father deserves the maximal punishment. This cultural attitude and judgment about patricide naturally conflicted with the law which would have reduced or denied criminal responsibility to one who is mentally ill. Mass communication pointed this out and called for forensic experts' opinion to discuss this. Finally, with pressure from the press, the judge changed the sentence to second degree homicide, effecting a compromise between cultural belief and the concepts of modern law. Later, we learned that the patient was sent to a custodial mental hospital for 6 years of confinement and treatment. This case of patricide represents how the Confucius educational system and public thoughts are so much influenced by the traditional approach to filial devotion.

The Buddhist's attitude toward suicidal behavior appears to be different from Confucianist thoughts. Buddhists think that human life is primarily one of stress. One should tolerate any difficulty of life from his childhood through his adulthood and should aim at happiness in old age. In other words, everyone in the world should share common distresses of life, serve others, and strive for enlightenment in his old age. In this way it becomes possible to be reborn as a human in the afterworld. Otherwise, if one cannot tolerate stress, if one becomes angry and fights or breaks human rules, one would be reborn in the form of an animal in the afterworld to compensate for his faults. One who destroys his own life would remain in a hundred-year-hell and would not be reincarnated in any form.[3]

Buddhists think that suicide occurs because of one's lack of tolerance or patience toward stress. Buddhists would try to help those who are so desperate that they would destroy themselves. The Buddhists have pity for them and try to rescue and guide them with mercy. They want to try to help those who are suffering without accusing them of misbehavior. Here, we can see again some sanction against suicidal behavior in Buddhistic concepts, although it is accompanied with sympathy, regret, and a feeling of mercy to the client which is not seen in Confucian doctrine.

In the contemporary society of Taiwan, Confucian educational influence and Buddhist-Taoistic beliefs are interwoven in the mind of the general population so that, within the cultural context, the general attitude toward suicidal behavior is seen as pitiful, regretful, shameful, and

[3] In addition, there is a saying among Taiwanese that the soul of a deceased by hanging could not be rescued from hell unless another person hangs in the same place within 3 years, upon which his soul would be replaced by the new one. However, in our community we do not see the traditional belief that the soul of the deceased by hanging would haunt and torment those in the immediate vicinity.

weak, as well as foolish. Such attitudes are directly influenced by the traditional culture. The Chinese generally would not think the suicidal act is courageous or brave, but also they would not think it should be condemned.

Suicide is not regarded as a crime in Taiwan, unlike other regions of the world where unsuccessful suicides may be legally confined to an appointed hospital. As has already been mentioned, the general attitude toward suicide is rather sympathetic; it is certainly not condemned and punished. However, there is one particular attitude that considers the significant other(s) as having contributed to the suicide. As a result, the close relatives of the deceased seek ways to protect themselves from other people's condemnatory attitude, especially by use of various projections. There is some evidence that the use of projection as a way of dealing with interpersonal difficulties became most prevalent during the after-migration period.[4] Since 1949, 2 million Chinese mainlanders have migrated to this island. At first, there was chaotic social disorganization, but in the past 2 decades Taiwan has undergone rapid development. An almost entirely new style of social life has been established, although the aftereffect of the migration still remains. Among the psychiatric symptoms of Taiwanese inpatients compared cross-culturally with Japanese and American patients, it has been found that outwardedly expressed hostility is more prevalent among Chinese patients than among patients of other cultures.[5] The outwardly directed hostility in verbal and behavior symptoms is also frequently seen among attempted suicides. Many of them, especially female patients, show extreme anger and temper outbursts prior to turning back their aggression on themselves. This has become a typical pattern of behavior among our patients and is seen much more frequently than other types of suicidal behavior such as masochistic or nihilistic behavior.

EPIDEMIOLOGICAL FINDINGS IN SUICIDE

Official reports of completed suicide in Taiwan during the postwar period showed an average rate of 15 to 16 per 100,000, which would indicate an

[4] Paranoid patterns and the effect of migration were studied and reported by the author and his colleagues (Rin *et al.*, Hsu, and Liu, 1958; Rin *et al.*, Wu, and Lin, 1962; Yeh, 1962).

[5] A cross-cultural study of psychiatric inpatients in Taiwan, Japan, and the United States has been carried out by Rin, Caudill, and Schooler (National Institute of Mental Health grant MH12733). In the preliminary analysis, it was found that Japanese patients show more inwardly suppressed symptoms such as depression, obsession, and *shinkeishitsu* (nervous temperament), while Taiwan Chinese patients show more outward hostility in their symptoms. Compared to these two Oriental

upper medium range of frequency in the list of countries reporting to the World Health Organization. During the past decade, however, the rate dropped to 8 or 9. Suicidal death is usually reported by family members to the police station; an on-call public prosecutor accompanies the forensic physician to make an investigation and certification. All of their records are filed and kept in the police department permanently, and, except for the official statistical report, the contents are not open to the public or for research surveys. Therefore, only the suicides reported in newspapers allow us to know what has happened in those cases.

In spite of the limited amount of information, we still can see from the newspaper cases such statistics as age, sex, precipitating factors, and methods of suicide.[6] The general figures reveal that younger females aged 15 to 24 (which make up 60 percent of all females) and males above 30 (especially 30 to 49, which make up 40 percent of all males) showed heightened rates of completed suicides, with the number of males exceeding females by 10 percent. Frustrated love affairs, marital discord, and conflict with a family member were reported in female cases, while a higher rate of criminal and legal activity and severe social maladaptation were given as the reasons of suicide for males. Both used sleeping pills and other poisons for suicide (90 percent of the total suicides). Younger persons (below age 29) seemed to commit suicide out of environmental or interpersonal difficulties more frequently, while older persons committed suicide more out of mental or physical illnesses. Among other findings, it was noted that the male Chinese over age 40 who had migrated showed a higher rate of suicide, while native Taiwanese between the ages of 30 and 39 also were a high risk group. The latter cases involved criminal and legal problems fairly often, but special attention should be given the former because of their dreadful experience of migration and broken homes.

In the data on attempted suicide among psychiatric inpatients (Rin, 1972), there was evidence that during the years 1952 to 1954, the years of mass migration, the mainland Chinese had a much higher incidence of suicide compared with the Taiwanese. Migrant housewives aged 30 to 39 were particularly affected and showed the highest rate of attempted suicide during that period. It is known that chaotic mass migration influenced the whole life of the family. Marital discord and other socio-

---

cultures, American patients tend to show more breaks with reality, *i.e.*, delusions and hallucinations. The above findings strongly suggest a positive relation between symptom cluster patterns and personality traits which are culturally determined.

[6] Rin *et al.* (in preparation *a*). There were 568 suicides and attempted suicides reported in five newspapers in Taipei during the year 1969 to 1971. Our most popular newspaper, *Lieh-ho-pao*, reported 364 cases from the Taipei area, and an analysis has been made of these patients. Two hundred and forty-eight out of 364 cases (68 percent) were committed suicides.

psychological difficulties became frequent. In the last 15 years, the symptoms resulting from migration have almost completely disappeared. For this reason, we can say that there was evidence of increased violence, aggression, and suicide which was a direct result of the anomic involuntary migration.

Although it is not an easy task to identify the year a rising rate of attempted suicides appeared, it is known that the number of suicides brought to emergency services of the large general hospitals in Taipei seemed to increase in 1968 to 1969. The author and his colleagues have analyzed the suicide attempts at Mackay Memorial Hospital during the year 1969 to 1971 and found that 1,286 cases of attempted suicides were collected by the Suicide Prevention Center Clinic.[7] The data showed identical trends in sex, age, precipitating factors, and method of suicide compared with the completed suicides reported in newspapers. The majority of attempted suicides were young females, aged 15 to 29, and native Taiwanese of lower socioeconimic background. These findings are shared by other Asian countries. However, the heightened rate of attempted suicides among the aged occurring in Japanese or Chinese communities in Occidental societies is not a part of our picture. The majority of cases took sleeping pills or other poisons in their attempt. Male patients showed more violent and severe destructive acts in suicide than female patients. The most frequent reasons for suicide were related to interpersonal conflict associated with love affairs, marital discord in the earlier stages of marriage, and clashes with family members through various kinds of incompatibility.

Special attention must be given to the major precipitating factors of suicide attempts by female patients. The most frequent instance was marital discord, which included the husband's extramarital affair, suspicion of the husband's infidelity, quarrels on miscellaneous matters of family life, etc. The second most frequent reason for the suicide attempt was a frustrated love affair in which again there was incompatibility on both sides, frustrated dependency needs, abandonment of love relations, competition with another girl to catch a boy, etc. The love affair usually involved a married man. Those cases attempted suicide as a method of holding the man's affection and obtaining economic support, especially because of pressures from the man's family. The third most frequent

---

[7] Rin *et al.* (in preparation *b*). This study is aimed at exploring sociopsychological factors of attempted suicides in Taipei. Data kept in the Suicide Prevention Center files at Mackay Hospital during the year 1969 to 1971 were analyzed. There were 2,105 registrations with suspicion of suicidal behavior, but, after screening out missing files, causes of accidents, and cases with suicidal ideas only, 1,286 cases of attempted suicides remained. Detailed analysis of the data is in preparation.

reason for suicide was conflict with the family in relation to dating or marriage. One specific situation was the girl who met objections from her parents because of her desired marriage with her lover. This involved a clash between the traditional family attitude toward marriage and the free choice of a marriage partner by the younger generation. The suicide attempts of young females because of such conflicts deserve special attention.

Hanging and drowning were the most common methods used in suicide until several decades ago. Usually hanging resulted in higher rate of mortality than drowning which generally resulted in approximately a 50 percent mortality rate. Nowadays, sleeping pills and other chemicals that are easily obtainable are used most often for suicide. Jumping from a high building has become more common as new construction of buildings in city areas has increased. The latter naturally shows higher mortality rate than the former. Use of insecticides or rodenticides and other poisons also results in fairly high risk of lethality. Such cases are more apt to come from rural areas.

Guns, explosives, burning, and banging of the head are fairly violent methods, as are cutting and slashing. However, the former four kinds of methods are not frequently found. Several cases of persons who used guns against love partners and the family and finally himself have been reported. For example, a 30-year-old single man shot a girl because of frustration in a one-sided love affair. Another man in his thirties shot a girl and her mother when his marital arrangement was disrupted by the girl's family. Explosives were violently used in a very similar occasion. A 33-year-old man killed his 20-year-old mistress and himself with explosives when his wife ran away from home. Another pair of young lovers committed suicide with explosives in a hotel room. A 60-year-old man exploded himself because of his fear of being sentenced for causing a forest fire.

Burning is a rare method. Such cases burned themselves in different ways and with apparently bizarre, psychotic symptoms. Banging of the head seemed to occur in a particular situation, such as clients attempting suicide while being confined in a mental institution or jail. Among our cases, gas intoxication played no role, in spite of the increasing usage of gas stoves in general households.

CONCLUSIONS

Causal factors and symptoms of suicide are correlated to the cultural context. The reasons for suicide usually centered around the family relationship in our culture. This was true in ancient history and it is also true today, although the style or pattern of problems involved has greatly changed. This chapter summarizes a review of suicide in the history of China and suicide in the contemporary culture of Taiwan and describes what has happened in the change of the pattern of suicide and in the attitude toward suicide.

It is striking that suicide and attempted suicide are over-represented by young females of lower class background who believe strongly in the old cultural tradition. For this the following explanations are given. Love affairs have become common among the younger generation, although it is generally a fairly new experience in our society. The model for it has been generally provided through mass communication devices; its source is mainly from Western culture. Young females with limited education are apt to clash with their boy friends and their family members because they have not yet grown mature enough to cope with love affairs. Suicide in today's society occurs more frequently because of conflicts in the family relationship. Moreover, the mode of suicide seems to be more overtly aggressive and goes against the old cultural attitudes. Hence, the submissive and masochistic attitudes shown in the past traditional society no longer remain. The older generation gradually has come to accept the younger people's love affairs. However, they still adhere to the traditional attitude and are embarrassed and ashamed with the free love behavior of their offsprings. A frustrated love affair is one of the most frequent reasons of suicide occurring among young females in Taiwan.

It is necessary to explore further the nature of the immature personality development in young females, as well as the socioeconomic changes which are taking place so quickly, such as mobilization, broken families, and lack of proper parental identification, all of which are seen more often in the lower classes. Moreover, many of the young female suicides come from mobile populations with rural family background. These people are drawn to the city area where rapid industrial expansion has taken place in the past several years. Another factor would be that young males are mobilized into the military, so that the proportions of young females exceeds that of the males among the population. Thus, suicidal behavior is seen to be closely related to the changing attitudes and economic system in a modernizing society, and the suicide act reflects the uncertainty of new behavior patterns and goals of life of the younger generation.

It was not until World War II that concubines became unusual in Chinese society. In a rich family, concubines were allowed to exist and institutionalized marriage operated as a system for the sake of succession of the family. In the postwar era, or perhaps even 2 or 3 decades earlier, monogamy became the standard marriage pattern and the nuclear type of family began to increase. Although concubines are now almost nonexistent in ordinary families, men still follow the old tradition of keeping mistresses outside the marriage. Some young females prefer the status of mistress in order to reach economic stabilization. Thus, common law marriage has been maintained in an altered form. Extramarital affairs of these partners often create conflicts with either their wives or their mistresses. Suicide by these women is quite common among our patients.

With the development of economic life and the increased number of nuclear families, traditional mother-in-law and daughter conflict seems to have diminished. However, we still find suicide cases that are the result of this problem. It is our observation that the background conflict between mother-in-law and daughter itself would not be a direct cause of suicide, but that such conflict usually results in discord between the married couple. Young husbands and wives often quarrel in situations where the wife felt seriously frustrated because the husband took the side of his mother, or he remained ambivalent between his mother and wife. Suicide was likely to occur with those wives who felt they were losing their husbands' affection.

A passing but extremely chaotic time with much social disorganization was caused by the mass migration of so many from mainland China to Taiwan. Stress and crisis were particularly seen in migrant families, and the suicide risk was very high among this group, especially among housewives in their thirties. This tells us that social disorganization strongly affects family life. As time has passed, the effect of the migration has gradually faded away and the suicide rate of both migrant and host groups has become equal. However, some migration aftereffects are still seen in the suicide case histories. The most violent type of suicide, with guns and explosives, is generally used by men in their thirties, more by migrants, often in homicide-suicide pattern. Burning was another type of violent method but was more common among psychotic persons.

REFERENCES

Bourne, P. G. 1970. Suicide in the Chinese of San Francisco. *Transcultural Psychiatric Research Review*, 7:210–212.

DeVos, G. A. 1962. Deviancy and social change: A psychocultural evaluation of trends in Japanese delinquency and suicide. In: R. J. Smith and R. K. Beardsley (Eds.), *Japanese Culture: Its Development and Characteristics*. Aldine Publishing Company, Chicago.

Kato, M. 1970. Self-destruction in Japan: A crosscultural epidemiological analysis of suicide. *Transcultural Psychiatric Research Review*, 7:14–15.

Okumura, N. 1943. Takasagozoku no jisatsu (Über den Selbstmord der

Takasago-Rassen; Urvölker in Taiwan). *Journal of the Medical Association of Taiwan*, 42:200–214.

Rin, H. 1961. An investigation into the incidence and clinical symptoms of mental disorders among Formosan Aborigines. *Psychiatria Neurologia Japonica*, 53, 480–500.

Rin, H. 1972. A study of attempted suicides among psychiatric inpatients. *Journal of the Formosan Medical Association*, 71:89–96.

Rin, H., Cheng, L. T., and Chen, T. How a newspaper tells us suicide stories. In preparation *a*.

Rin, H., Cheng, L. T., and Shieh, F. M. Attempted suicides in Taipei. In preparation *b*.

Rin, H., Hsu, C. C., and Liu, S. L. 1958. The characteristics of paranoid in present-day Taiwan. *Memoirs of the Faculty of Medicine, National Taiwan University*, 5:1–15.

Rin, H., Wu, K. C., and Lin, C. L. 1962. A study of delusions and hallucinations manifested by Chinese paranoid psychotics. *Journal of the Formosan Medical Association*, 61:46–57.

Yap, P. M. 1958. *Suicide in Hong Kong with Special Reference to Attempted Suicide*. Oxford University Press, Oxford.

Yeh, E. K. 1972. Paranoid manifestations among Chinese students studying abroad: Some preliminary findings. In: W. P. Lebra (Ed.), *Transcultural Research In Mental Health*. East-West Center Press, Honolulu.

seventeen

CHARACTERISTICS OF SUICIDES AND ATTITUDES TOWARD SUICIDE IN JAPAN

MAMORU IGA, PH.D.,
and KICHINOSUKE TATAI, M.D., M.P.H.

The purposes of this paper are 1) to describe Japanese suicides, 2) to analyze the suicide of Yukio Mishima as an example, 3) to discuss Japanese attitudes toward suicide, and 4) to draw some generalizations.

JAPANESE SUICIDES

Japan has been one of the leading nations in suicide rates. The uniqueness of Japanese suicides is found in their traditional pattern of suicide, types of suicides, and the current suicidal picture.

Japan's rates were 18 per 100,000 in 1901, then 19 in 1910 and 1920, then 22 in 1930, and 14 in 1940. It was at this time that Japan was engaged in a major war in China. In 1950, the rate climbed once more to 20, and to 25 in 1955. Since then the rate has declined to 21 in 1960 and 14 in 1967.

Pattern of Japanese Suicides

While suicide rates generally increase with age in Western countries, Japan shows double peaks for youth and aged people. Thus, the rate for males in

1952 to 1954 went from 26 for ages 15 to 19 to 60 in ages 20 to 24, then down to 24 in the middle ages 30 to 49, and back to 96 for ages 70 and over.

The suicide rate for Japanese females is the highest among modern nations. In 1952 to 1954, their rate was 36 for ages 20 to 24, and 22 for 25 to 29 age groups. They also show a double peak, with the rate declining to 16 in ages 30 to 49 and rising to 66 for ages 70 and over.

The rate for Japanese females 20 to 24 years of age was more than 6 times that for the American counterpart in 1963 (26 versus 4, respectively) and about 1.5 times as large in 1967 (13 versus 8, respectively). The rate for the 75-and-over group was about 10 times that of the American counterpart (57 versus 8, respectively, in 1963, and 66 versus 6, respectively, in 1967). The ratio of male to female suicide rates was 1 for Japan in 1955 (22 to 19), while all other major nations show much higher ratios for males (for example, Britain, 1.7; Denmark, 2.1; Sweden, 3.2; and the United States, 3.5). The 1 to 1 ratio did not change in 1968, in contrast to the average ratio of suicides in the United States, which is about 3 males to 1 female (Seiden, 1969, p. 13).

While suicide was the second major cause of death for Japanese males 15 to 29 years of age in 1966, it was the primary cause for the female counterpart. Thus, for males 15 to 29, accident accounted for approximately 45 percent of the deaths, while suicide was about 13 percent. For females 15 to 29, suicide was first with about 20 percent of the deaths, while accident was second with about 13 percent in ages 15 to 24, and cancer was second in ages 25 to 29 with 14 percent.

The ratio of successful suicide to attempted suicide is also about 1:1 for young Japanese females from 19 to 29 and for males 20 to 29, but for older males and older females, successful suicide rates are much higher than the rates for attempted suicides (Okazaki, 1958, p. 149). In contrast, the comparable ratio for American males is about 1 to 1, but for females it is about 1 to 10 (Okazaki, 1958, p. 148).

While in Western countries cities usually show higher suicide rates than do rural areas, there is little difference between them in Japan. While only three of 46 Japanese prefectures in 1955 showed markedly higher suicide rate for cities, the rural population showed a higher suicide rate in 17 prefectures. For the remaining 26 prefectures there was no consistent difference between the two areas. It is also to be noted that rural areas in the Kinki region (which includes Kyoto, Osaka, Hyozo, Nara, Wakayama, and Shiga prefectures) show the highest rates of suicide—higher than cities in the same region and also rural areas in the other regions. The suicide rate is not related with the rural-urban difference for young persons, but rural areas show higher rates for persons above 40 years old (Naka, 1966*a*, p. 107).

While most suicides in Western countries seem to occur during the daytime, most Japanese suicides occur at night (Okazaki, 1958, p. 55). The suicide-homicide ratio also shows a Japanese uniqueness. In 1950, the crude suicide rate was 19.6 in contrast with the homicide rate of 2.2. The ratio was about 9:1, in contrast with 4:1 for white males and females, and 0.1:1.0 for nonwhite males and females, respectively, in the United States (Tatai, 1952, p. 13). While the suicide rate appears to be inversely related to the violent crime rate in the United States, Japanese rates show a complicated picture. Their suicide rate increased from 17 to 61 per 100,000 in Japanese youth from 15 through 24 years of age during the years 1948 to 1955. However, their homicide rate was almost constant, between 15 and 16 for the same period. At the same time, their rate for other violent crimes such as rape kept pace with the suicide rate, increasing from 17 to 40.

In Western countries, suicide is generally not related to economic status, or, when it is, there seems to be a direct relationship. However, in Japan the relationship is inverse—the lower the socioeconomic status the higher the suicide rate. The suicide rate for the 20- to 24-year-old male is 129 for the unemployed, 77 for the employed, and 36 for the man employed by a big firm in 1955 (Naka, 1966*b*, p. 56). Since the unemployed includes college students, whose rate was about 31 that year, the rate for the unemployed excluding the students would be much higher than 129. When the average of the suicide rates of those engaged in all occupations, 15 years old and above, is regarded as 100, the index in 1965 for agriculture and fishing was 151, and that for mining was 144. In contrast, the indexes for white collar occupations were much lower: clerical (67), service (73), sales (77), and professional (80) (The Ministry of Welfare, 1966, p. 59). Naka found that suicidal victims in rural areas are generally from poor families and rural areas generally are much lower than cities in average annual income (Naka, 1966*a*, p. 126). Also young suicidal victims in rural areas are more likely ill persons or returnees from cities where they failed in work, both indicating economic difficulties (Naka, 1966*a*, p. 120).

Types of Suicides

The uniqueness of Japanese suicides is also indicated by their distribution in terms of method, motive, and participants.

Distribution in Method The dominant method of Japanese suicides up until the 1950's had been hanging; after that pills became the primary method. In 1955, suicides by poison, pills, and gas accounted for 39 percent of the total suicides in that country, followed by hanging (28 percent), drowning (13 percent), "killed by train" (11 percent), and others

(4 percent). Among college students in the same year, the distribution was sleeping pills, poison, and gas (71 percent); hanging (10 percent); drowning (5 percent); jump from height (4 percent); cutting (1 percent); and "railway and others" (8 percent). Some of these methods, which reveal important characteristics of Japanese suicides, will be briefly explained.

Dokuyaku Jisatsu (Suicide by Poison and Sleeping Pills) Suicide by rat poison had been a common method among Japanese people before sleeping pills became easily accessible. Ryuunosuke Akutagawa, a famous writer who killed himself with sleeping pills, is partly responsible for popularizing this method. The special significance that sleeping pills have to Japanese, who are strongly sensitive to the appearance after death, is evident in Akutagawa's note: "My first concern was how to die easily. Hanging satisfies this purpose, but imagining the ugliness of myself hanged dead, I felt by it. . . . I decided to use sleeping pills" (Kato, 1965, p. 230).

Jusui Jisatsu (Drowning) Around the end of the second century Ototachibana-Hime drowned herself to appease the Sea God so that her husband's ship would be saved in a stormy sea. In the 15th century, many Buddhists of Jyodo-Sect drowned themselves, following the teaching of *enri-odo gongu-jodo* ("forsake the filthy world, and joyfully seek for the Pure Land") (Nishimoto, 1966, pp. 342–43). This method was particularly prevalent among females during the Tokugawa Period.

Tooshin Jisatsu, or Minage (Jumping from Height) Leaping from a high place became a prominent type of Japanese suicide since 1903, when Fujimura Misao, a college student, jumped from the Kegon Fall, leaving a philosophical note in a form of Chinese poem. His suicide was extolled as the first suicide for the purpose of merging oneself into Nature. In the subsequent 8 years, there occurred about 200 completed and attempted suicides at the same place. When a college coed leaped into Mihara-yama volcano in 1933, 804 males and 140 females imitated her by jumping to their deaths at the same place.

Hara-kiri or Seppuku (Self-disembowelment) *Hara-kiri* is the most typically Japanese suicide, because it requires a much greater degree of fortitude than ordinary persons can muster. About *hara-kiri*, Tatai (1970) stated:

> "*Hara-kiri* began about 1,000 years ago, during the initial state of feudalism in Japan. The hara-kiri as an honorable suicide to avoid being captured. At first he stabbed a short sword into the left abdomen, moved to the right, and then pulled it out. Again he stabbed it into the epigastrium, and cut down vertically. Finally he gouged the throat by it. This act was a show of bravery because instant death was not expected. Since about 400 years ago, *hara-kiri* was used as an honored penalty death for the Samurai, while the commoner was hung

to death in the plaza. *Hara-kiri* then became a ritual; the condemned man stabbed a short sword into the left abdomen, cut to the right, cut up, and then pulled it out. Immediately after this act, his head was severed with a long sword by one of his friends who stood by, presumably to help him to an easier death."

Classification by Motive

Junshi (Suicide following the Master's Death) Until the middle of the 7th century, when a high status person died, his wife, retainers, and slaves followed him or were buried alive with him. Their spirits were believed needed to serve him in the afterlife. The forced *junshi* was banned in 659 and figurines were buried instead. A modern example of *junshi* was committed by General Nogi and his wife after the death of the Meiji Emperor in 1912.

Gisei-shi (Sacrificial Suicide) Sacrificial suicide is exemplified by Ototachibana-Hime, referred to above. All through the history of Japanese suicide, self-sacrifice has occupied a prominent place, although often the "self-sacrifice" was forced. For example, a victim who was called *hito-bashira* ("human pillar") was buried under the foundation of a bridge for the pupose of appeasing the river god and to facilitate the construction of the bridge. There were elements of involuntariness in some of the cases of the *kamikaze* (suicide) pilots during the last war. According to Dr. Kato, many of them used alcohol or amphetamines (*The Kashu Mainichi*, Nov. 10, 1970). This might have been for the purpose of numbing fear or stifling any elements of resistance or resentment.

Funshi or Munenbara (Suicide for Indignation or Mortification) Fun-shi or *munenbara* is *hara-kiri* based on dire resentment, hatred, and enmity. Although there is no way to know its proportion to total suicides, it is important because it symbolizes a society in which there is little available to inferiors who want to express their indignation toward superiors.

Kashitsu-shi or Sokotsu-bara (Suicide for Expiating Mistakes) Ka-shitsu-shi or *sokotsu-bara* symbolizes a society where a mistake may have to be paid for by death. "During World War II, a young naval reserve officer, a graduate of a commercial college, committed *hara-kiri* when he could not complete his assigned task within a given period of time" (Seward, 1968, p. 38). A school master committed suicide because the Emperor's portrait in his charge was burned. Whether he was responsible for the outbreak of the fire is not important, but the "negligence" that resulted in the burning of Emperor's portrait must, he felt, be redeemed even by suicide.

Kanshi or Kangenshi (Suicide for Remonstration) Suicide for remonstration is also typical of an authoritarian society, where an inferior often had to kill himself in order to communicate a criticism to his superior.

Even with suicide, there was no guarantee that his criticism would be acknowledged. This type of suicide apparently is not frequent in modern Japan, but in the senior author's research in 1968, one of the 72 completed suicides studied appears to have been classified.

Classification by Number of Participants Suicides committed by a number of persons together is called *shinju*, which is subdivided into *jyoshi* ("love pact suicide") and *oyako shinju* ("parent-child suicide"). Of 1,281 *shinju* in 1954, 72 percent were *jyoshi* and 22 percent were *oyako shinju*. Of *jyoshi*, 92 percent were heterosexual love pact suicides, and 5 percent were homosexual. Fifteen percent of *jyoshi* suicides were between husband and wife. *Jyoshi* includes *muri-shinju*, in which one partner forces the other to commit suicide or kills the partner to take with him. It is actually a murder-suicide. This type is estimated at about 12 percent of *jyoshi* (Ohara, 1965*a*, p. 229).

Although a case of *jyoshi* between a prince and his "incestuous" sweetheart is recorded in Kojiki (compiled in 712 A.D.), it did not become a popular phenomenon until the end of the 17th century. The increasingly rigid class stratification, the constrained code of behavior, and its enforcement with severe punishment prevented the free expression of human feelings. Love between unmarried persons became "immoral," to be punished by parent or employer. Even affection between a Samurai and his wife was disapproved because it would weaken the Samurai spirit, *i.e.*, the readiness to die for his master. A product of this social condition was an increase in *jyoshi*, especially between a commoner male and a brothel prostitute. Monzaemon Chikamatsu, a Japanese Shakespeare, glorified the love and suicide of suppressed persons in his innumerable plays, all of which had great influence upon modern Japanese. The tendency to glorify *jyoshi* is still a potent cause of Japanese suicides today.

In *oyako shinju*, a parent or parents kill their children first and then commit suicide. In Japanese thinking, *oyako shinju* is a merciful deed on the basis that it would be happier for children to die with their parents rather than to suffer in this harsh world without parental protection. In 1954, there were about 400 *oyako shinju*—more than one case per day. Of this type, 73 percent were committed by the mother, 3 percent by the father, and 3 percent by both parents. Of the *oyako shinju* committed by the mother, 66 percent involved one child; 24 percent, 2 children; 8 percent, 3 children; and 2 percent, 4 children. Those committed by the father or by both parents seem to involve a larger number of children than above (Ohara, 1965*a*, p. 269). The great frequency of *oyako shinju* among the Japanese suggest such important features of Japanese society as: 1) general poverty and a lack of social welfare services; 2) Japanese thinking that is characterized by *mujo-kan* ("view of the world as fleeting and everlasting change"), by an excessive emphasis on obligation and shame, and by a view of death as a salvation; 3) emphasis on group (*e.g.*, family) and the sacrifice of the individual; 4) extremely intense emotional attachment between mother and child and the tendency to regard children as parental possessions; 5) lack of spiritual support in times of frustration; and 6) the predilection for nonrational, esthetic responses along with the tendency to romanticize death (Ohara, 1965*a*, pp. 254–266).

Current Suicidal Activity

Despite the rapid decline in the suicide rates, suicide is still a major topic in current news in Japan. On November 25, 1970, Yukio Mishima, a Nobel Prize candidate for literature, committed *hara-kiri* with one of his followers. A few months later, a university student stole a national treasure sword from a show case at the Kanazawa Museum and committed *hara-kiri* there. In October 1970, a leader of a student movement at Waseda University poured gasoline over his body and burned himself to death (*Bungei Shunju*, Dec. 1970, p. 189). Half a month before, a similar suicide was committed by a high school student in Kobe (*The Kashu Mainichi*, Sept. 28, 1970). In Akita Prefecture, which is one of the low suicide rate prefectures, a 14-year-old girl and a 15-year-old boy, separately and within a 2-month period, poured gasoline on themselves and burned themselves to death (*The Shuukan Asahi*, March 13, 1970). In summer, 1969, four Japanese professors killed themselves "apparently despondent over university problems" (*The Los Angeles Times*, Sept. 20, 1969; *the Kashu Mainichi*, Oct. 14, 1969). One of them committed *hara-kiri* with a kitchen knife. In September of the same year, the director of Tokyo Medical and Dental University Hospital hanged himself "because of campus strife and his inability to handle it" (*The Los Angeles Times*, Sept. 20, 1969). Japan tops the world in the number of old women committing suicide. At least 10 Japanese aged 60 or over kill themselves every day (*The Los Angeles Times*, Oct. 7, 1969). These news items suggest that major factors making for a high suicide rate are still potent in that country. The 1963 and 1967 suicide rates for older Japanese are much higher than their counterparts in Sweden, which shows higher suicide rates for total population than Japan.

SUICIDE OF YUKIO MISHIMA: AN EXAMPLE OF JAPANESE SUICIDE

An immediate cause of suicide is a definition of the situation that is characterized by a goal-means discrepancy and an alienated conception of self, together with a self-destructive response to the definition. The response is largely determined by: a) the victim's attitudes toward life, death, and suicide; and b) the attitudes of others toward the victim and toward suicide in general. In this section, the suicide of Yukio Mishima, a Nobel Prize candidate for literature in 1970, will be analyzed in terms of his suicidogenic definition of the situation and his response to it.

Goal-Means Discrepancy

According to two popular magazines that published special issues on Mishima shortly after his suicide,[1] 11 (27 percent) of 41 critics attributed his suicide to the discrepancy between his ideal society and actuality, and 27 (65 percent) to the discrepancy between his ego ideal and self-conception. Three critics (8 percent) regarded his suicide as *jyoshi*, or love pact suicide, stemming from his homosexuality.[2] The two kinds of discrepancies may actually be two sides of the same phenomenon because the discrepancy between the conceptions of ideal and actual societies may be a "sociological" motive that provided "an ego-syntonic outlet" to an operant motive of suicide, *i.e.*, aggression resulting from the discrepancy between ego ideal and self-conception. Of 35 critics who evaluated Mishima's works immediately after his death, nine (23 percent) praised them as top class and deserving a Nobel Prize, while five (14 percent) labeled them as "very good." Six critics (17 percent) evaluated only his earlier works[3] as being good, and the remaining 16 (46 percent) expressed their disliking. Five of these criticized his works as superficial, and four others called him *kichigai* ("insane").

The general consensus among Japanese seems to be that Mishima was a genius, but his later works showed little variation or development despite the fact that he continued to be a superb critic (*The Shuukan Gendai*, 1970, p. 151). Probably, Vidal is right to comment that once Mishima became famous, he was quickly satisfied with "familiar patterns" and did not venture into new patterns of literary art (Vidal, 1971, p. 10). The decline in his creativity seems to be indicated by his growing sense of inadequacy of words, as expressed in *Sun and Steel* (Mishima, 1968). The sense probably produced a deep conflict within him; he was a person of

---

[1] *The Shuukan Gendai* (Dec. 12, 1970) and *The Bungei Shunju* (Feb. 1971). A few nonliterary figures (*e.g.*, actresses) and those whose evaluation of Mishima was not clear were excluded.

[2] With Hissho Morita, who beheaded Mishima before his own suicide.

[3] Include: *Confessions of a Mask* (1949), *Thirst for Love* (1950), *Forbidden Colors* (1951), *The Sound of Waves* (1954), *The Temple of the Golden Pavilion* (1956), and *Kyoko no Ie* (*The House of Kyoko*, 1959).

high self-expectation and a strong narcissistic temperament, together with good competency in criticism.

Personal Factors in Goal-Means Discrepancy

Major factors in Mishima's goal-means discrepancy may be analyzed in terms of a) narcissistic temperament, b) feudalistic philosophy of life, c) limited life experiences, and d) active nihilism as his attitudes toward life, death, and suicide.

Narcissistic Temperament The junior author of this article once participated in a panel discussion on television with Mishima. All other members were seated, and a comfortable but lively discussion was going on. When Mishima came in, he headed straight for his arranged seat without glancing at anybody in the meeting. After talking about the previously assigned topic, he left immediately without saying a word to anybody. This may symbolize his being entirely engrossed in his own self.

Mishima's narcissistic temperament is suggested by his personal background. He was born in Tokyo in 1925 as the oldest son of a high official in Japanese Government. Forty-nine days after his birth, he was separated from his parents and reared as an only child by his grandmother. She was a sickly and vain daughter of a judge of the Japanese Supreme Court, with a "rigid, indomitable, frantic and poetic" personality. She reared Mishima as if he had been a girl until he became 14 years old, when she died. He was then returned to his parents. Because of his sickliness, his childhood was spent in almost complete isolation and indulgence. His world was that of picture books and child stories (Okuno, 1970, p. 78).

These early personal experiences partly explain Mishima's narcissistic temperament. As the oldest son of a high governmental official there was an inflated self-concept in a society where "Government is divine, people base" (*kanson mimpi*). The oldest son in an upper class family in traditional Japan was always given specially favored treatment as the heir to the family line. Mishima was also reared as the only child by an indulgent and highly status-conscious grandmother. When Yukio was born, the family had six maid servants despite their grave financial difficulties. Yukio attributes this to his grandparents' vanity. His winning a citation from the Emperor as the highest ranking graduate from the Peers School must have been very ego-inflating, just as was his graduation with high honor from the most prestigious university in Japan. His employment in the Ministry of Treasury was important because a position in that Ministry is known as the royal road to success and power. In addition, the almost instant success he achieved when he launched on his writing career placed him at the height of his popularity at the age of 23. Generally, Mishima lived surrounded by adoration and adulation. These personal factors were reinforced by general cultural factors that produce narcissistic personalities in upper class Japanese children, *e.g.*, little discipline of the infant, constant attention given for need gratification, and exaggerated deference and flattery shown by inferiors, *e.g.*, merchants, artisans, gardeners, and servants.

Feudalistic Philosophy of Life "Feudal" is interpreted here as contrasted to both "folk" and "industrial." It is characterized by favorable attitudes toward rigid class stratification with: 1) the ruling class composed of governmental bureaucracy, priests, scholars, nobility, landlords, and militarists (or Samurai); 2) the existence of minorities occupying a marginal position, not fully integrated into the social system; and 3) education emphasizing "memorization and understanding of the ancient thought-ways" and the simulation of the elites' ideal patterns by subservient masses (Sjoberg, 1966, p. 49).

In infancy, Mishima was reared by his paternal grandmother, who was an epitome of Japanese feudalism. Education during his childhood and adolescence was at the Peers School. Its commencement ceremony was held in the special presence of Emperor and Empress. Past principals of the school were mostly generals and admirals; one of them is a national hero, General Nogi, who committed *junshi* ("suicide to follow a deceased master") with his wife after the death of the Meiji Emperor. The rearing and schooling seem to have formed Mishima's feudalistic philosophy of life.

Limited Life Experiences Generally, Mishima's childhood and adolescence were characterized by an atmosphere of rigidity, fanaticism, indulgence, and detachment from reality, all of which contributed to limited life experiences. As an adult he was strongly self-restraining in either heterosexual or homosexual associations (Date, 1970, p. 140), contributing to a smooth but unchallenging life. The too easy and unexciting life produced in him a yearning for s,toosui ("rapture"), *isshun no semei no nenshoo* ("a moment of burning life"), or *jyonetsu no kooyo* ("frenzied passion") (Mishima, 1968). His ideal life was "a world which has no tomorrow," for example, a promise of rendezvous under probable air raid conditions. The lesser the feasibility, the better (Miyoshi, 1970, p. 131).

The lack of complicated and intense life experiences may have influenced negatively his capability to understand and describe a great variety of emotions. Shiga Naoya, one of the great novelists in Japan, criticized Mishima for writing only of "dreams" (*Shuukan Gendai*, 1970, p. 87). Yoshiyuki Junnosuke criticized Mishima's description of the fishing village in his most realistic novel, *The Sound of Waves*, for its lack of realistic atmosphere (*Shuukan Gendai*, 1970, p. 153). Mishima himself denounced realistic writings. To him, the writer's life should be separated from his novel, which should describe a life as "should be" or "could be." Although his work may be a confession, the confession represents his interpretation and wish, which are never reality itself. This theory is reasonable, but all writers reveal their interpretations, whether they theorize or not. The difference among them is evaluated by how the interpretation and the wish are expressed in a literary form. The expression requires the composition of concepts. A larger number of concepts facilitate expression, and the amount of meaningful concepts accumulated largely depends upon the degree of variety and intensity of life experiences.

Mishima's limited life experiences are exemplified with reference to his feudalism. He knew the Samurai culture but not the merchant one. The former is characterized by an emphasis on *on* ("favor to repay"), *giri* and *gimu* ("lighter obligation" and "heavier obligation," respectively), the fanatic belief in the supremacy of his own group, and nonrational obedience to the lord including the sacrifice of own family members, lovers, and friends. The merchant culture, on the other hand, stresses *ninjo* ("humane feelings"), calculation for self-profit, and cooperation among family members and friends. Takashi Yasuda commented that Mishima did not understand the beauty of *wagoto* ("tender behavior"), *e.g.*, coyness displayed by a *kabuki* player performing a feminine role. He understood *hara-kiri* ("self-disembowelment") but not *jyoshi* ("love pact suicide"), which is an aspect of the merchant culture and requires treating the female as an equal individual (*Shuukan Gendai*, 1970, p. 162).

Not only did Mishima not know the merchant culture, but the Samurai culture with which he was familiar was that of the later Tokugawa period (1600 to 1868). At that time, the Samurai was an alienated figure, entirely dependent for his survival upon the rice stipend bestowed by his lord upon him. The cultivation of a spirit of self-sacrifice was the price for securing the master's protection. His anxiety caused by dependence was compensated for by his prejudice against, and maltreatment of, commoners and outcasts.[4] Since these people composed about 90 percent of the Japanese population, the Samurai was almost entirely insensitive to feelings of the great majority in his society.

In addition, the Samurai culture that Mishima knew was its ideal abstraction, disregarding any humanity underneath. The Samurai was a human being, too; he would have had similar basic needs and wishes just as others. The human side of the Samurai culture was present before the establishment of the rigid class stratification under the Tokugawa regime.

---

[4] For example, the *samurai* "might kill commoners with impunity" (Quigley and Turner, 1956, p. 11).

Samurai were then independent fighters who could support themselves on their own land and who could count on their own ability for gaining a better future. Because of their lesser alienation from life, they were more rational about life and death and freer in self-expression and enjoyment (Shiba, 1971, p. 100). Thus, the very narrow conception of feudalism and the lack of understanding of the non-Samurai culture and of the actual culture of Samurai as human beings became a handicap for Mishima as a writer.

Active Nihilism: Attitudes Toward Life and Death It is said that Japanese people act more on the basis of mood than on the basis of ideology. If we regard feudalistic nationalism as Mishima's ideology, his mood was "active nihilism." Mishima's activism was influenced by Wang-Yang-ming's philosophy that the ultimate significance of life lies in attaining the "great nothingness" and in *chikoo gooitsu* ("identity of knowledge" and "identity of action") through rejecting conceptual knowledge. Nihilism is indicated by his own observation that "the characters in the book [*Kyoko no Ie*] ran about in this direction or that as their individual personalities, their profession, and their sexual preferences command them, but in the end all roads, no matter how roundabout, lead back into nihilism" (Keene, 1971).

Although Mishima maintained that the Wang-Yang-ming's "great nothingness" may be regarded as the root of his active nihilism (Mishima, 1970*a*, p. 217), there is a great difference between the two. The great nothingness is, as Mishima himself described, "the root of creation and the fundamental truth beyond good and bad." When a person attains it, his action reaches "justice beyond life and death" (Mishima, 1970*a*, p. 216). There is nothing nihilistic about this philosophy. Oshio Heihachiro,[5] a scholar of the Wang-Yang-ming school and one of the few scholars whom Mishima respected, demanded in 1837, a time of terrible famine, that the government open its storehouses to the starving people of Osaka. The government officials refused, and in desperation Oshio and his men broke open the storehouses. Their triumph, however, was short-lived, and he dismissed his followers and killed himself (Keene, 1971, p. 5). In Oshio's mind, the great nothingness was the root of justice for which he died. On the other hand, what provided Mishima his basic mood was nihilism. The great nothingness for him was a root of an action characterized by "solitude, tension, and tragic resolution" (Mishima, 1970*a*, p. 56). The more apparently meaningless the action the better, because it is "purer and

[5] Both Oshio and Mishima committed *hara-kiri* at the age of 45. Mishima might have been influenced consciously or unconsciously by Oshio's death.

more unique" (Muramatsu, 1970, p. 54). It is a moment of rapture that Mishima wanted. His narcissism and nihilism were too strong for him to be concerned with ideology or justice. His nihilistic mistrust of humanity and distorted interpretation of the great nothingness appear to have limited his perspectives, contributing to the discrepancy between his ego ideal and self-conception.

Alienated Conception of Self

The four factors in Mishima's goal-means discrepancy—narcissistic temperament, feudalistic view of life, limited life experiences, and active nihilism—also made for his alienated position among Japanese writers and critics, who generally are hostile to their feudal tradition. Alienation here is interpreted as meaninglessness, loneliness, mistrust, powerlessness, idolization of physical beauty, and insensitivity to human feelings, all of which characterize Mishima's major works.

The most typical example is Fujiko in *Kyoko no Ie*. She was a daughter of an executive of a big company, of which her husband was an employee. She accompanied her husband to New York, where "all Japanese are her enemies." Her association with Americans was not satisfying because she could not impress them with her wit. Her husband was not helpful because he was interested in nothing but his own business. She became desperately lonely: "Her apartment room, confined by snow, looks like a prison. Loneliness, burning inside, flushes her face. Standing up with her cheeks in her hands, she walks around in the room. Finally, kneeling down in front of a window, she prays to God, in whom she does not believe: 'Please help me! Please save me! I will do anything if you relieve me of this loneliness.' " In order to get attention from somebody, she wants to attempt suicide; to break the loneliness, she sleeps with a White neighbor and hopes that her husband will become angry and punish her.

Fujiko's loneliness is a reflection of Mishima's feelings. Tsuyoshi Muramatsu, probably the closest friend of Mishima's, observed that Mishima "always made an effort to appear to be cheerful and to disguise sadness by joking, but he was easily hurt and very lonely" (Muramatsu, 1970*a*, p. 53). Mishima's sickly childhood under the indulgent and formal grandmother, with limited outside contact, produced a boring life. The boredom and the wish to escape from it are suggested by a poem of his childhood, which he composed at the age of 15:

> Every evening, I stood by the window
> Waiting for some disaster to occur—
> For the wicked, ferocious-looking dust storm of a calamity

To march in a big wave from beyond the horizon
Like a big dark rainbow.

As Fujiko represents Mishima's mistrust by regarding all Japanese in New York as enemies, Mishima himself felt that he had been betrayed by his seniors and friends one after another. He had no friends among literary colleagues (Ooka, 1971, p. 110). To him, even a happy family life was an "enemy" of human beings (Muramatsu, 1970, p. 53).

The boredom and mistrust produced a philosophy that life's only significance was in a moment of *toosui* ("rapture") and *kikikan* ("sense of imminent danger"). The central theme of his life and works is "a romantic impulse to death." A moment of rapture and the sense of imminent danger are best embodied in the Samurai spirit—to be ready, or forced to be ready, to sacrifice oneself for his lord.

Despite his fame for beautiful wordings, Mishima suffered from a sense of powerlessness with words. This sense inclined him to emphasize action as a substitute form of self-expression. To him, the only knowledge was an experiential one (Mishima, 1970*b*, p. 219). However, action did not give him an ultimate satisfaction because of his obsession with physical appearrance. In his view, beautiful actions, of which the most beautiful is suicide, require physical beauty, and physical beauty is contingent upon biological youthfulness. He believed that "when a man becomes 40 years old, there is no way to die beautifully" (*Shuukan Gendai,* 1970, p. 101). The beautiful body, which he developed by strenuous "body building" efforts for 10 years, produced after all only a strong sense of futility.

The combination of Mishima's sense of powerlessness and obsessive concern with youthful physical appearance is represented in his works. His protagonists became increasingly younger in his later works, for example, "I" in *Kinkakuji (The Temple of the Golden Pavilion,)*, the boy in *Gogo no Eiko (Towing in the Afternoon)*, and the boy who committed suicide in *Hoojo no Umi (The Sea of Fertility)*. At the same time, these boys represented increasingly more the sense of powerlessness toward words. Mishima's concept of beauty was not only a reflection of alienation, but the concept promoted it. For example, the more "I" of *Kinkakuji* became trapped by the beauty of the Golden Pavilion, the more alienated he became from fellow men and reality.

Most heroes and heroines in Mishima's works are engrossed with their own satisfaction and are insensitive to others' feelings. Noboru in *Shizumeru Taki (Sunken Waterfall)* seduced another man's wife. When she became entrapped by him, he forced her into committing suicide. Seiichiro in *Kyoko no Ie* was insensitive to his wife's despair. Etsuko in *Thirst for Love* seduced a man servant. When he yielded to her seduction, she killed him because she did not want to lose her identity.

Response to Alienation

The characteristics of Mishima's personal background—narcissistic temperament, feudalistic view of life, limited life experiences, and active nihilism—not only contributed to his alienation but also determined his response to it. When he was frustrated, his aggression found an outlet in an attack upon modern Japan, which did not satisfy his feudal mind, and the attack was expressed in a way which was most satisfactory to his narcissism, feudalism, and nihilism.

Mishima's response to alienation is represented in *Kyoko no Ie* (1959), which is one of his most cherished works, although, to his great disappointment, it received negative criticisms. It summarizes the philosophy of life presented in his previous works and foreshadows that in his subsequent works. Roughly, Mishima's works show a change parallel to the general trends in Japan since World War II: 1) period of the reconsideration of world views (1946 to 1952), 2) period of obsessive concern with love and sex, a tendency toward anomie (1953 to 1958), and 3) period of attempt at a solution (1959 to 1970) (Mita, 1967).

One of the responses is a compromise with reality. After spending money in providing a place for indulgence to young people, Kyoko (Mrs. Mirror) finally yielded to financial difficulties and returned to her husband whom she did not love. She expressed her resignation: "I am cured—cured from the illness that I must think this world is unreal—that the existence of this world is dependent upon our perception. It is solid, despite its amorphous appearance. It is built just like a drawer made by an expert, and it cannot be destroyed by a dream. Look at the God I have decided to believe. On one red glittering eye, there is written the word, obedience; and on the other, patience. The smoke coming out of two big nostrils writes in the air a word, hope. On the red dangling tongue, there is the word, happiness, and in the back of the throat, we can see in relief the word, future" (*Kyoko no Ie*, p. 525). This response provided an ingredient to his suicide as a resistance to social change.

The second response is suggested by three protagonists. Osamu is a modern Japanese Narcissus. Tired of being pursued by females, he sold himself to a homely usuress. In order to monopolize him, she killed him and then committed suicide, embracing his body. Osamu knew what was coming and accepted it with a masochistic pleasure. Shunkichi is a symbol of physical strength. After winning a boxing championship, he had his wrist broken by a gang. Later, he found a significance of life in working for an ultranationalist group. Natsuo is a symbol of creativity. When he received recognition as a promising artist, his life became meaningless. Bored with life, he rapidly became emaciated. One morning, the sight of a daffodil in sunlight suddenly triggered his awakening (mystic immersion into Nature), and he regained his energy. His returning to Nature was consummated by discarding his virginity with Kyoko and leaving Japan for South America. Thus, the three protagonists foreshadow violence, narcissism, masochism, mysticism, ultranationalism, and nihilistic defiance against convention, which were major components of Mishima's suicide.

ATTITUDES TOWARD SUICIDE AND SUICIDAL VICTIMS

Views of Life and Death

One of the basic philosophies of Japanese people is the Buddhist concept of *mujo-kan* (the view of life as ephemeral, determined by the principle of eternal change). The existence on this earth is *keso* ("false phase"); it does not provide the real home for man to rest. Our bodily life is a temporary lodging of our soul, and the biological life itself is meaningless. Not only is the present life a *keso*, but it also is a filthy field in which greedy and evil people fight against each other for a little gain. In addition, man must always suffer from the problems related to birth, aging, illness, and death. Love, hatred, and separation always produce sufferings. The ideal of *enri odo, gongu jodo* ("escape from this filthy world," "aspire for the pure land") is a core of the traditional Japanese personality.

Thus, the life on this earth is not only meaningless but filled with suffering. The only way to make it meaningful and enjoyable is through "enlightenment." People must learn that their sufferings result from their attachment to worldly things (*e.g.*, life, love, pleasure, etc.), which cannot last, and that the attachment is a product of the ignorance of reality. The reality is that not only external things but a person's conceptual self itself are shadows of his own desires. Only when he eliminates his conceptual awareness of the self and becomes "egoless" (*muga*) will his real self (soul) appear. In the real self, nature or natural law will emerge without any distortion, and there will be no craving for worldly objects or any more sufferings. The concept of *muga* is made for the negation of biological life in the Japanese mind. In his suicide note, Yukio Mishima wrote that *kagiri aru inochinara eien ni ikitai* ("If our biological life is limited, I would like to live forever") (*The Kashu Mainichi*, Nov. 28, 1970).

A most important characteristic of the Japanese view of life and death is in their conception of nature, which is expected to embody itself in the real self. To Chinese people, nature (heaven) is superordinate to the prince; the latter rules under the mandate of the former. Therefore, according to Mencius, if the prince violates "the way of Heaven," people have the right to chase him (Clyde, 1952, p. 56). In Japan, on the contrary, the feudal lord, Shogun, or Emperor is the Absolute, who can do nothing wrong. Therefore, to follow nature means to adjust to the norms of the established social system, *i.e.*, to "take proper place and serve society" (*bun o tsukushite yoo ni tatsu*) (Kaneko, 1941, p. 96).

Thus the traditional view of biological life among Japanese people is negative and that of biological death is accepting. At the same time there is a strong emphasis on success (*shusse*) and pleasure. The significance of life lies in obtaining success as measured by people's reactions. The failing person must bear shame and misery. A unique aspect of Japanese society is that a person's success and pleasure are almost entirely determined by one event—entrance examination into a good university. The combination of the negative view of life, on the one hand, and the emphasis on success and fun, on the other hand, contributes to suicide on two levels: first, the intensity of the wish for success and fun makes for a greater discrepancy between aspiration and self-concept in the failing person; second, the negative view of life impresses the failing with the desirability of escaping death, so that he may rid himself from competition, whether by resignation or by suicide, without disturbing the social order.

Attitudes Toward Suicide

The teaching by Doogen, the founder of the Soto Zen Sect, that realization of the fullest meaning of life comes through self-sacrifice for social service and through the negation of intellectual apprehension (Tsunoda *et al.*, 1958, pp. 238, 251, 255) has been interpreted as approval of suicide in the eyes of most Japanese. Confucius' concept of *Tao* ("Way" or "Natural Law") and Mencius' concept of *Gi* ("great cause"), which are to be upheld at the expense of biological life, also have contributed to Japanese suicide. Since *Tao* and *Gi* are equated with "taking one's proper place" in the established social order, when the social structure is rigid, there is almost no means of protest against superiors. "Suicide has been always an accepted means of protest" in Japan (Flinn, 1969, p. 20).

Today, the Japanese attitude toward suicide is changing. Despite this, 27 percent of the high school and 28 percent of the college students whom Ohara studied in 1963 thought that "suicide is good" (Ohara, 1965*b*, p. 112). A survey by the Kyoto University Psychology Department found that 25 percent of the senior students at junior high schools in Kyoto had had a suicidal wish (Ohara, 1965*b*). A study of 1,229 junior high school students in Osaka found that 10 percent of the male and 17 percent of the female students had experienced suicidal impulses. About 9 percent of them said that suicide was good. The major reasons given for suicidal impulses were examination problems, schoolwork difficulties, and "being scolded" (Ohara, 1965*b*).

Evidence of the propensity toward suicide is also found in the senior author's research of 72 Kyoto University students who had committed suicide during the 13 years from 1956 to 1969. Thirty-three of the 72 were majoring in the physical sciences (11 in science, 11 in engineering, 8 in agriculture, and 3 in medical science). On the questionnaire that was given to all newly admitted students, 10 of these 33 students listed as their favorite reading works generally regarded as "suicide literature." Physical science students are usually considered as less liable to suicide because of their less critical attitudes toward society and self, less romantic attitudes toward life and death, and their relatively more secure future prospects in Japan. Therefore, the finding that nearly half of the students who committed suicide during the 13-year period were in physical sciences and that about one-third of them chose "suicide literature" as their favorite reading when they entered the university was highly suggestive.

Three of the 10 preferring suicide literature chose Arthur Schopenhauer, who maintained that suicide was the greatest treasure for humans. Two chose Ryuunosuke Akutagawa, who praised suicide as beautiful and who committed suicide himself. One of the two wrote in his last note: "Now my mind is peaceful. . . I have never felt such satisfaction before. I feel every thing was predestined this way. The charm of death is beyond all arts. Sunset is beautiful. As Akutagawa said, the strings of my mind vibrate." Five loved the literature by Osamu Dazai, who committed suicide himself and revealed his feeling about suicide in one of his representative novels: "Sister. I give up. I go ahead. I don't know why I have to live. I don't understand it. . . . Man should have the right to die as well as to live" (Dazai, 1969, p. 284).

The accepting attitude toward suicide is even justified in the name of individual rights and democracy. Professor Sonohara stated: "There are two views of suicide: (1) the negative view that suicide is a religious and moral evil and (2) the positive view that suicide is an expression of individual rights and freedom. The former is prevalent when the authoritarian control is strong and the latter when social control declines. Since the liberal ideology of individual rights has been established, the latter has become dominant" (Ohara, 1965*b*, p. 113). Suicide may be an expression of minimal individual rights and freedom, but the development of the liberal ideology of individual rights has no intrinsic relationship with suicide; it will more likely lower suicide rates. However, Professor Sonohara's justifying attitude toward suicide is revealing. We need "to deromanticize death and suicide" (Shneidman, 1969, p. 28) and to look into "socially patterned defects" (Fromm, 1954) as a factor in the high suicide rates in Japan.

Attitudes Toward Suicidal Persons

Only 9 percent of the university students in Kyoto regard suicide as a social problem. For a majority of respondents suicide is a personal problem. Nineteen percent of the students castigated suicidal victims as "cowardly," 20 percent criticized them as "lacking in thinking," and another 20 percent maintained, "Let them alone." These figures seem to support Dr. Ohara's criticism of Japanese people for their indifference to the victim involved in *oyako shinju* ("parent-child suicide") (Ohara, 1965*a*, p. 267). The indifference may be explained in terms of insecurity and a lack of concern with social welfare.

Insecurity of Japanese The indifference to other people's problems is rooted in a general insecurity among Japanese people. When a person is insecure, he may be exclusively concerned with his own security or he may feel too helpless to offer assistance to others. The insecurity is further represented by the fact that "even in dissent, Japanese avoid speaking with clarity, vigor and personal force" and they have to show their dissension only in a group (Riesman and Riesman, 1967, p. 197). Even in a group, if they know that others are not speaking out, they will not either. Highly educated persons are expected to be more expressive than others because of their better social connections, greater capability to communicate, and because of their confidence in problem solving. However, even the highly educated Japanese shows a noticeable "dread of power" (Fischer, 1963). The dread of power—both authority and violence—is the root of Japanese insecurity, and it is produced by a number of factors. First, Japanese people have not in the past been allowed to possess effective means of self-defense (*e.g.*, gun, sword). Second, Japanese government has been more concerned with national order and glory than individual welfare. Since politicians have been interested primarily in the use of local bosses for political gains, there have been close ties between politicians, policemen, and bosses at the sacrifice of general citizens. Third, Japanese cannot count on others for help against authority or violence because of the "ancient Japanese reluctance to help anyone in trouble, for fear of becoming obliged to the victim" (Trumbull, 1958, p. 74).

Lack of Concern with Social Welfare One of the suicidal subjects in the senior author's 1968 research characterized in his note the typical Japanese personality as: 1) *shimaguni knojo* ("insular personality"), fighting against each other even for a little gain, 2) inhuman exploitation of inferiors under pseudo-familistic capitalism, and 3) *hooken-sei* ("feudalism") which stifles individuality, depriving the individual of the capacity to solve his own problems, of confidence in his own capability to develop, and of any ability in self-expression. These characteristics suggest the lack of concern with social welfare. The lack of concern with others is exemplified in a statement made by a Japanese professor in Riesman and Riesman (1967, p. 276): The "discrepancy between the intransigent concern for beauty and cleanliness inside and the complete unconcern outside" (shows lack of concern for the other). The degree of selfishness, rudeness, and inconsiderations shown in public conveyances in Japan is said to be "unsurpassed" (Kawasaki, 1969, p. 86).

Japanese leaders set examples of the unconcern for public welfare. Riesman and Riesman (1967) also pointed out that while successful Americans seek from philanthropy or from their role expectations, "to give back some of the 'take' from industrial achievement, there is very little concern for the public welfare" among Japanese businessmen (p. 78). In politics, voting masses are generally ignored in elections, which are "by custom dominated by personal connections rather than policies" (Kawasaki, 1969, p. 194). The successful candidates are usually local bosses, and when a candidate is not a local boss, he most often will "rely on a certain election boss who secures block votes" (Kawasaki, 1969). When politicians are elected, they are given "a free hand to consolidate their positions to their advantage with a mixture of bribes and threats" (Riesman and Riesman, 1967, p. 56). Most Japanese politicians of note are said to have no necessity of buying food at all because "they constantly receive presents of seasonal food items, canned food, imported wines and spirits, from their friends and followers" (Kawasaki, 1969, p. 168). Governmental officials also often "end up filling an entire room with presents received from numerous associates for business contacts" (Kawasaki, 1969, p. 167). It is professors that are expected to lead public opinion for social change. However, despite their dissatisfaction about politicians and despite their often professed Marxian ideology, Japanese professors are "indifferent on the whole to political activities" (Riesman and Riesman, 1967, p. 163). In short, Japanese elites generally show little concern with the public.

The unconcern with public welfare is rooted in the basic Japanese values of particularism and traditionalism. Among Japanese people, there is no transcendental rightness or wrongness; justice is tied up with status (Riesman and Riesman, 1967, p. 251). "Everything is done in terms of who one's teacher or sponsor is and in terms of friendship and connections" (Riesman and Riesman, 1967, p. 40). "Japanese expect special private favors in return for forming personal ties with others," making them "moral cowards" in relation to social problems (Kawasaki, 1969, pp. 106, 200). In spite of the modernization and alleged democratization of Japan, there still is little development of universalism (Lifton, 1967, p. 275), and even for the best intellectuals, "it is difficult for Japanese to be universalistic" (Riesman and Riesman, 1967, p. 30). Consequently, they have little sense of fair play (Kawasaki, 1969, p. 104) and little concern with underdogs (Riesman and Riesman, 1967, p. 278).

The lack of universalistic principle is expressed in Japanese opportunism or "situational realism." Zen Gakuren (Federation of Student Self-Government Association) activists change into organization men as soon as they go into business (Riesman and Riesman, 1967, pp. 299, 346). The left-wing students are called "apple-red–red only on surface (Ishizaka, 1968) because they are in reality highly conservative, since "their aim is to preserve present prosperity and peace and the pleasures and opportunities that go with them" (Riesman and Riesman, 1967, p. 297).

Traditionalism, like particularism, provides Japanese people with their basic criteria for evaluating behavior. Even radical students at Zen Gakuren meetings, who are expected to rebel against the establishment, "behave in an identical way as the Right Wing" (Riesman and Riesman, 1967, p. 301). Since Japanese tradition is anchored to status hierarchy, Japanese people "care what some people think but not what the subordinate thinks" (Riesman and Riesman, 1967). The insensitivity to the feelings of people in need seems to stem from this.

Japanese personality today is characterized by a mixture of traditionalism and present orientation. However, their present orientation does not increase their concern with social problems (Iga, 1970). The typical Japanese are hedonistic and nihilistic. The traditionalistic principles "have largely yielded to the spirit of 'enjoy today,' for tomorrow who knows" (Kawasaki, 1969, p. 193). They seem to be motivated more by a materialistic view of the world with a "shortage of moral courage and discipline" (Riesman and Riesman, 1967, p. 199). Thus, the general Japanese attitude toward persons in need is more or less indifference and avoidance. This does not mean that they are by nature cold hearted. The mechanism of "psychic numbing" (desensitizing oneself to other's sufferings) (Lifton, 1967, p. 32) seems to stifle their sensitivity, primarily because of their own insecurity and sense of helplessness in the authoritarian society.

DISCUSSION

This chapter first described Japanese suicides, analyzed the suicide of Yukio Mishima, and then discussed Japanese attitudes toward suicide and suicidal victims. These three sections point to two independent variables in high suicide rates in Japan: authoritarianism and culture conflict.

Japanese society is still highly authoritarian in various senses. First, Japanese people are strongly conscious of status differences, which provides the basic frame of reference to the Japanese mind. Both authoritarian aggressiveness and submissiveness are marked. Japanese people perceive social relations as power relations, producing an intense desire for success (*shusse*). They show a strong inclination toward moralistic condemnation of the person who fails in performing role expectations. Under a patriarchal authoritarianism, it is young, female, and poor people that will suffer most.

Why does authoritarianism produce a high suicide rate? External regulations in an authoritarian social structure produce fatalistic suicides, in apparent contradiction to some sociologists, who hold an inverse relationship between external regulations and suicide rate (Henry and Short, 1954; Maris, 1969). When external regulations are strong, hostility is to be directed internally. The contradictory views suggest that external regulation itself is not a factor in suicide, but the degree of the internalization of external regulations is. Here, DeVos' concept of role narcissism is important. "Role narcissism" is defined as "complete identification with one's social role" as expressed by an "emphasis on an idealized, stringent self-discipline and sense of dedication to role which is to take priority over natural human feelings" (DeVos, 1964, p. 8). When the young and the female are socialized to "role narcissism" under strong external regulations, and when they fail to satisfy their role demands, they may perceive no way out of shame and guilt, in addition to the fear of social punishment. Since poverty is an indication of failure in the society where success and pleasure are rewards for talent and effort, the poor may be condemned, or they condemn themselves for the failure, particularly for failing in satisfying parental wishes. Self-blame is expected in the society where the Oedipus complex is normal. Fromm pointed out the correlation between the patriarchal family, irrational authority, and intense emotional mother-son attachment (Fromm, 1954). DeVos discussed the moral masochistic attitude of the Japanese mother in child disciplining; this attitude produces strong guilt in Japanese (DeVos, 1960).

The Japanese version of authoritarianism also produces a highly narcissistic, arrogant, but dependent personality, as represented by Yukio Mishima. When this type of personality is placed in the situation that demands downgrading his self-image, he may prefer death. The concept of role narcissism applies to this type of person, too. Authoritarianism also affects the general public's attitude toward the suicidal victim. Because of their authoritarian submissiveness, insecurity, and helplessness, they tend to avoid being involved in other people's troubles, giving the final push to the victim toward suicide.

Thus, authoritarianism affects goal-means discrepancy, self-concept, and the perception of the general public's attitudes toward the victim, producing a suicidogenic definition of the situation. In order for the definition to evolve into a suicidal act, there must be cultural sanctions favorable for the act. As the third section of this paper discussed, the Japanese people's attitude toward life is negative and tends to lower their commitment to life on this earth. On the other hand, their attitudes toward death and suicide are accepting. There is even a tendency to romanticize suicide. These attitudes are also consistent with authoritarian totalism, in which only those who adjust to the existing social order and who contribute to group goals may prosper. Those who fail to adjust and contribute should eliminate themselves from competition, so that social integration and group development may not be hindered.

Thus authoritarianism produces a suicidogenic definition of the situation and response. However, authoritarianism alone does not explain current suicides in Japan, where a rapid social change is taking place. The importance of culture change with reference to suicide is proved by the fact that the suicide rates in regions that are exposed to Western cultures to a greater extent (*e.g.*, Kinki, 29; Tokai, 25; and Kanto, 23) suicide rates are higher than in Tohoku (20) or Hokkaido (21).

However, culture change alone does not provide a sufficient explanation either. Tokyo, with culture change probably faster than others, does not show the highest suicide rate in Japan. In fact, its suicide rate is much lower than that of the prefectures in the Kinki region. The most important factor seems to be the combination of a high degree of the retention of traditional culture (and consequently a high degree of "role narcissism") and extensive culture change. This assumption is supported by the finding that the rural areas in the Kinki prefectures show the highest suicide rates—higher than cities in the same area and also rural areas in the other regions. Kinki is the region that retains the most traditional form of Japanese culture, as represented by Kyoto and Osaka. At the same time, it is the area that is extensively exposed to the impact of modern cultures through Osaka, Kyoto, Kobe, and Nara. Wakayama, another prefecture in Kinki, is not only adjacent to the Osaka metropolis but it is the prefecture that produced the largest number of emigrants to the United States, Canada, and Brazil. The direct and indirect influences of the emigration on the remaining members of the community seem to be extensive. The finding that older people show a higher suicide rate in rural areas than in cities seems to suggest the greater difficulties that older people have in adjusting to social change there—the disorganization of the traditional family without counterbalancing social services.

In addition to the conflict between traditional and modern cultures, Kinki people experience another level of culture conflict, too. It is between the merchant culture that dominates Osaka and Kyoto (called *kamigata*) with a high value on *ninjo* ("humane feelings"), self-profit, calculation, and practicality, on the one hand, and, on the other hand, the Tokyo culture characterized by bureaucratic and absolutistic authoritarianism with the overlay of Western civilization (Iga, 1971). Tokyo culture is an offspring of the Samurai culture, which emphasizes *on* ("favor"), *giri*, and *gimu* ("lighter obligation" and "heavier obligation," respectively), the fanatic belief in the supremacy of one's own group, and nonrational obedience to superiors. The Samurai who laid the foundation of Tokyo culture in the Meiji Restoration were emotionally convinced that "their views are unadulterated truth" and to them "the respect for an opponent's views made little sense" (Keene, 1960, p. 118). On the other hand, people in Kinki in many respects have been proud of their *kamigata* culture, which had flourished when Tokyo was a remote barbarous land. Kyoto had been the capital of Japan for more than 1,000 years before Tokyo became the capital in 1868.

The two levels of culture conflict have produced confusion, lack of confidence, anxiety, and diffuse aggression in Kinki people. The diffuse aggression is represented by the fact that Kyoto—the most traditional city in Japan—is a major center of radicalism in that country. It is the center of a strong teachers' union movement and it had a socialist mayor and a socialist governor long before Tokyo did.

REFERENCES

Clyde, P. H. 1952. *The Far East*. Prentice Hall, New York.

Date, M. 1970. Watashi dake ga shitte iru sonohi no shinsoo (The truth of the day which I alone know). *Shuukan Gendai*, Dec. 12, 136–141.

Dazai, O. 1969. *Works of Dazai Osamu*. Shincho-sha, Tokyo.

DeVos, G. A. 1960. The relation of guilt toward parents to achievement and arranged marriage among the Japanese. *Psychiatry*, 23:287–301.

DeVos, G. A. 1964. Role narcissism and the etiology of Japanese suicide. Paper read at the International Conference of Social Psychiatry, London.

Fischer, J. 1963. The Japanese intellectuals: Cliques, soft edges, and the dread of power. *Harper*, Sept., 14–24.

Flinn, K. 1969. Suicide in Japan. *Columbian Fathers Mission*, July.

Fromm, E. 1954. Individual and social origins of neurosis. *American Sociological Review*, 9:380–384; 1954. In Kluckhohn *et al*., *Personality in Nature, Society and Culture*, pp. 515–522. Knopf, New York.

Henry, A. F., and Short, J. F. 1954. *Suicide and Homicide*. The Free Press, Glencoe, Ill.

Iga, M. 1970. Studies of social problems by Japanese scholars. *Rice University Studies*, 56(4):173–187.

Iga, M. 1971. Kyoto and university student suicide. *Psychologia*, 14(1): 15–24.

Ishizaki, T. 1968. Zaikai goju-nen wasure nokori (Memory of 50 years in the financial world). *Bungei Shunju*, Nov., 164–172.

Kaneko, D. 1941. *Nihon bukkyo shikan* (Historical view of Japanese Buddhism). Iwanami Shoten, Tokyo.

Kato, H. 1965. Jisatsu stairu no hensen (Shift in suicide style). In: K. Ohara (Ed.), *Gendai no Esupuri: (L'Espirit d'Aujourd'hui: Suicide), Kaishaku to kansho* (Interpretation and appreciation), Nov., 226–237.

Kawasaki, I. 1969. *Japan Unmasked.* Charles E. Tuttle, Rutland, Vt. and Tokyo.
Keene, D. 1960. The man in the Japnese mask. *The New York Times Magazine*, Nov. 6.
Keene, D. 1971. Mishima. *The New York Times Book Review,* Jan. 3.
Lifton, R. 1967. *Death in Life.* Random House, New York.
Maris, R. W. 1969. *Social Forces in Urban Suicide.* Dorsey Press, Homewood, Ill.
Ministry of Welfare, Japanese Government. 1966. *Jinko Dootai Tokei* (Statistics of Population Dynamics).
Mishima, Y. 1968. *Taiyo to Tetsu (Sun and Steel).* Kodansha, Shincho-sha edition, Tokyo.
Mishima, Y. 1970*a*. *Kyoko no Ie (The House of Kyoko)* (1959). Shincho-sha edition, 1970.
Mishima, 1970*b*. *Koodo-gaku Nyumon (Introduction to Study of Action).* Bungei Shunju, Tokyo.
Mita, S. 1967. *Gendai Nihon no Seishin Koozo (Psychological Structure of Modern Japan).* Koobundo, Tokyo.
Miyoshi, Y. 1970. Dashi okurete ita shitsumon (Questions left unraised). *Shuukan Gendai*, Dec. 12, 130–135.
Muramatsu, T. 1970. Watshi wa sore o yochi shite ita (I foresaw it). *Shuukan Gendai*, Dec. 12, 44–55.
Naka, H. 1966*a*. Toshi to Nooson no Jisatsu (Suicide in urban and rural areas). In: Koosaka and Usui (Eds.), *Nihonjin no Jisatsu (Suicide of Japanese People)*, pp. 98–128.
Naka, H. 1966*b*. Seinen no Jisatsu (Suicide of youth). In: Koosaka and Usui (Eds.), *Nihonjin no Jisatsu (Suicide of Japanese People)* Sobunsha, Tokyo, pp. 55–82.
Nishimoto, S. 1966. Waga Kuni no Bukkyo to Jisatsu (Buddhism and suicide in our country). In: Koosaka and Usui (Eds.), *Nihonjin no Jisatsu (Suicide of Japanese People)* pp. 333–335.
Ohara, K. 1965*b*. *Gendai no Esupuri: Jisatsu (L'Esprit d'Aujourd'hui: Suicide)* Shibundo, Tokyo.
Ohara, K. 1965*b*. *Gendai no Esupuri: Jisatsu (L'Espirt d'Aujourd'hui: Suicide*). Shibundo, Tokyo.
Okazaki, A. 1958. *Jisatsu no Kuni: Nihon no Kiroku (Country of Suicide: Record of Japan).* Toyo Keizai Simpo-sha, Tokyo.
Okazaki, A. 1960. *Jisatsu no Shakai-Tookei-teki Kenyu (Social Statistical Study of Suicide).* Nihon Hyoron-sha, Tokyo.
Okuno, T. 1970. Mishima Yukio nyuumon (Introduction to Mishima Yukio). *Shuukan Gendai*, Dec. 12, 77–81.
Ooka, S. 1971. Ikinokotta monoe no shoogen (Witness to those who remain alive). *Bungei Shunju,* Feb., 110–114.
Quigley, H. S., and Turner, J. E. 1956. *The New Japan.* University of Minnesota Press.
Riesman, D., and Riesman, E. 1967. *Conversations in Japan.* Basic Books, New York.
Seiden, R. H. 1969. *Suicide among Youth: A Review of the Literature, 1900–1967.* National Clearinghouse for Mental Health Information, U.S. Government Printing Office, Washington, D.C.

Seward, J. 1968. *Hara-kiri, Japanese Ritual Suicide*. Charles E. Tuttle, Rutland, Vt.

Shiba, R. 1971. Tenno Bushido, Guntai (Emperor, Samurai Code of Behavior, and Army). *Bungei Shunju,* Feb., 94–109.

Shneidman, E. S. 1969. *On the Nature of Suicide*. Jossey Bass, San Francisco.

Sjoberg, G. 1966. Folk and Feudal Societies. In: J. L. Finkle and R. W. Gable (Eds.), *Political Development and Social Change*, pp. 45–53. Wiley, New York.

Tatai, K. 1952. Recent trend of suicide in Japan. *Bulletin, Institute of Public Health*, Sept.

Tatai, K. 1970. Japanese Suicide. *VITA, Official Newsletter for the International Association for Suicide Prevention*, 6:3, Dec.

Trumbull, R. 1958. Japan turns against the Gyangu. *The New York Times Magazine*, Nov. 30.

Tsunoda, R., de Bary, W. T., and Keene, D. 1958. *Sources of Japanese Tradition*. Columbia University Press, New York.

Vidal, G. 1971. Mr. Japan: Review of *Sun and Steel* by Yukio Mishima. *The New York Times Review*, June 17, 8–10.

Index